Strengthening South Korea–Japan Relations

East Asia's International Order and a Rising China

Dennis Patterson and

Copyright © 2024 by The University Press of Kentucky

Scholarly publisher for the Commonwealth,
serving Bellarmine University, Berea College, Centre
College of Kentucky, Eastern Kentucky University,
The Filson Historical Society, Georgetown College,
Kentucky Historical Society, Kentucky State University,
Morehead State University, Murray State University,
Northern Kentucky University, Spalding University,
Transylvania University, University of Kentucky,
University of Louisville, University of Pikeville,
and Western Kentucky University.

All rights reserved.

Editorial and Sales Offices: The University Press of Kentucky
663 South Limestone Street, Lexington, Kentucky 40508-4008
www.kentuckypress.com

Parts of chapter 2 are based on updated work originally published in *International Area Studies Review* (2018), volume 21, number 1, pp. 9–27.

Cataloging-in-Publication data is available from the Library of Congress.

ISBN 978-0-8131-9921-4 (hardcover)
ISBN 978-0-8131-9922-1 (paperback)
ISBN 978-0-8131-9923-8 (pdf)
ISBN 978-0-8131-9924-5 (epub)

This book is printed on acid-free paper meeting
the requirements of the American National Standard
for Permanence in Paper for Printed Library Materials.

Manufactured in the United States of America.

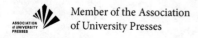

Member of the Association
of University Presses

Strengthening South Korea–Japan Relations

Contents

Abbreviations   vii

Figures and Tables   ix

Preface   xiii

1. Introduction: The East Asian Alliance System and the Problem of South Korea–Japan Relations   1

2. The Origins of the East Asian Alliance System and Its Impact on South Korea and Japan   19

3. China's Rise and the Asia Pacific's International Order   43

4. South Korean and Japanese Views of China and the United States   71

5. Public Attitudes and Relations between South Korea and Japan   91

6. Territorial Disputes, Human Rights, and Court Case Challenges in South Korea–Japan Relations   115

7. US Leadership and the Evolution of Interstate Relations in the Asia Pacific   145

8. The Challenge of Maintaining the Liberal International Order in the Asia Pacific   163

Acknowledgments   189

Notes   191

References   201

Index   211

About the Authors   225

Abbreviations

BRI	Belt and Road Initiative
CPTPP	Comprehensive and Progressive Agreement for the Trans-Pacific Partnership
CUES	Code for Unplanned Encounters at Sea
EEZ	exclusive economic zone
GDP	gross domestic product
GSOMIA	General Security of Military Information Agreement
GSS	General Social Survey
IPEFP	Indo-Pacific Economic Framework for Prosperity
MOU	Memorandum of Understanding
NPT	Nonproliferation Treaty
RCEP	Regional Comprehensive Economic Partnership
SLOC	sea lines of communication
THAAD	Terminal High Altitude Area Defense
TPP	Trans-Pacific Partnership

Figures and Tables

Figures

Figure 2.1 The East Asian Alliance System 23

Figure 2.2 Growth in South Korea's International Trade and GDP per Capita 31

Figure 2.3 Expansion of South Korea's Working-Class Wealth and Political Rights 32

Figure 2.4 Japan's Diplomatic Missions, 1955–2005 37

Figure 2.5 Changes in Japan's International Status, 1960–2005 38

Figure 2.6 Korea's Diplomatic Missions, 1948–2015 39

Figure 3.1 Chinese Military Expenditures 50

Figure 3.2 Military Expenditure Shares 52

Figure 4.1 Japanese Feelings toward China, 1978–2018 75

Figure 4.2 Japanese Feelings toward the United States, 1978–2018 81

Figure 4.3 South Koreans with Favorable vs. Unfavorable Views 87

Figure 5.1 Japanese Perceptions of South Korea, 1978–2018 95

Figure 5.2 South Koreans Favoring Japan vs. China 102

Figure 5.3 South Korean Views of Japan 104

Figure 5.4 Japanese and South Koreans Viewing Bilateral Relations as Bad 106

Figure 6.1 Contrasting Views of the South Korean Supreme Court Decision 131

Tables

Table 2.1   Sources of Economic Aid Received by South Korea, 1960–95   25

Table 2.2   Japanese Exports: Value, Growth, and Percentage of GDP   29

Table 2.3   Diplomatic Successes of South Korea's Presidents in the Pre- and Post-transition Periods   40

Table 3.1   China's Importance as a Trading Partner for South Korea and Japan   49

Table 3.2   Average Growth Rates in Military Expenditures   51

Table 4.1   A Decadal Analysis of Japanese Feelings of Closeness to China and the United States   76

Table 4.2   South Koreans Who Selected Either the United States or China as the Country to Which They Feel Closest   83

Table 5.1   A Decadal Analysis of Japanese Respondents' Feelings of Closeness to or Distance from South Korea   96

Table 5.2   Countries Most Favored by South Koreans   99

Table 5.3   South Korean and Japanese Views of Each Other's Leaders   107

Table 5.4   The State and Importance of South Korea–Japan Bilateral Relations   109

Table 5.5   Reasons for Japanese and South Korean Negative Views of Each Other   111

Table 5.6   South Korean and Japanese Opinions on Actions Needed to Improve Bilateral Relations   113

Table 6.1   Most Important Reasons South Koreans and Japanese Hold Negative Views of Each Other   122

Table 6.2   Comfort Women and Building Better South Korean–Japanese Relations   127

Table 6.3   Japanese and South Korean Perceptions of Historical Issues and Bilateral Relations   128

Table 6.4   How South Koreans and Japanese View Trade with Each Other   133

Table 6.5	South Korea and Japan as Military Threats to Each Other 138
Table 6.6	How South Korea and Japan Should Respond to the South Korea Supreme Court Decision Requiring Compensation for Forced Labor 139
Table 6.7	Contrasting South Korean and Japanese Views on the Forced Labor Issue 141
Table 6.8	South Korean and Japanese Views of Countries of Economic Importance 142
Table 7.1	Support for and Concerns about the Trump Administration 156
Table 7.2	Favorability of and Confidence in US Presidential Administrations 157
Table 7.3	South Korean and Japanese Views of the United States and US Presidents 158
Table 7.4	South Korean and Japanese Perceptions of Affinity and Importance 160
Table 7.5	Trilateral Cooperation and Perceptions of Threat and Alliance Importance 161

Preface

Former Montana senator and US ambassador to Japan Mike Mansfield once said that the relationship between the United States and Japan is the "most important bilateral relationship in the world, bar none." This statement, made at a time of heightened tension in United States–Japan relations, was meant to get leaders in Washington and Tokyo to lower the temperature that had been raised on trade and economic issues so that they could focus on strengthening this long-standing alliance. Since this statement was made, the United States and Japan have generally overcome these economic tensions and continued to build a strong and effective alliance-based partnership that not only allowed for the expansion of trade and commerce throughout the globe but also helped maintain the liberal international order in the Asia Pacific, creating the conditions that led to more prosperity for more people than at any time in human history. For these reasons, this statement from Mansfield is unassailably true.

The liberal international order in the Asia Pacific was not engendered and sustained strictly by the trade and commerce that grew so dramatically since the end of the Pacific and Korean Wars. Indeed, creating and maintaining peace and stability in this region for so many decades also required military alliances and deployments, and the United States was primarily responsible for creating and maintaining these alliances and military deployments throughout the Asia Pacific. In spite of its central role, the United States did not accomplish these outcomes alone: it was assisted by the two military alliances it created and sustained with Japan and South Korea. The importance of the alliances' efforts to maintain peace and stability in the Asia Pacific cannot be overstated, but we also need to understand that the origins of the United States' postwar military commitment rests with its alliance with South Korea when it pushed the North Korean army back above the thirty-eighth parallel. Since that time, the United States has maintained its military presence on the peninsula to help South Korea maintain its territorial integrity.

We can then say that the military alliance and diplomatic relations between the United States and South Korea are also among the most important bilateral relationships in the world. When we take these two sets of bilateral relations and combine them into a set of triangular relations with the United States at the apex and South Korea and Japan at the base, we quickly notice that another set of bilateral relations is of equal importance to those formed by the United States' separate relations with South Korea and Japan. This is the bilateral relationship between South Korea and Japan, which was established as an informal partnership rather than a formal alliance like those the two nations have long had with the United States. Nonetheless, outside the formal relationships that the United States maintains with Seoul, Tokyo, and many other capitals around the globe, this bilateral partnership between South Korea and Japan is, like the other two mentioned above, one of the most important bilateral partnerships in the world, and this is not just because it is the third bilateral relationship in this set of triangular relations but also because, as the base of the East Asian alliance system, it grows in importance with each passing day.

In spite of its importance, the South Korea–Japan partnership has always faced challenges, but from the end of the Korean War to the last two or three decades, it has functioned reasonably well at the base of this alliance system. Many important changes have occurred in the Asia Pacific in the last few decades. Perhaps most important is the rise of an increasingly powerful and economically influential China that has been not only altering the dynamics of interstate relations in the Asia Pacific but more importantly building its growing influence around an alternative set of norms and institutions that threatens the long-term significance of the liberal international order that has helped maintain the peace and stability of that region for many decades. China's rise in influence has been a partner to intermittent spikes in tension between South Korea and Japan. Tension in South Korea–Japan relations is nothing new, but in the last few decades these spikes have involved challenging unresolved issues of historical significance. Moreover, when this recent rise in tension is combined with the growing importance of South Korea–Japan bilateral relations in the context of a rising China, a focused analysis on the dynamics of this essential partnership becomes more significant.

We hope this volume lives up to the importance of the topic we investigate.

1

Introduction

The East Asian Alliance System and the Problem of South Korea–Japan Relations

In the postwar period, no part of the world experienced a more dramatic transformation than Asia.[1] In this part of the world, more than any other, we witnessed more people moving out of poverty into relative prosperity, greater expansions of international commerce and trade, and increasing numbers of citizens able to live their lives in peace and security under conditions of relative political freedom. What makes these developments even more remarkable is that the Asia Pacific was once a region defined by poverty,[2] civil and interstate conflict that resulted in widespread death and destruction, and some of the most incompetent and repressive political regimes on the planet. Repressive political regimes still exist in the region, but, with few exceptions,[3] the political systems of the countries that make up the Asia Pacific, ranging from democratic to authoritarian, are stable and generally responsive to public needs, and their economic systems are among the world's largest and most productive.

How the bulk of this region's nations transformed themselves into the economic powers with stable and effective political systems they are today is an important story that has been told on a country-by-country basis as well as from the perspective of the region at large.[4] The result of such efforts is a rich scholarly literature that has most often focused on domestic factors, particularly the domestic economic policies that many nations in the Asia Pacific employed to promote high levels of economic growth.[5] To be sure, this body of scholarly work has involved important debates, and we have learned much about the economic rise of the many nations that make up the Asia Pacific. Nonetheless, extant scholarship has still not given appropriate weight to another set of supporting factors that clearly facilitated the economic and political transformations we have witnessed throughout the Asia-Pacific region since the end of the Pacific and Korean Wars.

The reference here is to international factors, specifically the fact that interstate relations in the Asia Pacific have been defined by a decades-long environment of relative peace and stability that helped South Korea, Taiwan, Japan, China, and multiple Southeast Asian nations focus on those development policy mixes that accelerated their economic growth rates, expanded their international trading relations, and ultimately elevated the prosperity levels of their respective populations. The environment of peace and stability that has characterized interstate relations throughout the Asia-Pacific region since the end of the Pacific and Korean Wars was made possible in large part because of the system of alliances the United States created in Northeast Asia,[6] specifically what we will refer to throughout this volume as the "East Asian alliance system."

This alliance system is composed of a set of triangular relations among the United States, South Korea, and Japan, and it is defined specifically by the alliance that has existed between the United States and South Korea since the end of the Korean War, the alliance between the United States and Japan that was set up during the Allied Occupation, and an informal partnership between Seoul and Tokyo that was established in 1965. The United States sits at the apex of this relationship triangle and is connected to South Korea and Japan by its separate bilateral alliances with these nations. These alliances include both diplomatic and military/security components, the latter of which involve the stationing of US troops on South Korean and Japanese soil as reminders of the United States' commitment to defend these nations in the event any hostile power violates their territorial integrity. The informal partnership that exists between South Korea and Japan, on the other hand, forms the base of this relationship triangle and involves no formal bilateral alliance but rather what Victor Cha (1999, 36–58) has referred to as a "quasi-alliance."

This set of triangular relations forms the underlying architecture of the East Asian alliance system, and for many decades it has functioned as an international public good benefiting the larger Asia-Pacific region.[7] Specifically, as the relationship triangle's apex power, the United States put in place a security umbrella that helped prevent destabilizing regional arms races while, at the same time, protecting sea lines of communication (SLOCs) that have facilitated the massive growth of trade and commerce that have occurred throughout the region since the end of the Pacific and Korean Wars. This environment of peace and stability freed the nations of the region from the burdensome level of military expenditure that would have been necessary without the security umbrella the East Asian alliance system provided. This in turn allowed these nations to devote more resources to their own economic development, which then facilitated the rapid levels of economic growth that so many countries in this region experienced, ultimately making the Asia Pacific the world's largest and most dynamic region in terms of international trade and commerce.

The East Asian alliance system has endured for more than six decades, but since the end of the Cold War, the liberal international order this alliance system helped establish and maintain has come under an increasing amount of stress. This stress, both in the alliance system itself and in the international order it helped establish and sustain, comes principally from an evolution in power relations that has been occurring in the Asia Pacific for the last two to three decades. This evolution is being driven primarily by the sustained levels of rapid economic growth that China has experienced for several decades and also by the Chinese leaders' use of their country's increasingly abundant economic wherewithal to develop its military capabilities and expand its influence not simply in the Asia Pacific but also throughout the entire globe.

After former leader Deng Xiaoping implemented a series of market reforms in the late 1970s, China began experiencing a sustained period of rapid economic growth, which led to it becoming the world's second-largest economy, overtaking Japan for this position in 2010. Clearly, China has been able to achieve such levels of rapid economic growth because of the marketization and other economic reforms designed and implemented by its leaders, but it is also true that China's economic reforms were promulgated under a very supportive international environment.[8] Again, the reference here is to the liberal international order that the US-led East Asian alliance system established and maintained, which acted as an essential public good that kept the region's sea lines of communication open, allowing trade and commerce to expand freely throughout the region. This means that China—like South Korea, Japan, and other nations in the Asia Pacific—benefited from being able to implement carefully designed economic growth and trade expansion policies because of the environment of relative peace and stability that the US-led alliance system helped keep intact throughout the postwar period.

While the actual impact of China's rise to great power status is the subject of ongoing debates, a consensus has emerged among many scholars and analysts that the projection of Chinese military power in the East and South China Seas, as well as other foreign policy actions it has taken throughout the Asia Pacific and around the globe, is indicative of its long-term goal to create and lead alternative regional and international orders that better serve its domestic and international interests.[9] At best, China's rise and projection of power constitute a significant challenge to the East Asian alliance system and the liberal international order it has helped maintain in the Asia Pacific. However, while China's rise and the vision it promotes form the principal challenge facing members of the East Asian alliance system, other factors internal to the alliance system itself also undermine its effectiveness. These challenges stem from the long-term weaknesses that have existed in the South Korea–Japan "quasi-alliance" and from the exacerbation of these weaknesses by the United States' inconsistent and sometimes wavering commitment to the region.

These inconsistent levels of commitment have always concerned leaders in South Korea and Japan, but the negative implications of the United States not maintaining strong and ongoing levels of engagement with its allies have weakened the alliance system's ability to help maintain the region's overall peace and stability. To be sure, different presidential administrations have promoted different levels of engagement with the United States' Northeast Asian allies, with some administrations having alternative foreign and domestic policy priorities that diverted their strategic focus away from the Asia Pacific. For example, when the George W. Bush administration focused its attention on the Middle East and Afghanistan as part of its effort to wage a global war on terrorism after the September 11, 2001, attacks, the result was a reduced level of attention to the challenges the United States and its allies in Seoul and Tokyo faced in the Asia-Pacific region. This and other examples of shifts in levels of US engagement have rendered the United States' commitment to the region akin to a pendulum that has swung back and forth from a strong, focused commitment to its South Korean and Japanese allies, and the challenges of interstate relations in the Asia Pacific, to a less engaged and at times even hands-off approach.

Consider that, in response to the George W. Bush administration's enormous resource deployments to conduct the Iraq and Afghanistan Wars, the Obama administration in 2011 announced the "pivot to Asia." In this foreign policy shift, the United States made clear that, although it would continue certain aspects of the war on terror, its engagement in the Asia-Pacific region would significantly increase, leaving no doubt that the country would reengage with its South Korean and Japanese allies and the Asia-Pacific region overall. This recommitment was in part designed to mitigate the destabilizing influence of North Korean provocations and to help the United States and its allies in Seoul and Tokyo counter the rising economic and military power of China. This "pivot" was also an important part of not simply strengthening the United States' bilateral ties to South Korea and Japan but also helping these two allies find the common ground necessary to keep the base of the triangle of relations that makes up the East Asian alliance system on a more solid footing.

Barack Obama's "pivot" to the Asia Pacific presents a stark contrast to the approach to this region—and to other US allies throughout the world—taken by the Trump administration. While acknowledging Obama's concerns with a rising China and an increasingly provocative North Korea, this administration's overall approach involved an "America First" emphasis, which it applied to allies and adversaries alike. This different approach to US foreign policy elevated the importance of economic issues, particularly the elimination of the United States' bilateral trade deficits where they existed, which in turn put pressure not just on Beijing, which runs a large bilateral trade deficit with the United States, but also on leaders in South Korea and Japan, whose nations had also been running large imbalances.[10] Moreover, the Trump administration called on its Japanese and South Korean allies to increase their defense contributions, which significantly raised concerns about the United States' long-term security commitment to them as essential American allies.

It is true that having Seoul and Tokyo commit more resources to their mutual defense is not problematic in and of itself, but when the extremely high contributions Trump demanded were combined with his administration's lowered levels of engagement, the result was a weakened East Asian alliance system, which clearly redounded to the benefit of China. To be sure, the negative consequences of the Trump administration's approach were most likely not intentional, given that his administration did see China as a threat and, consequently, toughened the United States' trade stance by raising tariffs on many Chinese exports. Nonetheless, the Trump administration's demands for exorbitantly high South Korean and Japanese defense contributions, combined with its lowered levels of engagement with Seoul and Tokyo as essential partners in the East Asian alliance system, provided China with more opportunities to promote its own long-term goals in the Asia Pacific with less resistance.

The Trump administration's "America First" foreign policy approach resulted in much lower levels of cooperation on challenges of mutual interest and, thus, increased the distance between the United States and its allies in Seoul and Tokyo.[11] These negative developments in turn provided leaders in Beijing with more opportunities to manipulate the rules and norms that have governed the international order in the Asia Pacific and around the globe for many decades. As Jin Yinan, a professor at the National Defense University of the People's Liberation Army, observed, "as the U.S. retreats globally, China shows up" (Daalder and Lindsay 2018, 76). While motivated by a desire to improve the US position vis-à-vis its economic and trading relations, with both adversary and ally alike, the Trump administration's approach to American allies has not simply reduced the United States' leadership in the Asia Pacific and throughout the globe but also weakened the East Asian alliance system itself, rendering coordinated action between Seoul and Tokyo in response to regional problems—and also to problems in their bilateral partnership—much more challenging than they had been in the past.

Despite this negative assessment, the new Biden administration has brought more promise that the United States will step up and reengage with its allies in the Asia Pacific and around the globe, not simply to strengthen its current international partnerships but more importantly to reform and rebuild its long-standing alliances so that the liberal international order that has brought peace and stability to the Asia Pacific and elsewhere can survive current challenges posed by a rising China. Clearly, much changed during the four years of the Trump administration, but the promise of renewed American leadership does not mean that a return to the past— that is, a foreign policy informed by the days of US hegemonic domination of the Asia Pacific—is either advisable or even possible. What it does mean is that strengthening the current alliance system will also require its reform so that it better reflects the region's evolving political and economic dynamics.

Clearly, rebuilding and reforming the East Asian alliance system necessitates consistent US engagement and regional leadership because, without this element, it is increasingly likely that the Asia Pacific's evolving power dynamics will result in more opportunities for China to increase its influence and more easily reshape the liberal international order to better serve its interests. This is a course that will ultimately result in what current Singaporean prime minister Lee Hsien-Loong (2020, 53) refers to as the endangering of the "Asian Century" and all of the benefits it has provided to the United States and its allies. At the same time, the United States does not need to force either South Korea or Japan to choose between itself and China to overcome the US leadership deficit in the region. Rather, the countries need to not only strengthen the triangular relations that have long formed the architecture of this alliance system but also reform them so they operate with much more consultation and inclusiveness. Leaders in Seoul and Tokyo will need more flexibility both to strengthen their respective roles within the East Asian alliance system and to manage their own economic relationships with China while navigating this rising power's demands and challenges.

When we state that reforming the alliance system does not comprehend the United States forcing South Korea and Japan to choose between China and itself, we are not in any way implying that both South Korea and Japan should go their own ways, particularly in a manner that weakens the connections they have with the United States and with each other. Again, this is because a new, China-led international order in the Asia Pacific will be a partner to much more uncertainty than that associated with the current alliance system and because, as also stated above, an international order that is led by China will be structured around rules that elevate the exclusive interests of this increasingly influential and powerful country and the Communist Party that directs domestic and international behavior. These likelihoods then behoove leaders in Seoul and Tokyo to remain partners in the East Asian alliance system, firmly committed to the hub-and-spoke system that forms the foundation of this US-led international order, while at the same time finding a path that maintains continuity in these roles while allowing them to manage their deep economic ties with China.

This represents a course of action that is littered with challenges but none more pressing than the East Asian alliance system's weakest link, the partnership between South Korea and Japan, which became significantly strained a few years ago because of unresolved historical issues. This problem rests on a discrete number of unresolved issues that have divided these two US allies for many decades. These issues trace their origins to the period of Japan's occupation of the Korean Peninsula—which began in 1910—and its treatment of Koreans during this time, which became increasingly repressive throughout the years of the Pacific War. The specific issues that remain unresolved will be discussed in detail in the chapters that follow, but we note here that their salience in South Korea–Japan relations has played like a leitmotif, not simply weakening the effectiveness of their bilateral partnership when leaders in Seoul and Tokyo have been forced to address them but also accruing advantages to China in its efforts to rewrite the rules of the international order that have molded interstate relations in the Asia Pacific since the end of the Pacific and Korean Wars.

The point here is that resolving these issues that have historically challenged the health of the South Korea–Japan partnership—or at a minimum keeping them from resulting in heightened tensions between Seoul and Tokyo—is a necessity if the United States and its two allies are to strengthen the East Asian alliance system and endure the challenges represented by an increasingly influential China. Clearly, no scholar or analyst who has examined the challenge of South Korea–Japan relations will question the importance of addressing this problem of history, but simply asserting that this problem must be resolved for the reformation and strengthening of the East Asian alliance system does not mean that the data and arguments presented in the chapters that follow automatically contribute to our understanding of interstate relations in Northeast Asia. Indeed, the significance of any scholarly research effort rests with the insights and intellectual value it provides and the ability of the conclusions it supports to discernibly advance our understanding of such problems and ultimately of their solutions.

We are not the first to study this problem of South Korea–Japan relations and their importance for a robust and effectively functioning East Asian alliance system. To be sure, a growing body of scholarship exists, and we will evaluate this scholarship in the chapters that follow. In this evaluation, we will acknowledge that existing scholarly works have advanced our knowledge of this problem of South Korea–Japan relations and that the analyses we complete in the remainder of this volume have benefited from many of these contributions. Despite this, we will also reveal how existing scholarly work is characterized by certain intellectual gaps that our investigation addresses, resulting in a more complete understanding of how to think about these unresolved problems of history and build closer relations between Seoul and Tokyo so the East Asian alliance system can become stronger and continue to preserve the liberal international order that has molded interstate relations throughout the Asia Pacific for so long.

The intellectual gaps that we address below trace their origins to three unresolved issues in the scholarly literature, the positive impacts associated with the East Asian alliance system itself, the challenges posed by a rising China, and the importance of domestic political influences in South Korea–Japan relations. Concerning the first of these gaps, this issue rests with how scholars and analysts have treated the beneficial impacts of the East Asian alliance system itself. Specifically, the reference here is to the weight scholars have given to the supportive environment provided by the East Asian alliance system and the ways in which maintaining this environment molds the decision calculus of South Korean and Japanese leaders as they face their respective countries' futures in this region's interstate relations. Clearly, most scholars and analysts have acknowledged that this set of triangular relations has provided an environment of relative peace and stability in the Asia-Pacific region and that this in turn has allowed the remarkable expansions of trade and commerce that facilitated the high levels of economic growth and elevations of citizen prosperity we witnessed have in this region since the end of the Pacific and Korean Wars. No one has doubted or ignored these positive impacts, but simply acknowledging the positive role played by the East Asian alliance system does not really capture—and in fact unintentionally understates—how strongly South Koreans and Japanese, leaders and citizens alike, are committed to remaining part of this alliance system, problems in their bilateral partnership notwithstanding.[12]

In some ways, the benefits that accrued to South Korea and Japan— as well as other nations of the Asia Pacific, including China—have almost been taken for granted in the current body of scholarship. If the benefits that nations derived from the liberal international order this alliance system helped establish and maintain were given their appropriate weight, the continuation of this US-led alliance system would always be the principal factor influencing the strategic decisions made by leaders in Seoul and Tokyo. However, scholars and analysts assessing South Korea–Japan relations have not assigned this level of importance to the benefits that the alliance system has provided, and we know this because of how some scholars have mapped the strategic decisions that leaders in South Korea and Japan have and will continue to make as they face the challenges that exist in their own bilateral partnership, a rising China, and the role played by the United States as the alliance system's apex power. Specifically, many scholarly works have either implicitly or explicitly assumed that a course of action that involves South Korea and Japan abandoning their partnership with each other or their alliances with the United States can be weighted alongside strategic choices to maintain this alliance system in response to China's rising influence and past inconsistencies in the United States' commitment to the region.[13]

In contrast to this, we proceed from the notion that this assumption, implicit though it may be in the current scholarly literature, represents an intellectual gap in existing scholarship not because there is no possible scenario under which South Korea or Japan would willingly abandon the East Asian alliance system—there are possible, although very unlikely, scenarios that could lead to this extreme outcome[14]—but because leaders in Seoul and Tokyo will not simply consider abandoning the East Asian alliance system as part of their normal strategic decision-making unless they are absolutely forced to do so. Doing so would be tantamount to ending the liberal international order that has provided them with the numerous benefits they have enjoyed for so many decades. Moreover, any alternative international order would be attendant to much more uncertainty in terms of its effect on Seoul's and Tokyo's essential interests and, as we demonstrate in detail below, would clearly be reoriented to serving the expansionist interests of China as the region's new apex power.

Preceding from this assumption means that the analyses we provide in the chapters that follow must first provide a clear demonstration of the extent to which these two US allies have benefited from the East Asian alliance system, providing leaders in both nations with strong incentives to maintain the system and their essential roles within it. Only by making clear not simply how Japan and South Korea have benefited from this US-led alliance system but also how the benefits obtained by each country have involved high levels of economic growth, rising levels of domestic prosperity, and the growing international influence they both enjoy today can we conclude that, regardless of the challenges they face in their bilateral partnership or the pressure they experience from their economic relations with China, leaders in Seoul and Tokyo will always prefer the triangular relations of the East Asian alliance system to any alternative, China-led order. This is the task we undertake in chapter 2.

The second intellectual gap in existing scholarship that we address rests with how scholars and analysts have evaluated the impacts associated with an increasingly influential and assertive China, both in the Asia Pacific and around the globe. That China's rise has begun an evolution in the Asia

Pacific's power dynamics has been lost on no one who has investigated the South Korea–Japan partnership in the context of the Asia Pacific's interstate relations. Nonetheless, while it may be somewhat of an oversimplification, we can conclude that much of the early scholarly work on the impacts associated with China's rise has revolved around discerning China's ultimate intentions. Generally, these debates concern whether China is a revisionist power that seeks to rewrite the rules of the international order and remake the institutions that have governed this order throughout the postwar period or whether it is a status quo power committed to working within the rules and institutions of the current international order.

A large portion of this debate has investigated the motives behind China's new assertiveness in the region and around the globe, and this has involved the gathering of empirical evidence to support one view or the other. Clearly, these debates hold many insights and much intellectual value, and we will consider these contributions in our discussion of the scholarly literature. More important for our purposes, however, is that scholarly opinion on the impact of a rising China on the Asia-Pacific region, and the entire global system of interstate relations, for that matter, has been undergoing a shift. Specifically, recent publications increasingly reflect the view that China's rise will challenge the liberal international order that the East Asian alliance system has helped maintain since the end of the Pacific and Korean Wars because Chinese leaders have increasingly made clear that they intend to reshape existing rules and norms to better serve their interests. To have a more complete understanding of the impacts associated with an increasingly influential China, we will need to incorporate this more recent scholarship on China's vision for an altered international order into our discussion of the scholarship on its growing influence.

It is true that the vision for the international system the current Chinese leadership is intent on creating is being promoted with language embedded in such concepts as equality and inclusivity. Indeed, China's foreign minister noted in 2013 that his country would participate more "proactively in international affairs [for] a fairer and more responsible international system" (Rolland 2020b). While such language suggests that China's intentions are benign, if not salutary, the true test of its intentions will not be found in the language it employs, neither that used by its leaders in speeches nor that contained in the policy documents its Communist Party–led government produces, but rather in its actual foreign policy behavior, particularly in the Asia-Pacific region. We must conduct an empirical investigation that compares actual Chinese behavior in the Asia Pacific to the principles that are embedded in its vision, while also evaluating the results of this comparison to the challenges that China's actual behavior poses for member nations of the East Asian alliance system and their efforts to strengthen the triangular relations that underpin this system.

To accomplish the above, we begin with a mapping of China's economic and military rise and then turn to the scholarly literature that has assessed the intentions and impact of a China that has ascended to great power status. This discussion will naturally rely on ongoing scholarly debates about Chinese intentions, be they revisionist or status quo, but we will also focus on more recent scholarly assessments of China's vision for the alternative international order it is proposing to create. After assessing this literature and the evidence it offers, we then compare China's vision to its actual international behavior, again, with a focus on the Asia Pacific. What distinguishes our analysis of China's actual international behavior is that we add an additional dimension to our assessment, one that directly relates to how Chinese foreign policy behavior is directed toward not simply South Korea and Japan as individual nations, but more importantly these two nations as allies of the United States with respect to their roles as members of the East Asian alliance system.

A focus on this additional dimension is motivated by the incentives that Chinese leaders face in their efforts to implement their vision for an alternative order in the Asia Pacific as well as around the entire globe. Specifically, regardless of whether Chinese intentions are in fact benign because it is in fact a status quo power, or whether it is a rising power intent on remaking the current liberal international order, the truth is that it is in the interest of the Chinese leadership to undermine the East Asian alliance system and the set of triangular relations that forms its essential architecture. This does not mean that China is willing to risk direct war with the United States to accomplish its alliance-weakening objective, at least at this point in time, but rather that there is a clear relationship between the strength of the East Asian alliance system and the ease with which China can realize its vision for an international order in the Asia Pacific that is more conducive to its interests.

For that reason, a direct way for Chinese leaders to enhance the achievement of their goals is to use those unresolved issues of historical significance to divide South Korea from Japan and increase the diplomatic distance between them so that the result is a challenged and poorly functioning relationship between these two partner countries in the US-led East Asian alliance system. Indeed, as long as unresolved historical issues remain salient problems in South Korea–Japan relations, they will disrupt bilateral relations between these two US allies and extend the advantage to China in achieving its goals in the Asia Pacific. These unresolved problems of historical significance in South Korea–Japan relations are available for use as a policy asset by the Chinese leadership to achieve its aim to remake the international order in the Asia Pacific and around the globe. These are the topics that we will address in chapter 3.

The third contribution of our investigation starts with the fact that both South Korea and Japan are democratic countries, which means that their leaders will not be able to fabricate workable solutions to the challenges they face in their bilateral relations without the support of their respective publics for the contents of any agreement they work out. Because of this, we dedicate a significant portion of our investigation to public attitudes in both South Korea and Japan, covering a breadth of substantive areas that separate Seoul from Tokyo and assessing how the distribution of public opinion on unresolved issues of historical significance will act as either a constraint on efforts to hammer out compromises on outstanding issues or as an incentive to pursue a course of action that will not necessarily strengthen this partnership and could, in fact, result in a weakened relationship.

The examination of public opinion data in South Korea and Japan will cover how the South Korean and Japanese people view first the United States, as the current leader of the East Asian alliance system, and then China, as the region's rising economic and military power whose intention is to remake the liberal international order that has existed in the Asia Pacific for many decades. Public attitudes toward the United States and China and their roles in the region will be covered in chapter 4. This discussion will be followed by an investigation in chapter 5 of how respondents in South Korea and Japan view each other. This investigation will cover how the publics in each country view the other member of this partnership, the state of their bilateral relations, and the overall importance of their partnership in the East Asian alliance system.

Overall, the results of this investigation will show that public opinion has historically not been very supportive of efforts to find acceptable solutions to the unresolved historical issues that increase tensions in their

14 *Strengthening South Korea–Japan Relations*

partnership and weaken the East Asian alliance system. Evidence for this is witnessed in respondents' negative views of the other country and also in their lack of support for their leaders' attempts to broker compromises that are essential to ameliorate the destructive tendencies of unresolved historical issues. To illustrate this more clearly, we map public attitudes in South Korea and Japan on these unresolved issues of historical significance in chapter 6. The public attitudes we investigate relate specifically to the ongoing problems of disputes over contested territory, the tragedy of South Korean comfort women, and the issue of forced labor during the Pacific War and recent actions taken by South Korean courts relative to this outstanding issue. Our purpose in mapping the attitudes of South Korean and Japanese respondents on these issues is not simply to compare the perceptions of South Koreans versus Japanese on such unresolved problems, but more importantly, to determine if there are areas of common understanding that could allow leaders in both countries to begin to build some workable solutions that would be acceptable to the publics in both of these US allies.

This mapping of public attitudes on outstanding issues of historical significance will be followed by an examination in chapter 7 of how the Japanese and South Korean publics view the state of interstate relations in the Asia Pacific, particularly the competition that exists between the United States and China and the meaning that this competition bears for the future of the East Asian alliance system. Specifically, this effort will involve a close examination of how respondents in South Korea and Japan view the United States as the alliance system's apex power and how these attitudes compare to their perceptions of China as the region's rising power and potentially the new apex power. Recent data on the current Biden administration will naturally be included, but this examination will also include data pertaining to the Japanese and South Koreans' views on the United States' two previous presidents, Donald Trump and Barack Obama. This examination of public opinion data will reveal how the perceptions of the Japanese and South Korean publics have changed over time, and it will also highlight how these public opinion data indicate that South Koreans and Japanese have been consistent in wanting not just a stronger commitment to their alliances from US administrations but also an effort that reforms and strengthens the East Asian alliance system overall.

It is true that the examination of public opinion data we complete in these four chapters is more extensive than what we witness in other scholarly studies of South Korea–Japan relations that include analyses of survey data. While this difference is not insignificant, what distinguishes our scholarly examination of public opinion data, their relationship to South Korea–Japan relations, and the importance of US leadership in the Asia-Pacific region, is not simply how broad it is but rather how the patterns of attitude distribution we map in the chapters that follow touch directly on many of the important challenges that will have to be addressed if the East Asian alliance system is to remain an effective source of peace and stability in an Asia Pacific characterized by evolving power relations. Specifically, we take several distributions of public attitudes on important issues in South Korea–Japan relations and the influence of the United States versus China in the Asia Pacific and determine what these patterns say about possible ways to reduce the tension associated with unresolved historical issues between Seoul and Tokyo. We will also highlight what these attitude distributions suggest about the kind of action that the United States needs to take to strengthen the bilateral partnership between Seoul and Tokyo and improve the functioning of the East Asian alliance system overall.

Our examination of the perceptions of South Koreans and Japanese on these important matters is driven by the idea that any investigation of public attitudes on salient issues reveals whether an extant distribution of opinion will operate as a constraint on leaders from taking certain actions or an incentive for leaders to pursue specific policy courses. While most public opinion studies of South Korea–Japan relations have identified many more constraints, our examination does uncover areas of common understanding, which can help leaders in Seoul and Tokyo identify policy paths that could lead to compromises acceptable to the South Korean and Japanese publics. In this effort, we will not gloss over areas where public attitudes act as constraints on certain policy actions, but we will show that the negative attitudes that exist among the South Korean and Japanese publics do not foreclose on leaders in these two nations finding publicly acceptable solutions to problems in their bilateral relations.

Given the prevalence of negative perceptions that South Korean and Japanese respondents have of each other, this may seem like an overly optimistic evaluation of our public opinion analysis. Nonetheless, we find that this optimism is justified not simply because our analysis identifies areas of common understanding but also because it reveals that public attitudes in South Korea and Japan are not immutable and have responded in clearly identifiable ways to regional developments. This is very important because it is in the statics and dynamics of the views held by the publics of South Korea and Japan that we can understand how leaders in Seoul, Tokyo, and Washington can proceed to address the challenges they face in both South Korea–Japan relations and the overall robustness of the East Asian alliance system. If public attitudes were immutable and unresponsive to exogenous developments, it would be very difficult for leaders in Seoul and Tokyo to overcome the constraints that extant negative views present. This would not only lead to the problem of unresolved historical issues continuing to weaken the triangular relationships that form the East Asian alliance system's underlying architecture but also make it much less likely that the United States and its two Northeast Asian allies could begin reforming and ultimately strengthening the East Asian alliance system, preserving the peace and stability the region has experienced for so many decades.

The identification of constraints and opportunities that the attitudes of the South Korean and Japanese publics present to their respective leaders takes us to this volume's final topic, that of how the United States can help its two Northeast Asian allies improve their bilateral relations and then work with their respective leaderships to reform and strengthen the East Asian alliance system so it can withstand the pressures it has been enduring because of China's rising economic and military power. This will be the subject of an epilogue that constitutes the manuscript's eighth and final chapter, which begins with us emphasizing that strengthening the alliance system will require that its set of triangular relations be thoroughly reformed. The East Asian alliance system cannot be adequately strengthened by a simple restoration of past patterns that initially defined the alliance system's triangular relations, and this is because of the profound changes that have taken place in both South Korea and Japan and in the Asia Pacific's overall interstate relations throughout the last several decades.

In addition to China's rise, there is another aspect to how interstate relations in the Asia Pacific have changed dramatically, necessitating reforms rather than a simple restoration of the United States' previous role as the alliance system's apex power. The historic hierarchies that long existed in the alliance system's triangular relationships have undergone profound changes in the last two to three decades. The first of these is manifested in the changes that have been occurring in the inequalities that long-defined relations between Japan and South Korea. This relationship has evolved from a very notable hierarchy, with South Korea being the significantly weaker partner, to one of virtual equality, where South Korea is no longer the alliance system's most dependent power (Kim 2017). In addition to this, the extreme hierarchy that historically existed between the United States and each of its allies in Seoul and Tokyo has evolved, and these three allies have become much more equal, even though the United States remains the alliance system's apex power. These changes in the alliance system's hierarchies must be taken into consideration if the set of relationships that underpin the system is to be reformed in a way that will allow it to endure as the principal supplier of peace and stability in the Asia Pacific.

Emphasizing that the alliance system needs to be reformed is not tantamount to being clear about exactly what reforming it entails, particularly if the United States, South Korea, and Japan are to overcome the challenges they face with respect to one another and with respect to the liberal international order that the alliance system has created and maintained. The Biden administration has announced a commitment to rebuilding its alliance partnerships in the Asia Pacific—and also around the globe—but for this effort to succeed, discussions of how to reform and reinvigorate this alliance system will have to focus on two aspects of the current administration's approach—and that of any succeeding presidential administration—to reestablishing its leadership in the Asia Pacific and strengthening the East Asian alliance system.

The first aspect is the reform efforts directed specifically at the triangular relations of the alliance system itself—that is, the actions the United States can take to help rebuild the partnership between South Korea and Japan. It also refers to the specific ways that the United States can reform and then strengthen its separate bilateral relationships with each of its Northeast Asian allies. Reforming the East Asian alliance system in these two ways is necessary to rebuild its strength so it can function effectively in an age of growing Chinese influence throughout the region. Accomplishing this, however, will not be sufficient for the United States, South Korea, and Japan to be effective in maintaining the alliance system's regional influence and, thus, the ability to ensure the Asia Pacific's peace and stability in the future. A second aspect of US efforts to reinvigorate its regional leadership involves employing all of the diplomatic, economic, and military resources of the alliance system's members to stem the growing influence of China in the region and without provoking a war with this rising power. In our discussion of this aspect, we focus on the actions the United States, South Korea, and Japan will need to take and these actions' diplomatic, military/maritime, and economic components, all of which are necessary to enervate the growing regional and global influence of China.

2

The Origins of the East Asian Alliance System and Its Impact on South Korea and Japan

The East Asian alliance system has helped maintain an environment of relative peace and stability in the Asia-Pacific region for many decades, and, during this time, we have witnessed many nations in the region undergoing profound socioeconomic transformations. These transformations were driven first by immense expansions of commerce and trade, both among nations of the region and with others around the globe. The expansions of international trade facilitated some of the highest levels of economic growth witnessed in the postwar period, which greatly benefited the United States' two oldest allies in the region, South Korea and Japan, as well as such other Asia-Pacific nations, including China. It is interesting that the socioeconomic transformations that so many of this region's nations experienced was an unintended consequence of the East Asian alliance system because its establishment was premised on security calculations made by the United States to stem the rise of Communist influences in the Asia Pacific.

The United States' security concerns were necessitated by two sets of events in the aftermath of the Pacific War, the first of which rested on the relationships the United States had with China and Japan during that war and the dramatic changes in these relationships shortly after the surrender of Japan in 1945. The reference here is to the replacement of China with Japan as the United States' principal regional ally after the Communists defeated the Nationalist Government in China in 1949. The second set of events refers to the inability of the United States and other actors, particularly the Soviet Union and the United Nations, to agree to a formula that would result in a peaceful reunification of the Korean Peninsula, which was occupied by the Soviet Union in the North and the United States in the South. This failure to reunify the Korean Peninsula led to North Korean forces crossing the thirty-eighth parallel in June 1950 to reunify the peninsula by force. After three years of fighting, the Armistice of 1953 was promulgated, and the United States pledged to defend the government in Seoul against further invasions, maintaining troops on South Korean soil to that end.

These security conditions are the genesis of the East Asian alliance system, which is composed of two arms.[1] The United States–Japan arm of this alliance system began with the profound political change that occurred in China when the Communists defeated the Nationalists, which then precipitated a reverse course in the United States' approach to maintaining peace and stability in postwar Asia. Essentially, the United States elevated occupied Japan as its principal ally in the postwar Asia Pacific, which was no simple task because it forced leaders of the Allied Occupation to rethink their pursuit of thoroughly reforming Japan, particularly their use of deep, cartel-busting reforms that further weakened an already enfeebled Japanese economy. This economic problem led Occupation authorities to cease imposing widespread and somewhat punitive reforms on Japan and begin a rehabilitation process that involved, among other things, providing economic aid rather than breaking up the country's massive industrial and financial combines so that Japan could restart its manufacturing sector and restore other economic operations. Under Douglas MacArthur, the authorities also sought to hasten the end of their occupation of Japan, encouraging all former combatants to hammer out peace treaties with their former enemy and pursue reparations that were much more moderate than Japan's former combatants had been demanding.

The United States initiated the establishment of the Japan-US arm of the alliance system, starting the process whereby diplomatic and security treaties were drafted, signed, and promulgated between Japan and the United States as well as other nations that either had been occupied by Japan or had been one of its former combatants. Formal hostilities between Japan and its wartime combatants, as well as the Allied Occupation of the country itself, ended with the signing of the San Francisco Treaty. In September 1951, forty-eight nations agreed to the terms of this treaty, but addressing the security challenges that were emerging in the Asia Pacific would require one more agreement between the United States and Japan, one that was directly focused on the future security of Japan and the region.

The reference here is to what is known officially as the Treaty of Mutual Cooperation and Security between the United States and Japan, which was signed subsequent to Japan regaining its full sovereignty and provided the basis on which US-Japan security relations would evolve over the ensuing decades. This Security Treaty pledged both countries to resolve all conflicts in a peaceful manner and also required the United States to come to the aid of Japan in the event of violations of its territorial integrity or other threats to its security. To this end, the United States designed and implemented a Status of Forces Agreement in which it maintained military bases on Japanese soil. Initially, the Security Treaty and Status of Forces Agreement were very unpopular in Japan, especially in Okinawa, where the bulk of US forces were located and remain to the present day.[2] In spite of this, the US-Japan side of the East Asian alliance system increasingly earned the support of both leaders in Tokyo and the Japanese people because it helped maintain the stability of interstate relations in the Asia Pacific and provided the Japanese government the freedom it needed to rebuild its devastated economy and reconnect with the world.[3]

The South Korea–US arm of the East Asian alliance system began very differently than the US-Japan arm. South Korea, and the entire Korean Peninsula, for that matter, had been a colony of Japan since 1910,[4] and just before Japan's official surrender in 1945, the northern part of the Korean Peninsula became occupied by the Soviet Union, while the remaining portion south of the thirty-eighth parallel became occupied by the United States and its allies. Unlike in Japan, where the US Occupation worked with an operating Japanese government to implement significant reforms, the United States established a military government in the part of the Korean Peninsula it occupied, ignoring the appeals and protestations of the People's Committees that existed in all of the South's provinces. Resistance to the US-led military government was particularly strong in places like Cheju Island, and this resistance led the United States to use force to suppress the opposition it encountered.

The military government was replaced with the first postwar republic in 1948 under the leadership of President Rhee Syngman, whose government faced dire economic conditions and survived only because of significant US largesse. However, with very little hope of a peaceful reunification on the peninsula, in June 1950, North Korean forces crossed the thirty-eighth parallel in an effort to reunify the peninsula by force. The North's invasion quickly pushed US and South Korean forces back to the southernmost part of the peninsula, establishing a defensive line known as the Busan Perimeter. The perimeter initially held out against numerous Northern assaults, but it could not endure without substantial US reinforcements. While not all personnel in US defense and diplomatic circles argued in favor of a military response, President Harry Truman responded to President Rhee's appeals for assistance with a UN Security Council resolution in support of an international police action led by a large US military force.

The tide of the war changed quickly, especially after MacArthur's amphibious landing at Incheon.[5] However, with US-led forces pushing the North Koreans back to the Chinese border at the Yalu River, a large contingent of Chinese ground troops, combined with Soviet military aid and air support, intervened and pushed Allied forces back below the thirty-eighth parallel. North Korean and Allied forces moved each other back and forth for a time, but the battle line ultimately settled at the thirty-eighth parallel in a virtual stalemate.[6] This stalemate led to the negotiation of the Armistice of 1953 and a cessation of hostilities on the peninsula. It also resulted in the beginning of the US–South Korean arm of the set of triangular relations that formed the East Asian alliance system.

When the Armistice of 1953 was promulgated, South Korea was not simply devastated by the North's invasion; it was also isolated internationally and completely dependent on the United States for its security and economic aid. Moreover, to be certain that North Korea would not be tempted to repeat its efforts to reunify the peninsula by force again, the United States formalized its military relations with Seoul, effectively beginning in 1950. Naturally, this military alliance was implemented as an insurance policy to reassure the North that any new attempt to violate the South's territorial integrity would result in a strong military response, but it was also established because the United States wanted to connect this bilateral relationship to the one it had with Japan. This would complete the establishment of the East Asian alliance system so the United States could establish a clear perimeter beyond which the spread of communism would not be allowed.

A graphic representation of the set of triangular relations that constitute the East Asian alliance system is provided in figure 2.1. As the figure illustrates, the United States occupies the top angle as the alliance system's apex power, while the bottom two angles are occupied by South Korea and Japan. The sides of this relationship triangle represent the United States'

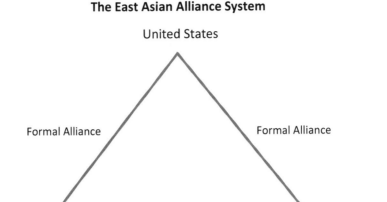

Figure 2.1. Source: Authors.

formal alliances with South Korea and Japan, which are presented in the figure as solid lines. The base represents the connection between Seoul and Tokyo, and as we see from the figure, it is not solid. Despite many common interests in the region, the South Korea–Japan relationship has been fraught with tension because Koreans were subjected to a thirty-five-year uncaring and increasingly brutal colonial regime established by Japan in 1910. Thus, no leader or citizen in South Korea would have chosen to have a relationship thrust upon them by the United States.

Because of this, the informal partnership between South Korea and Japan represented the weakest part of the newly established East Asian alliance system, which behooved the United States to help improve relations between Seoul and Tokyo. Many factors motivated the United States to push for a thaw in South Korea–Japan relations, among them the idea that an alliance system in which two members' bilateral relations were defined not simply by mistrust but also by near-outright animosity would be far less effective at thwarting the aggressive efforts of the region's Communist powers than one where relations were functionally amicable, even if only in a perfunctory way. In addition to this, the United States was also motivated to improve bilateral relations between South Korea and Japan

24 *Strengthening South Korea–Japan Relations*

because of the combination of the costs of the Pacific and Korean Wars and the increasingly high burden of having provided financial aid in the past to Japan and of sending growing aid amounts to South Korea was becoming unsustainable, undermining its ability to lead the East Asian alliance system.[7]

Options for the United States to accomplish this goal were limited, but the most logical place to begin rested with getting Japan to increase its engagement with South Korea and getting South Korea to accept closer ties with Japan. Japan was entering a period of economic rebound that would ultimately lead to an extended number of high-growth years, and, as a result, American officials believed it made sense for Tokyo to assume a larger financial burden in support of the East Asian alliance system. The US thinking on this matter was reinforced by the fact that South Korea was in dire need of economic help and required aid amounts that exceeded what the United States could continue to provide on its own. Moreover, South Korea's economic dependence was so deep that President Rhee Syngman used the aid from the United States to help fill in the substantial deficits that existed in his country's national budget (Kuznets 1977). Without substantial amounts of financial aid, President Rhee would not have been able to keep his government functioning.[8]

The problem the United States faced in its effort at reconciliation was that any attempt to reconcile with Japan was unacceptable to the Rhee administration, which initially thwarted US plans to have Japan assume larger shares of the financial aid that South Korea would receive. This problem frustrated US officials for a short time but became moot in May 1961 when a military coup placed General Park Chung-Hee in South Korea's Blue House. General Park did not harbor the same level of animosity that his predecessor, President Rhee, had held toward Japan,[9] and this made him agreeable to US desires for South Korea and Japan to mend relations and reestablish economic ties. With prodding from the United States, then, full economic and political relations between South Korea and Japan were reestablished, and this process began with the Treaty on Basic Relations between Japan and the Republic of Korea, signed in 1965, where Japan extended South Korea $300 million in the form of reparations, an additional $200 million in long-term credits, and a commitment for foreign direct investment from Japanese businesses that was close to the amount of reparations Japan would send to South Korea as part of this treaty. The result was an enormous initial sum of money extended to the South

The Origins of the East Asian Alliance System and Its Impact 25

Korean government that elevated Japan's status as an important provider of economic aid to Seoul.

The data in table 2.1 track how the sources of economic aid received by South Korea changed over time. We see that, in 1960, nearly 100 percent of economic assistance to South Korea came from the United States. Five years later, the US share declined by twenty-five percentage points, but the United States did remain South Korea's top provider of economic assistance for a number of years. By the middle of the 1970s, however, the US aid contribution to South Korea had continued to decline to just under 40 percent, reflecting the implementation of the Reconciliation Treaty with Japan. As expected, Japan came to provide more than one-third of South Korea's economic assistance while aid from other sources, including multilateral programs, assumed nearly one-quarter of the economic assistance Seoul received. These trends continued over the next two decades as US shares declined dramatically while the shares contributed by Japan continued to grow. By 1995, Japan was providing over 85 percent of the economic assistance South Korea received, with the remainder coming from sources other than the United States.

The implementation of this Treaty on Basic Relations, and the consequent rise in aid from Tokyo, did not render relations between these two US allies overtly friendly. Indeed, there were numerous protests against the Reconciliation Treaty, and there was also ongoing anxiety that South

Table 2.1. Sources of Economic Aid Received by South Korea, 1960–95

	United States		Japan		Others	
	Amount	Percentage	Amount	Percentage	Amount	Percentage
1960	248	99.32	0	0.00	1.71	0.68
1965	164.75	73.13	50.45	22.39	10.09	4.48
1970	132	56.17	91.33	38.86	11.7	4.98
1975	113	39.56	97.39	34.10	75.23	26.34
1980	47	22.48	125.6	60.08	36.44	17.43
1985	7	6.03	84.6	72.83	24.56	21.14
1990	4	1.36	240.63	81.67	50	16.97
1995	0	0.00	356.96	87.43	51.34	12.57

Amounts in the columns are in current US (millions) dollars and amounts in the Others column include economic aid from multilateral sources.
Source: Compiled by the authors from Organisation for Economic Co-operation and Development (OECD) official development assistance data.

Korea would again become a colony of Japan, but this time as an economic vassal state. Nonetheless, from this point on, leaders in Seoul and Tokyo made remarkable progress in building a workable bilateral partnership, which helped keep the East Asian alliance system intact despite the periods of increased tension that occurred from time to time. One reason for this was the fact that, from its inception to the end of the Cold War, the East Asian alliance system was put together in a strictly hierarchical manner.[10] Because the United States was the alliance system's apex power, South Korea and Japan typically followed its lead in their foreign policy decisions, something that was reinforced by these allies' dependence on the security umbrella provided by the United States (Roehrig 2017). In addition to this, there was also a significant hierarchy between South Korea and Japan, with the former being the alliance system's very junior power.

Both South Korea and Japan were economically and militarily dependent on the United States, but each's level of dependence was not the same, particularly as the postwar period progressed. Both South Korea and Japan received aid from the United States, and both required access to the US market for their exports. However, given that Japan entered a period of rapid economic growth earlier than South Korea, its dependence on the United States for economic aid declined more quickly. Also, as shown in table 2.1, South Korea became increasingly beholden to Japan as Tokyo assumed larger shares of the aid South Korea received. This economic dependence kept South Korea on the lowest rung of the alliance system's ladder of hierarchy (Kim 2004), but like Japan, South Korea also came to benefit from the security umbrella provided by the United States and the supportive economic environment provided by the US-led liberal international order. This environment facilitated South Korea's own period of rapid economic growth, which led to it experiencing higher and higher levels of prosperity for its citizens as well as a rise in international influence, which ultimately changed its relationship with Japan from one of hierarchy to one of relative parity.

South Korea's and Japan's Rise to International Influence

As stated above, despite the internal and external challenges it has and continues to face, the East Asian alliance system has held together and provided an environment of peace and stability throughout the Asia Pacific for many decades. This environment gave both Japan and South Korea the opportunity to accrue significant benefits, allowing them to implement domestic economic development policies that then led to significant expansions of international trade and long periods of rapid economic growth. The stories of Japan's and South Korea's postwar economic transformations are well known, but the scholarly literature on their respective economic successes has generally followed the developmental state tradition and, thus, focused on the state structures and the economic development policies these countries' leaders designed and implemented (Johnson 1982). This means that the environment of international peace and stability within which Japan and South Korea experienced their high levels of economic growth has not really been given its due. In the discussions that follow, we highlight the positive role it played in Japan's and South Korea's rise to international influence.

Both Japan and South Korea entered the Cold War period, suffering extensive damage due to the Pacific and Korean Wars. Before its surrender in 1945, Japan had been utterly destroyed by Allied bombing campaigns. There are different estimates, but most agree that over one hundred thousand residents were made homeless with every incendiary bombing campaign completed over Japan's largest cities (Kawai 1960; Reischauer 1970). Because of their cultural significance, only two cities, Kyoto and Nara, were spared the destruction the other urban areas experienced, and all of the nation's merchant fleet was destroyed by Allied ships and submarines. The same is true for South Korea because of the North's invasion, but there is another aspect to the challenges leaders in Seoul faced in the wake of the Korean War. Japan's colonial government supported industrial development in the northern part of the peninsula while making the South the colony's breadbasket. This placed most of Korea's manufacturing facilities north of the thirty-eighth parallel, which meant that the productive capacity in Korea at the time of the Armistice of 1953 was in the North and not the South. Thus, with the addition of the devastation that was partner to the North's invasion, whatever industrial capacity South Korea had was destroyed when the armistice was promulgated.

Despite the inauspicious conditions both of these US allies experienced in the wake of the Pacific and Korean Wars, Japan and South Korea entered into long periods of rapid economic growth that transformed their economic structures and led to substantial increases in levels of prosperity for the average Japanese and South Korean. These developments also resulted in each country experiencing a rise in international influence. For Japan, this economic transformation actually began in the late nineteenth century when Japanese modernizers transformed their country from a

28 *Strengthening South Korea–Japan Relations*

centrally controlled collection of medieval fiefdoms into a modern nation-state with an industrial economy and an increasingly powerful military. Because of this transformation into a modern nation-state, Japan clearly had the potential to rebuild itself after the war, but its recovery was not automatic, especially in the opening years of the Occupation period when Japan's economy was moribund and nearly 100 percent dependent on aid from the United States.

Japan's postwar economic resurgence began with the manufacturing booms it experienced after the start of the Korean War. This does not mean that its economic growth was monotonic; according to the Economic Planning Agency, Japan went through eight business cycles between 1960 and 1990 inclusive.[11] In spite of its cyclic nature, Japan's postwar economic resurgence is noteworthy because the country came to hold many of the world's most notable technologically advanced and leading-edge companies and its population continually enjoyed growing and widespread economic prosperity. Moreover, its high levels of economic growth led Japan to become the world's second-largest economy—a status it enjoyed until its position was overtaken by China in 2010—and one of the world's providers of economic aid to developing nations.

There are many indicators of economic development that we could examine to show how dramatic Japan's economic resurgence was. Indeed, indicators such as rates of economic growth and changes in the structure of the Japanese economy throughout the postwar period reveal the dramatic scope of Japan's postwar economic resurgence (Patrick and Rosovsky 1976). What is more important, however, is the extent to which the international environment of peace and stability created and sustained by the East Asian alliance system facilitated Japan's economic transformation. We noted above that one of the benefits of this alliance system was that it protected sea lines of communication (SLOCs), which in turn allowed for the dramatic expansion of international trade that occurred throughout the Asia-Pacific region. The East Asian alliance system made this incredible expansion of international trade and commerce possible, facilitating Japan's many years of high levels of economic growth, which, as all who have studied Japan's postwar economic resurgence have noted, was an export-led phenomenon.[12]

Data on the expansion of Japanese exports are provided in table 2.2, which covers the period from 1950 to 2015 and is divided into five-year increments. The data show that rates of export growth did decline over time but nonetheless remained positive except for the last year, 2015

The Origins of the East Asian Alliance System and Its Impact   29

Table 2.2. Japanese Exports: Value, Growth, and Percentage of GDP

Year	Export Value ($ Billions)	Growth	Percentage of GDP
1950	$0.83		
1955	$2.01	242%	
1960	$4.05	201%	9.14
1965	$8.45	209%	9.20
1970	$20.03	237%	10.36
1975	$63.99	319%	12.27
1980	$145.10	227%	13.13
1985	$194.35	134%	13.89
1990	$320.17	165%	10.22
1995	$488.88	106%	8.97
2000	$519.27	129%	10.62
2005	$666.35	129%	14.01
2010	$857.11	130%	12.52
2015	$773.03	90%	17.69

Source: World Bank (various years).

(Wood 1992). Indeed, until the mid-1980s, Japan's exports grew at over 200 percent each five-year period. We also see that, for the period of time covered by this series, exports as a percentage of the country's gross domestic product (GDP) grew substantially. Growth in Japanese exports slowed from 1985 to 2015 but still registered positive rates of expansion that averaged over 100 percent for this thirty-year period.

As the data in the table also suggest, from this time to the present, exports did assume an increasingly large share of Japan's GDP. Indeed, from 1960 to 1985, exports were 11.33 percent of GDP, but this grew to 13.25 percent after 1985, averaging nearly 18 percent since 2015. These data make clear the importance of the expansion of trade opportunities for Japan's overall economic performance, but this relationship is reinforced when we compare the expansion of Japanese trade with the dramatic rise that occurred in its per capita GDP. Most notable is that increases in trade and per capita GDP occurred parallel to each other, which allows us to conclude that GDP growth in postwar Japan was indeed facilitated by the expansions that occurred in Japanese exports. Moreover, the expansion of Japanese trade would not have been as dramatic as it was without the environment of peace and stability engendered and sustained by the East Asian alliance system.[13]

When we examine economic development data for South Korea, we can see how its economic resurgence was similar to that of Japan, and we

30 *Strengthening South Korea–Japan Relations*

can also see that the liberal international order provided by the US-led alliance system was an important factor that helped make South Korea's economic transformation possible. As stated above, South Korea was devastated by the North's invasion and, after the Armistice of 1953, ended up with an economy that was in utter ruin. It is also important here that, unlike Japan, South Korea had not transformed itself into a modern nation-state, let alone one with an incipient but modernizing industrial economy, as Japan had done. This means that the conditions that defined South Korea's entrance into the divided Cold War world were even more inauspicious than those faced by Japanese leaders eight years earlier. In fact, some US foreign policy leaders felt South Korea should be abandoned because it would never produce anything on its own that any other nation would want to import. Fortunately, as witnesses to South Korea's current economic status know well, such dire predictions proved to be false.

According to adjusted 2019 data, South Korea's economy was ranked twelfth in the world, something that is remarkable because, well into the 1970s, South Korea was still behind such countries as the Philippines in terms of its level of economic development. Data on South Korea's economic growth are presented in figure 2.2, where the left-hand y axis reveals the total amount of its international trade and the right-hand y axis reveals growth in its per capita GDP. Data in figure 2.2 on the left-hand y axis indicate that South Korean international trade experienced modest growth in the first two decades after the Korean War but then grew at increasingly high rates. Specifically, from the end of the Korean War to the mid-1960s, growth in South Korean trade remained relatively flat, but trade began to grow modestly over the next fifteen years. From 1985 to 2010, growth in South Korean trade began to accelerate, where increases in the levels of South Korean trade expanded dramatically.

Throughout this period of time, we also see that growth in South Korean per capita GDP paralleled South Korea's growing engagement in the world trading system, as is indicated by the figure's right-hand y axis. Specifically, in the 1960s, South Korea was undoubtedly a poor country as its per capita GDP was less than $200. In the following decade, South Korea remained a relatively poor country even though its per capita GDP more than doubled to just less than $500. By the 1980s, however, South Korea had become more prosperous as growth accelerated, producing a per capita GDP of over $5,000. Although it suffered economic declines in the next two decades because of the Won Crisis of the mid-1990s and the

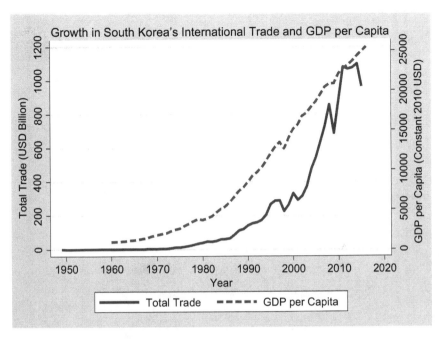

Figure 2.2. Source: OECD International Development Statistics.

financial crisis of 2008,[14] South Korea's per capita GDP has continued to increase, and in 2016 it increased to nearly $28,000.

The relationship between trade expansion and growth in per capita GDP very much resembles the patterns we provided above with respect to Japan in that they both grew in tandem. While we cannot say with absolute certainty that South Korea would not have experienced the rise to international influence it experienced without its membership in the East Asian alliance system, we can demonstrate that it was South Korea's growing levels of international trade—which were facilitated by the international order that the alliance system helped maintain—that encouraged the profound transformation in the country's political-economic system. Evidence for this connection begins with the fact that not only did South Korea possess a large supply of increasingly skilled and educated labor but, more importantly, labor was South Korea's abundant factor of production, which economic studies of the South Korean economy indicate was never in short supply (Amsden 1992; Kuznets 1977). Perhaps the best evidence for this is the fact that the South Korean economy was not able to absorb all available labor early on in the aftermath of the Korean War because, in 1960, as much as 20 percent of South Korea's industrial and agricultural labor force was unemployed (Reeve 1963).

South Korea's labor force continued to increase throughout the next several decades, and as both GDP and trade expanded, South Korean labor became increasingly absorbed into the labor market, and workers experienced increments in their wages. This occurred even though compensation levels for workers were strictly controlled by the South Korean government, and labor movements for wage increases were often strongly and sometimes violently suppressed. The importance of these developments is reinforced by the data in figure 2.3, which reveal the dramatic and ongoing growth that occurred in the country's real GDP per worker.[15] South Korean workers became more prosperous over time, which in turn provided them with more wherewithal to become politically active and more capable of advocating for their essential interests.

This growing pressure from South Korean workers resulted in them obtaining increased political rights, as indicated by the corresponding rise in democracy, also captured in figure 2.3.[16] Specifically, Korean workers

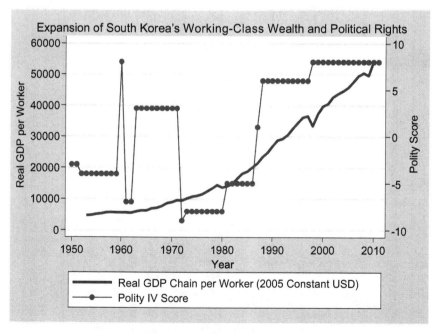

Figure 2.3. Source: OECD International Development Statistics and Polity IV.

secured a limited expansion of political rights in the 1980s, corresponding to the wealth gains they had been experiencing from the country's growing international trade. However, this expansion of political rights was at its greatest when the country transitioned to and consolidated its democracy. Again, this process would not have been possible without labor, as the country's abundant factor, experiencing the economic gains it did from the rapidly growing international trade.[17] When trade expands, it benefits the owners and users of a nation's abundant factors, and as stated above, in South Korea this meant labor (Stolper and Samuelson 1941). Consequently, South Korean labor became more prosperous as trade expanded, allowing workers to advocate for more political rights, which then increased pressure on the government to open up and ultimately become more democratic.

The expansions of international trade and rising levels of economic prosperity that both Japanese and South Koreans experienced throughout the postwar period are important phenomena in and of themselves, but they also point directly to the central question we address in this volume: specifically, whether the economic transformations experienced by South Korea and Japan would have occurred to the extent that they did without the environment of peace and security that the East Asian alliance system helped provide. We turn to the evidence for this relationship in the final section of this chapter.

The Supportive Impact of the East Asian Alliance System

Both Japan and South Korea implemented domestic economic development strategies that encouraged the continued expansion of exports, which also, over time, led to their exported products becoming increasingly high in their capital and technological contents. Clearly, the policies that were put in place encouraged the high levels of economic growth that both countries experienced. It is also clear that the positive impacts associated with the economic development policies designed and implemented by leaders in South Korea and Japan were made possible at least in part by the supportive international environment put in place and maintained by the US-led East Asian alliance system. This assertion makes intuitive sense given that the economic rise of these two countries occurred under the liberal international order put in place in the aftermath of the Pacific and Korean Wars. Nonetheless, pointing only to an obvious temporal relationship between these allies' economic transformation and the nature of the international order under which their transformations occurred still begs the question of whether or not the East Asian alliance system facilitated South Korea's and Japan's dramatic economic developments. To address this outstanding question, we focus on the export-led component of the development strategies of leaders in South Korea and Japan.

It is well known that, throughout both the Cold War and post–Cold War years, the Asia Pacific experienced a dramatic expansion of trade and commerce, and this expansion occurred among the nations of the region itself and with other nations around the globe. Naturally, the relative peace and stability the alliance system provided through the US-led security guarantee and its protection of SLOCs supported the efforts of nations in the region to expand their trading relations. This is not to suggest that the building of trading relations was automatic; it did require certain efforts on the part of leaders, and both South Korean and Japanese leaders devoted much effort to expanding the economic relationships of their respective countries. The reference here is to both countries establishing and then expanding their formal diplomatic connections, which research has shown is highly important in nations' efforts to build trading relations. This is especially true for Japan and South Korea, which were forcibly cut off from the rest of the world in the immediate aftermath of the wars they fought.

A certain body of scholarly literature on the relationship between trade and diplomacy is known as the "trade follows the flag" perspective (Pollins 1989a, 1989b). The idea that "trade follows the flag"—that is, that nations use the tools of diplomacy for economic reasons—is not new, and these connections have been measured and calibrated, indicating how changes in "state-to-state diplomatic relations" have affected trade flows between these nations (Pollins 1989b; Patterson and Choi 2018, 2019). Brian M. Pollins identified very strong empirical connections, allowing him to conclude that diplomacy significantly boosted trade between nations with formally established diplomatic relations and that this was true even when he controlled for all the standard economic factors that traditionally go into explaining nations' levels of international trade.

There are many reasons that "trade follows the flag" (Pollins 1989b), but there is strong evidence that diplomatic relations are a very important factor in both establishing and increasing flows of goods between pairs of nations who have formal diplomatic relations. This is because diplomatic relations help reduce the "fixed entry costs" exporters encounter when entering the market of a new nation (Ferguson and Forslid 2014). Given these relationships, it is expected that trade levels will increase between nations who have established formal diplomatic relations.[18]

There is little doubt that decisions that concern the establishment of trading relations involve the type and quality of goods to be exported or imported as well as their price. However, such economic and product-specific factors are not the only ones that nations factor into consideration of whether or not to establish trading relations with new nations or to expand trade with existing partners. To ensure that they can continue to operate in mutually beneficial ways for the long term, nations entering into a trading relationship will want some assurance that the other country will be economically reliable and unlikely to be involved in political or social disruptions that will negatively affect economic relations. Having such assurances will minimize risk and help guarantee that a country's business interests are protected. The best method to provide such certainty is to ensure that the lines of communication remain open by establishing and maintaining formal diplomatic relations.

Again, we are not saying that diplomacy is the only factor determining the direction and level of trade that occurs between pairs of nations. To be sure, trade between nations will also depend on certain geopolitical factors, such as whether or not a nation is a member of a free trade area or whether there is a common language between the traders, filling a role similar to that played by the English language in the economic relations of the Commonwealth nations or other languages shared by nations with a similar colonial past.[19] There is also the impact of a nation's membership in a currency union, and perhaps the most important example of this factor would be the European Union, where transactions take place among member states in euros.[20] Finally, there is distance, which affects the costs associated with moving goods and services across countries, continents, and oceans. Rather, our point is that having diplomatic relations is not simply an important factor but perhaps the principal force behind the initiation of trading relations between two nations and the increase in volumes of trade where such relations already exist.[21] Along these lines, Andrew Rose (2007) found that the establishment of an embassy led to trade increasing by 120 percent and that the creation of additional consular offices within a country increased bilateral trade by 6–10 percent for each office established.[22]

At the end of the wars they fought, Japan and South Korea were initially cut off from the rest of the world. Japan's case of international isolation began with its loss of sovereignty during the Allied Occupation, which meant that its leadership could not implement any independent foreign policy initiatives that did not meet with the approval of MacArthur. South Korea was also completely isolated not just because the Armistice of 1953 resulted in it being completely dependent on the United States but more importantly because, as a former colony of Japan, it had no formal diplomatic relations when Japan surrendered. As a result, to expand their respective levels of international trade and thus effectively implement their export-led economic development strategies, both South Korea and Japan would have to reconnect themselves with nations from which they had been cut off.

The first step in this process involved leaders in both countries establishing or reestablishing formal diplomatic relationships with potential trading partners. Such diplomatic efforts were necessary not simply because Japan and South Korea needed to connect with nations from which they had been cut off but more importantly because, without such formal diplomatic relationships, the implementation of their export-led economic development policies would have faced significant barriers. In light of the data provided above, we know that both Japan and South Korea experienced massive expansions of international trade, and we also know that both experienced periods of rapid economic growth that fueled both nations' rise to the positions of international influence they enjoy today. What we have not examined is the extent to which leaders in Seoul and Tokyo were successful at reconnecting their initially isolated nations with the rest of the world. To map the diplomatic gains of Japan and South Korea in the aftermath of the wars they fought, we use the Correlates of War's "Diplomatic Exchange Data" (Bayer 2006; Singer and Small 1966; Small and Singer 1973). We examine two measures in particular: first, a count of each country's formal diplomatic relationships and, second, a measure of how both Japan's and South Korea's diplomatic successes translated into their standing in the world.[23]

Looking first at Japan, we know that all the formal diplomatic connections Japanese leaders had established were ended when hostilities in both the European and Pacific theaters in World War II ceased in 1945. All foreign and domestic policymaking in Japan was conducted under the Allied Occupation, which lasted until Japan regained its sovereignty in 1952. Throughout the last years of the Occupation, Japanese leaders had been working with the United States to rehabilitate itself as a peaceful and

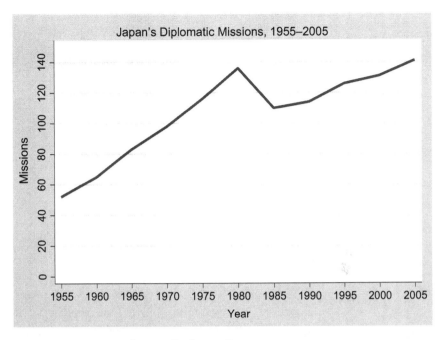

Figure 2.4. Source: Diplomatic Exchange Data.

democratic nation, part of which meant reconnecting with nations that were part of the US-led bloc of allies in the emerging Cold War. The formal diplomatic relations established by Japanese leaders are plotted in figure 2.4, which indicates that, by 1955, Japan had established formal diplomatic relations with fifty nations.

Japan's formal diplomatic connections more than doubled over the next three decades, but, as the graph also indicates, its relations with other nations did drop a small amount in the 1980s. This was the period of Japan's bubble economy, during which the value of land in Tokyo alone was reputedly more expensive than the land in all of the United States and Canada (Wood 1992), and, as a result, many of its poorer diplomatic partners were forced to close their offices in its capital city. After the bursting of the bubble economy in 1989, Japan's formal diplomatic connections recovered to reach a high point in 2009, the last data point we have reported in this series. The data presented in figure 2.5 measure Japan's international status, and we note that, according to the Correlates of War's "Diplomatic Exchange Data," Japan's international status was already quite high by 1955. This relatively high level of international status as Japan entered the Cold

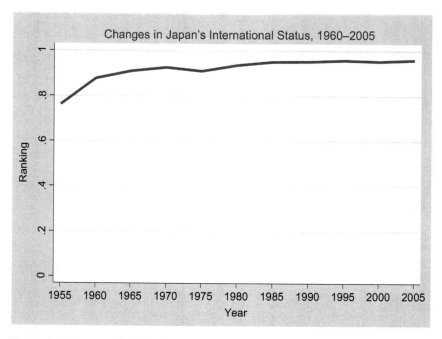

Figure 2.5. Source: Diplomatic Exchange Data.

War world continued to grow over the next decade and has remained high throughout the remaining years for which these data are available.

Like Japan, South Korea experienced a dramatic increase in its formal diplomatic relations throughout the years of the Cold War, but its rise to international influence began very differently. Because it was colonized by Japan from 1910 to 1945, it joined the family of nations with very few formal diplomatic relationships. Once it regained its sovereignty in 1948, its president, Rhee Syngman, began the process of establishing diplomatic relations with selected nations,[24] although his efforts were interrupted by the invasion of North Korea in June 1950. Nonetheless, over the next several decades, South Korea's place in the world changed dramatically because of the increase in the number of embassies that its leaders established throughout the world.[25] As the data in figure 2.6 indicate, from 1955 to the end of the decade, South Korea more than doubled the number of embassies it established, but it also sent a half dozen consuls abroad as well as two representatives to international organizations. In the 1960s, however, South Korea's diplomatic presence in the world grew even more dramatically, as President Park Chung-Hee nearly tripled the number of

The Origins of the East Asian Alliance System and Its Impact   39

Figure 2.6. Source: Diplomatic Exchange Data.

embassies that existed in foreign capitals.[26] As the data in figure 2.6 also make clear, after a very short stall, growth in South Korea's formal diplomatic contacts continued, albeit at a slower pace. By the end of the 1980s, South Korea maintained embassies in over ninety nations, a growth of nearly 3,000 percent from the end of the Korean War.

The diplomatic successes of South Korea's presidents are listed in table 2.3, where they are divided into two periods: the period prior to its democratic transition and the period after this transition.[27] The data in the table tell us that South Korea's presidents experienced different levels of success when it came to establishing formal diplomatic relations with the nations of the world. In the pre-transition period, Park Chung-Hee was the most successful of South Korea's presidents in reconnecting his country to the world diplomatically (Lee 1963). Chun Doo-Hwan continued this trend of diplomatic expansion, as did his successor, Roh Tae-Woo, who was the first democratically elected president since the Park Chung-Hee era.

By the time the country completed its transition to democracy—a period that corresponded with the winding down of the Cold War—the country had achieved over 80 percent of the diplomatic contacts it currently

40 Strengthening South Korea–Japan Relations

Table 2.3. Diplomatic Successes of South Korea's Presidents in the Pre- and Post-transition Periods

Presidents	Embassies	Consuls	Representatives	Total
Pre-transition				
Rhee Syngman	9	4	2	15
Yun Bo-Sun	0	0	0	0
Park Chung-Hee	55	20	0	77
Choi Gyu-Ha	0	0	0	0
Chun Doo-Hwan	17	4	1	22
Post-transition				
Roh Tae-Woo	8	3	1	12
Kim Young-Sam	4	2	1	7
Kim Dae-Jung	6	8	1	15
Roh Moo-Hyun	9	9	0	18
Lee Myung-Bak	4	4	1	9
Park Geun-Hye	1	1	0	2

Source: Compiled by the authors from the Ministry of Foreign Affairs and Trade's "Diplomatic Missions Established by Year."

maintains. The end of the Cold War offered opportunities for South Korea's democratically elected leaders to continue connecting to nations with which it had yet to establish diplomatic relations.[28] As the data in table 2.3 indicate, most of South Korea's new diplomatic contacts in the post-transition period came under the leadership of somewhat left-of-center presidents, Kim Dae-Jung and Roh Moo-Hyun.[29] The diplomatic successes that South Korea's leaders achieved resulted in a concomitant rise in its international status. By 1960, South Korea had only 10 percent of the number of embassies in Seoul as did the United States in Washington, DC, the country with the most diplomatic posts in its national capital at the time these results were calculated. This changed dramatically over the next ten years, however, as South Korea's international status ranking grew by sixty percentage points. There was a drop in the middle to late 1970s,[30] but the data in the figure tell us that South Korea's international status continued to increase, reaching over 90 percent of the world's number one diplomatic power by the early 1990s.

As we stated above multiple times, Japan and South Korea experienced significant increases in their economic growth, dramatic expansions of international trade, and increasing levels of prosperity for their respective populations throughout the postwar period. Clearly, the economic development policies designed and implemented by Japanese and South Korean leaders contributed to these outcomes. This is perhaps why it has been the development policies and state structures that have received the most attention from scholars who have investigated the economic rise of Japan, South Korea, and other nations in the Asia Pacific. The dominant theme of extant scholarship has been how the high levels of economic growth South Korea and Japan experienced were driven by policies that encouraged export expansion, but these studies did not address the question of how these two nations successfully implemented export-led development policies when they entered the divided world of the Cold War in near isolation and having only recently regained their sovereignty.

The answer to this question is that leaders in Japan and South Korea engaged in foreign policy efforts that reconnected their nations to the world by establishing formal diplomatic relations with numerous countries around the globe. The growing number of diplomatic connections were vitally important for their respective nations' economic development because they were an essential part of these leaders' efforts to expand the number of nations with which they traded, which was the only way they could realize the goals of their export-led economic development policies. In other words, Japan's and South Korea's export-led policy efforts succeeded because their respective leaders increased the number of countries with which they could trade by establishing and maintaining formal diplomatic relations with those countries.

This connection between diplomacy and trade then behooves us to focus our attention back on the East Asian alliance system—specifically, the fact that it created and maintained an environment that facilitated the expansion of international trade that South Korea and Japan increasingly engaged in throughout the postwar period, which in turn drove the high levels of economic growth both countries experienced. Again, this alliance system helped accomplish this by functioning as an international public good that protected SLOCs, allowing for a free flow of goods that continued to grow in substantial amounts throughout the Cold War and post–Cold War years. The East Asian alliance system, as an international public good, has had a facilitating impact because it has been protected by the security umbrella that the United States provided, not just to its Asia-Pacific allies but also to all nations around the globe that wanted to grow their international trade portfolios.[31]

For the East Asian alliance system to continue functioning in the positive way it has in the past requires first and foremost a clear and steady US commitment to the region, especially in light of its role as provider of the region's security umbrella and also in light of the positive influence it has had on leaders in South Korea and Japan and their ability to solve the challenges they face in their bilateral relations. Moreover, the robustness of the East Asian alliance system and its ability to continue as a source of long-term peace and stability in the Asia-Pacific region has presupposed that the liberal international order this alliance system established will continue without any challenge to the rules and norms that have guided its essential operations for so many decades. As stated above, this is no longer true as an increasingly powerful China has not only created a change in the Asia-Pacific's power dynamics but also made clear its intention to change the current rules and norms that have molded interstate relations in the region for many decades in a way that renders them more conducive to Beijing's interests.

What is interesting is that the United States' security umbrella and the postwar Asia Pacific's environment of peace and stability, which the East Asian alliance system helped provide, facilitated China's economic and military resurgence. Nonetheless, because the country's current leadership is intent on remaking the postwar liberal international order that the United States led throughout the postwar period, we turn next to China's rise and the challenges its ascendance poses to the set of triangular relations that form the underlying architecture of this alliance system.

3

China's Rise and the Asia Pacific's International Order

South Korea and Japan are the oldest and most dependable allies the United States has in the Asia Pacific, and their six-decade alliances have not simply endured; they have also remained robust partnerships that helped maintain peace and stability in this region for many decades. To be sure, the individual roles played by South Korea and Japan in the East Asian alliance system have not been the same, because, as explained above, the circumstances that led to each's alliance with the United States were different. Moreover, their informal partnership with each other in the East Asian alliance system has involved many challenges, and these challenges have certainly varied over time, which sometimes resulted in increased and even damaging levels of tension between Seoul and Tokyo. Nonetheless, bilateral relations between South Korea and Japan have stayed intact and continued as the base of the East Asian alliance system's set of triangular relations.

Since the turn of the century, however, China's growing economic and military influence in the region—and around the globe, for that matter—has posed a direct challenge to the East Asian alliance system and rendered a smoothly operating South Korea–Japan partnership more difficult than at any time in the past. This is not just because China's rise initiated an evolution in the region's power dynamics, elevating its influence at the expense of that of the United States,[1] but more importantly because China's current leadership has formulated an evolving vision for global interstate relations that it intends to implement to reform the current liberal international order and perhaps even to replace the order that the United States and its allies put in place after World War II (Rolland 2020a, 2020b; Tellis 2020). What is important for our purposes is that, as China continually employs its growing economic wherewithal and military power to realize its alternative international vision, no part of the world will be more

44   *Strengthening South Korea–Japan Relations*

directly affected than the Asia Pacific. Consequently, even short of China replacing the current liberal international order with its alternative vision, its growing power and influence have already resulted and will continue to result in ongoing challenges to the East Asian alliance system, particularly its most fragile link, South Korea–Japan relations.

China's rise and its vision for an alternative international order has prompted many scholars and analysts to assess what these developments mean for the reality of global interstate relations and the interests of the United States as the apex power of the East Asian alliance system. The debates have tended to focus on whether China's intentions are truly revisionist and intended to replace the postwar liberal international order or whether they are status quo in that its international rise will occur more or less in concert with existing norms and institutions. This has been an important debate that is partner to many insightful discussions that undoubtedly inform our assessment of China's rise to great power status. We will acknowledge these contributions so that our assessment builds on this scholarship, but we will also note the limitations that exist in current scholarly work as we evaluate the impacts of China's rise, particularly on the South Korea–Japan arm of the triangular relations that form the East Asian alliance system.

Our discussion of China's growing regional influence and its vision for a new international order will focus first on a growing body of literature dedicated to understanding this vision and its implications for the US-led international order in the Asia Pacific. Recent scholarly work notes that China's leaders have been developing and promoting an international vision that is evolving and being constantly updated by both Chinese scholars and Communist Party officials. We will naturally examine these Chinese contributions, but we will also examine assessments made by scholars and analysts in the United States, South Korea, and Japan. Of particular note in this examination is the contrast that exists between the Chinese explanations of the concepts that form their country's alternative vision and international goals and the non-Chinese assessments that not only have attempted to derive meaning out of these concepts but have also explored how to square these concepts with China's international behavior and what changes and continuities we can expect in the future.

While certainly varied in tone and substance, Chinese elaborations on their country's vision for an alternative international order have emphasized not just the conceptual basis of their evolving vision but also the conviction that this vision's foundational concepts will lead to great improvements in interstate relations compared to the outcomes that have occurred under the current system. In other words, Chinese analysts argue that their alternative vision will lead to an international order that is more just and equitable for a greater number of the world's nations. Non-Chinese analyses tend to agree that the concepts underlying China's vision, while laden with Chinese cultural and civilizational references, do imply an international system that is generally more representative and just than that which exists under the current order. On the other hand, non-Chinese scholars and analysts do not share the same level of optimistic enthusiasm as Chinese leaders express about the salutary results of realizing this vision.

Non-Chinese analysts do not all agree on the impacts that will be associated with a China-led international order, but they do share several points of agreement. Specifically, non-Chinese analysts note that, under Xi Jinping, Chinese leaders have become increasingly vocal in their criticisms of the current international order the United States and its allies have led for many decades. They add to this that Chinese leaders have become increasingly vocal about their desire to shape the global discourse along the lines of China's vision for a significant revision of the current liberal international order. In addition to these points, non-Chinese analysts also agree that the vision Beijing is promoting has been carefully couched in language that speaks to treating nations more equitably and justly than the current system ostensibly does. This does not mean that these analysts express no doubt that a new China-led order will result in an international system that matches the goals contained in their evolving vision; there is much skepticism that any of the positive outcomes Chinese leaders promise will in fact occur.

Our purpose then is to determine what impact ongoing Chinese efforts to implement their vision for an alternative international order will have on the East Asian alliance system, and South Korea–Japan relations in particular, as well as on the long-established liberal international order that has helped maintain peace and stability in the region for so many decades. While there is no singularly correct way to approach this question, we will do so by examining the actual international behavior of China. Specifically, we will investigate how specific foreign policy actions of China have affected Japan and South Korea as individual nations and how each's bilateral relations with Beijing have been affected by China's growing influence in the Asia Pacific and around the globe. We will also focus on how South

Korea and Japan have responded to China's growing economic and military power, noting the differences in their reactions and the effects those responses have had on their bilateral partnership. Moreover, we will also discuss what Seoul's and Tokyo's responses to China's growing power and influence implies for the United States' attempts to renew and strengthen its leadership in the Asia-Pacific region.

In this investigation, we are interested in evaluating China's foreign policy behavior toward South Korea and Japan, particularly with respect to how Chinese leaders respond to incidences of rising tension between these two US allies. Specifically, we will note and evaluate any and all of Beijing's direct or indirect actions that have helped raise tension in the South Korea–Japan partnership and China's exploitation of this increased tension to promote its own interests in the region. This assessment will be guided by the assumption that, regardless of whether China's international goals are reformist and complementary to the norms and institutions that make up the current liberal international order or are manifestly intended to replace them entirely, China's international behavior in the Asia Pacific is assisted by increased tension in South Korea–Japan relations. This is because challenges in the partnership between Seoul and Tokyo weaken the East Asian alliance system overall, and nothing helps leaders in Beijing advance their international vision more than a weakened East Asian alliance system.

Indeed, a weakened alliance system will provide less resistance to China's efforts than one that is robust, where all alliance partners can put up a common response to China's efforts to undermine the current liberal international order in the Asia Pacific. Moreover, the most direct way for the Chinese leadership to weaken this alliance system is to focus the attention of leaders in Seoul and Tokyo on the challenges that exist in their own bilateral relations, which can result in increased diplomatic distance between them. Beijing can best accomplish this by exploiting the most volatile issue in South Korea–Japan relations, the problem of unresolved historical issues. This problem has received much scholarly attention, but it has not been discussed as an important part of China's realist strategy to drive a wedge between Seoul and Tokyo so it can more easily proceed with its efforts to revise the international order in the Asia Pacific to better serve its own interests.

We begin our discussion of China's efforts to increase the distance between South Korea and Japan and undermine the East Asian alliance system overall with a review of China's rise to great power status.

China's Rise to Great Power Status under the East Asian Alliance System

There are many reasons that China has been an important regional and world power throughout the postwar period. Indeed, it has been the world's most populous country for many years, it has veto power on the United Nations Security Council and, in 1964, it joined the group of nations that are nuclear powers. However, before China entered the long period of rapid economic growth it continues to experience, it was a very poor nation with limited ability to influence international affairs in the profound way that it currently affects interstate relations in the Asia Pacific. This changed because of the market reforms that Chinese leader Deng Xiaoping put in place, which since that time have fueled the rapid economic growth that in turn allowed for the strengthening of its military power. As a result, and particularly in the past two decades, Beijing's ability to influence interstate relations in the Asia Pacific and, ultimately, remake the liberal international order that the United States and its allies established at the end of World War II has grown dramatically.

Economic growth in China began to accelerate almost immediately after the implementation of Deng's market reforms, but as stated above, the country remained poor for quite a while afterward. Indeed, in 1990, China's per capita GDP was a meager $317.88, which was more than $40 behind India's per capita GDP and just 9 percent of Russia's. Ten years later, China's per capita GDP had grown substantially, becoming double that of India's and increasing to over 50 percent of Russia's. However, from this time at the turn of the century, growth in China's per capita GDP has accelerated even more, and the prosperity of its people has begun to rise dramatically. From 2000 to 2010, China's per capita GDP quadrupled to over $4,500, and seven years later, it nearly doubled to $8,826.99. After 2010, economic growth continued at a rapid pace, often at double-digit rates, but even with rapid economic growth, China is still a long way from catching up with the United States and Japan in terms of GDP per capita.[2] China's 2019 per capita GDP of $10,261.70 is still less than 15.7 percent of that of the United States at $65,298.51 and just one-fourth of Japan's.[3]

In addition to rapid economic growth, the years after the market reforms were implemented witnessed a significant expansion of China's international trade. In 1995, China exported just under $150 billion in products and registered imports at just less than that amount ($132 billion).

Twenty-two years later, in 2017, its exports had grown to $2.26 trillion while its imports had grown at nearly as dramatic a rate, reaching $1.84 trillion. This remarkable level of growth in China's international trade is partly the result of the economic development policies its leaders designed and implemented. Nonetheless, China's domestic economic development policies alone are not sufficient to account for the dramatic increases in its international trade volumes. The dramatic expansion of China's international trade was also made possible by the postwar period's peaceful and stable international environment in the Asia Pacific and around the globe. This is important not simply because of the facilitating role played by the East Asian alliance system in maintaining this supportive international environment but also because China's trade growth helped put it in a more advantaged economic position with respect to South Korea and Japan.

China, once dependent on both South Korea and Japan for trade and aid, has reduced these twin dependencies by using its long period of rapid economic growth and development to diversify its growing trade portfolio. We see from the data in table 3.1 that China occupied small percentages of the trade portfolios of both Japan and South Korea in 1992. Indeed, Japanese and South Korean exports to China in that year were well below 5 percent of their overall exports. The same is true for imports from China, which were less than 5 percent for South Korea but slightly higher for Japan at 7.26 percent. Twenty-four years later, however, the importance of China in the trade portfolios of these two US allies had changed dramatically. In 2016, imports from China represented over one-fourth of all of Japan's imports, while its exports to China had grown over four times, to 17.65 percent of all Japanese exports. For South Korea, by 2016, over 20 percent of its imports were from China, and over one-quarter of South Korean exports went to China. These trends indicate that Japan and South Korea have become much more dependent on the Chinese market both as a source of imports and as a destination for their exported products and services.

The data in the lower portion of the table reveal how China's dependence on Tokyo and Seoul for exports and imports has changed over the same period of time. In 1992, China received nearly 20 percent of all its imports from Japan, and it also exported over 13 percent of all its goods and services to Japan. In 2016, this reliance on Japan for imports had dropped significantly, as China more than halved its dependence on Japan from 19.60 percent to 9.17 percent. For the same period of time, China

Table 3.1. China's Importance as a Trading Partner for South Korea and Japan

	1992	2016
Japan		
Imports from China	7.26%	25.79%
Exports to China	3.51%	17.65%
South Korea		
Imports from China	4.56%	21.41%
Exports to China	3.46%	25.12%
China		
Imports from South Korea	3.25%	10.10%
Exports to South Korea	2.83%	4.47%
Imports from Japan	19.60%	9.17%
Exports to Japan	13.75%	6.16%

Source: World Bank (various years).

also halved the percentage of products that it exported to Japan from 13.75 percent in 1992 to 6.16 percent. For South Korea, changes over time, while mixed, still led to Seoul becoming more dependent on Beijing economically. Chinese imports from South Korea tripled between 1992 and 2016, while Chinese exports to South Korea nearly doubled. China's dependence on the South Korean market, however, did not grow nearly as much as did South Korea's dependence on the Chinese market. While China's dependence on imports from South Korea nearly tripled between 1992 and 2016, they still remain only 10 percent of China's overall imports. Also, Chinese exports to South Korea nearly doubled over the same period of time, but they remain relatively small, occupying less than 5 percent of China's overall exports.[4]

It is clear from the data provided above that China's rapid economic growth, which was driven in large part by its expanding volume of international trade, not just in the Asia-Pacific region but also around the entire globe, has resulted in it gaining a more economically advantageous position vis-à-vis South Korea and Japan. China's growing economic advantage in the Asia Pacific becomes even more notable when we consider that, in the last two decades in particular, leaders in Beijing have been devoting more of their country's expanding economic wherewithal to growing its

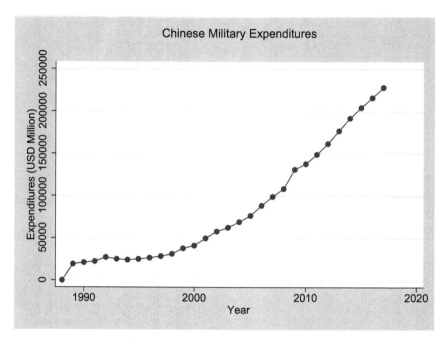

Figure 3.1. Source: World Bank.

military capabilities. As we see from the data in figure 3.1, China's military expenditures were relatively modest throughout the 1990s, during which time they grew in relatively small increments. After 2000, however, growth rates in China's military expenditures rose substantially, as the data in the figure make clear, and when we compare Chinese expenditures to those made by Japan and South Korea, we see clearly the profound difference that this growth has had.

The data in table 3.2 compare average growth rates in military expenditures for these three countries for the 1990s and the first decade of the 2000s. We see from this comparison that South Korea's military spending increased an average of 3.5 percent and that Japan's increased as well but at a much lower rate of less than 1 percent. For both periods of time, increases in China's military spending were nearly three times that of South Korea and over nine times greater than Japan's. These differential rates of increase in military expenditures led to predictable changes in spending balances among China, South Korea, and Japan. Total military expenditures for these three countries are presented in the form of a bar graph in figure 3.2.

Table 3.2. Average Growth Rates in Military Expenditures

	South Korea	Japan	China
Overall	3.5%	0.7%	9.4%
1990s	3.0%	1.5%	7.4%
2000s	3.8%	0.2%	10.6%

Source: Stockholm International Peace Research Institute.

We see that, in the late 1980s and early 1990s, Japan contributed the most to total military expenditures for these three countries. However, given that Japan's rates of expenditure remained quite low while South Korea's and China's expenditures grew modestly for the former and dramatically for the latter, it is not surprising that China's military spending assumed the largest share of military spending for these three East Asian countries. Indeed, as the data in the figure indicate, China's share has continued to expand at such rates that, by 2016, its military expenditures were more than double those of South Korea and Japan combined.

China's increased military spending has allowed it to make significant improvements in its military hardware and to expand not just the number and quality of its military bases but also their functional importance. Concerning its military hardware, China has produced and deployed three aircraft carriers, and it is currently in the process of producing a fourth, which will be its largest and will contain its most sophisticated weaponry, with more aircraft carriers being planned. China's fleet of carrier-based fighter aircraft were initially knockoffs of the Russian-made Sukhoi 33 aircraft with some domestically produced improvements in radar and weapons systems. The designs of these J-15 aircraft are decades old, but China has been replacing them with the Chengdu J-20 aircraft, a fifth-generation, long-range, stealth-capable fighter plane, the first of which came into service in 2017. In addition to this advanced aircraft's fighting capabilities, the Chengdu J-20 also has aerial refueling capabilities, which gives it the ability to engage in long-range combat missions.

These and other improvements in Chinese military capabilities have been partner to numerous land reclamation projects in which China has turned many of the South China Sea's shoals, reefs, and islands into military installations. The result of its efforts is that China now possesses a growing

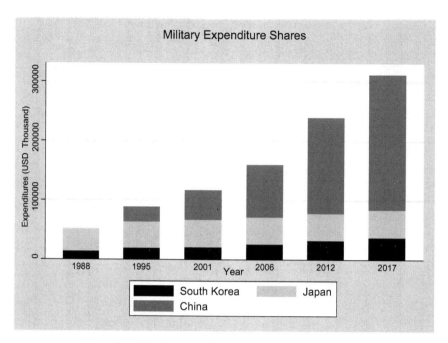

Figure 3.2. Source: World Bank.

number of military installations throughout the South China Sea, including barracks, radar stations, weapons encampments, ten-thousand-foot runways, and aircraft hangars. China's efforts in reclaiming this land and constructing different types of military facilities have until recently progressed with little resistance from the United States,[5] and this is also true of Chinese military expansion to other parts of the globe—specifically, beyond the East China and Yellow Seas. The Naval Division of the People's Liberation Army has already initiated a number of naval support projects in more than ten countries, particularly countries that have ports on the Indian Ocean and adjacent bodies of water (Erikson 2019). Among the more notable of these projects is China's development of a military facility in Djibouti on the Horn of Africa and, after extensive negotiations with the government of Pakistan, one in Gwadar on the Gulf of Oman.[6]

China's Vision for a New International Order

The questions that China's rise to great power status raise involve more than simply asking what its leaders plan to do with their country's growing economic and military influence, both in the Asia Pacific and around the globe. Indeed, they also involve assessing the impacts that China's international behavior has already had on the East Asian alliance system and exploring what the results of this assessment portend for the future of the US-led liberal international order that has been in place for many decades. There have been numerous attempts to answer these questions, particularly those involving the long-term goals of China's current leaders, and efforts by scholars to address such issues thus far have included references to historical analogies because of the concepts and language being employed in Chinese discussions of their country's alternative international vision.

Because references to history typically require extensive qualifications that often reduce the directness of comparisons being made across different time periods or other clearly defined contexts, conclusions derived from such approaches can be suggestive but do not lend themselves to solid, evidence-based generalizations. In the case of investigating the goals behind China's growing influence in the region and around the globe, this may be less of a problem principally because China's role as an Asia-Pacific power has deep historical roots that its leaders make frequent reference to in their evolving vision for an alternative international order that more directly supports China's strategic interests.

Indeed, from the beginning of the Ming dynasty, founded in 1368, to the late eighteenth and early nineteenth centuries when multiple European powers increasingly encroached on Chinese sovereignty, Asian international relations were governed by a unique system in which imperial China was the apex power. The word *governed* is used intentionally here because the Asia-Pacific region during this multicentury period was not structured in the same way as the Westphalian system of nation-states used in Europe and the West from the seventeenth century on. Rather than being composed of formally equal and sovereign nation-states that interacted with one another in an anarchic system to advance their individual interests, international relations in a large part of the Asian region throughout this time were defined by a tribute system where member states were, by definition, subservient to a hegemonic imperial China. Under this system, the interests of the member countries were not formally separate from those of China, while at the same time, each was required to pay tribute to the emperor and his court in exchange for the peace and stability that Chinese economic and military power provided (Kang 2010).

This tribute-based international system brought peace and prosperity to the region under Chinese suzerainty for many centuries, but with growing pressure from more-powerful European countries in the nineteenth century, Chinese hegemony and, ultimately, Chinese sovereignty were undermined, bringing the system to a slow, and, for China, ignominious end. The decline of China led to destructive wars and the temporary rise of Japan as the region's new hegemon, but the destruction of the Chinese tribute system did not see the restoration of peace and stability until the end of the Pacific and Korean Wars when the East Asian alliance system, under a strategic umbrella maintained by the United States, was put into place (Roehrig 2017). While Chinese sovereignty was restored with the surrender of Japan, its status as the region's center of civilization and dominant cultural, economic, and military power was not. Indeed, China was for many decades a secondary power, but this changed, particularly in the last two to three decades, when it began its rapid climb to great power status.

As an ascendant regional and global power, China has clearly become more active in promoting its economic and security interests, and since the appointment of Xi Jinping to the position of Chinese Communist Party (CCP) general secretary in 2012, it has also become increasingly vocal about having more influence on how the postwar international order is structured and operated.[7] This latter effort has involved a growing number of Chinese criticisms of the US-led postwar international order, which have increasingly included statements of Beijing's vision for an alternative international order as well as the impacts its vision will have on the current US-led liberal international order. As stated above, these developments have resulted in numerous scholarly debates, one of which involves determining whether China is a revisionist or status quo power.[8] In these debates, the former label suggests that China's rise will not simply challenge the current liberal international order but more importantly remake the norms and institutions that have underpinned this system of interstate relations for many decades. The latter label holds that China's rise will be peaceful and will occur in accordance with the rules and norms that currently structure interstate relations in the Asia-Pacific region as well as around the globe.[9]

These debates have produced many important insights, and, while most are not focused directly on the East Asian alliance system from the perspective of the essential role played by healthy relations between Seoul and Tokyo, they still inform our assessment of what China's growing regional influence means for the liberal international order that this system has helped maintain for many decades (Johnston 2003; Kastner and Saunders 2012). Our assessment of the impacts of China's rise begins with the point that China's rise has already been attendant to profound implications for the region's power dynamics and, in particular, the roles played by the United States, South Korea, and Japan in their bilateral and triangular relations as members of the East Asian alliance system.[10] Indeed, the influence of China in the Asia Pacific is a fait accompli that will continue to increase as it becomes more powerful and increasingly assertive in promoting its interests, and this means that stable relations between Japan and South Korea, essential for the East Asian alliance to continue as the overarching international architecture in the region, have already been negatively affected.

Before examining how China's rise has negatively affected the informal partnership that exists between Seoul and Tokyo, we must first examine Beijing's alternative international vision and the criticisms its leaders have leveled against the existing liberal international order. This effort begins with us making the point that Chinese criticisms of the US-led international order are nothing new and have been made by many of China's leaders (Chu 2020; Rolland 2020b). Most Chinese complaints have centered on perceptions that the United States and its allies have been interfering in matters that Chinese leaders see as their country's internal affairs and that are thus off-limits. Of particular concern are issues surrounding the status of Taiwan, Beijing's efforts to change the political dynamics in post-1997 Hong Kong, and anything that has touched on China's human rights record. Complaints from Chinese leaders about these issues have not diminished in recent years, but they have been joined by an additional chorus of Chinese declamations over the flaws in the current international order and the claim that the realization of China's alternative international vision will provide solutions to what is wrong with the current international arrangements (Schweller and Pu 2011).

Chinese criticisms of the liberal international order established in the wake of World War II mention not just that the system is dominated by the United States and its allies—what Chinese leaders refer to collectively as biased Western powers—but also that these nations are wont to impose their "Western" values on China and other nations rather than allowing them to govern themselves in obeisance to their own values. Moreover, leaders in Beijing complain that China has been denied a voice in any discourse that could address such systemic issues, denying Beijing the chance to share the benefits of its own experience given what it has accomplished over the last several decades and to help create a more just and equitable international system. To correct this situation, scholars and party leaders in China have begun to evolve a vision for an alternative world order that is informed by their country's economic achievements, which when implemented will allow China to help solve world problems, like climate change and global poverty, which Chinese leaders claim current international leaders cannot solve.[11]

It is true that, in the last four decades, China has experienced consistently high levels of economic growth, which have helped its leaders solve the enormous poverty problems they faced in the past and elevate the prosperity levels of the Chinese people. China's increasing economic wherewithal has also provided its leaders with the resources necessary to grow its military power and put the country on the path to great power status. These achievements are notable to be sure, but leaders in Beijing are championing them not just as significant national accomplishments that developed countries should recognize but also as hallmark developments that are uniquely Chinese—that is, specifically derivative of China's cultural and civilizational roots. As a result, references to China's culture and unique wisdom underpin its vision for an alternative international order, which its leaders assert will result in a more just and equitable world, particularly for developing nations.

In a special report on China's efforts to design and implement an alternative to the current US-led liberal international order, published in January 2020,[12] researchers at the National Bureau of Asian Research identified a number of concepts that are at the heart of Beijing's vision of an international order its leaders assert will be more peaceful, stable, and just. The concepts that constitute the ideational foundations of China's evolving international vision have been, and will continue to be, subjected to a process of nearly constant updating and revision not just by CCP officials but also by scholars selected by the party, whose main purpose is to elaborate on, and revise when necessary, China's alternative vision so that the nations of the world will be more receptive to it (Rolland 2020b).

The foundational concepts of China's vision speak to a unique Chinese identity and experience that derives not just from its cultural and civilizational superiority but also from its actual economic accomplishments over the last several decades. As suggested above, these two sources are not separate: the former, China's cultural assets and civilizational superiority, have been the principal driver of the latter, China's notable economic accomplishments. As a result, the concepts that form the ideational foundations of China's vision are then endowed with more practical meaning by leaders who promote them as being the wellsprings of China's rapid economic growth and, thus, economic ascendance. It is the combination of these cultural assets and economic experiences that leaders in Beijing want to share with the developing world so that these nations can enjoy the same prosperity and benefits that have accrued to the Chinese people under CCP leadership.

This is the vision Chinese leaders are promoting, but parallel with China's promotional statements are aspects of its international vision that are not spoken of by party leaders and scholars. These generally unspoken qualities of China's alternative international vision, however, do come into relief when the vision's ideational foundations are examined more deeply and China's foreign policy behavior is scrutinized more closely. Some observations note that a China-led international order will very likely be an extension of how leaders in Beijing manage their country's domestic affairs (Denmark 2020; Rolland 2020b), which suggests that China's alternative international order will be based on a reinvigorated Confucian ideology where the CCP remains unchallenged at the apex of power in Beijing and, by extension, at the top of the international order with which its leaders intend to replace the current US-led system (Foot 2020; Goh 2020; Rolland 2020a; Singh 2018).

CCP documents that discuss this vision employ numerous positive-sounding diplomatic concepts to capture certain aspects of the vision they are promoting (Rolland 2020b). These concepts include but are not limited to such salutary references as amity, mutual benefit, inclusiveness, joint contributions, and shared benefits.[13] Many of these concepts are purposively employed to suggest the benefits that will accrue to nations who accept China's alternative international vision, but to understand more clearly what this order actually means for the international order in the Asia Pacific maintained by the United States and its East Asian allies, we must look more closely at the vision's umbrella concept, *Tianxia*, or all/everything under heaven.

The concept of all under heaven is vague with respect to what it implies for the nations of the world, but we can say that it comprehends an international system with identifiable features. Some of these features are promoted vocally and with no hesitation by leaders in Beijing, while others—those that are in no way less associated with Tianxia—are not front and center in China's promotion efforts. Specifically, Chinese leaders repeat often and loudly that Tianxia conceives of a world order that is stable and peaceful, almost in a utopian way. At the same time, leaders in

Beijing do not hesitate to note that this stable and peaceful world under Tianxia will also be more just and equitable, especially for poorer nations that have not as yet experienced the benefits of development. What party leaders and appointed scholars have not announced is that the underlying architecture of Tianxia is composed of a rather rigid hierarchy with the apex of power located in Beijing. Indeed, Tianxia is a concept that has deep historical roots and recalls the period of time when not only was China at the apex of power in a Confucian-style tribute system but it was also the system's dominant civilization and guiding culture.

Having China replace the current liberal international order with one that, no matter how peaceful and stable, places the CCP at the top of its power pyramid will naturally raise suspicions in the United States and among its allies. This is why leaders in Beijing have emphasized some features of its vision but not others, and it is also why part of Beijing's efforts in this area have begun with it acknowledging that the nation-state will remain as the basic unit of the reformed international order it seeks to lead (Callahan 2008; Dreyer 2015). Moreover, focusing on these internal contradictions of Beijing's international vision helps us understand why Chinese leaders emphasized their commitment to having peaceful relations and a mutually beneficial coexistence with those Western powers that dominate the current liberal international order and why they propose building "a community of shared interests, destiny, and responsibility" (Shiu 2020, 46).

In addition to putting forth its promotional rhetoric, China has taken certain international actions that its leaders hold up as demonstrating its singular intention to create a more peaceful and stable international order that brings the benefits of its own economic development to as many nations as possible. The most notable illustration of this commitment to share its economic development successes with other nations is its Belt and Road Initiative (BRI), which nations may choose to join.[14] For nations that choose to participate in this initiative and experience the economic development benefits that the Chinese people have enjoyed, as leaders in Beijing claim, these nations must first engage in consultation with BRI officials. They will then proceed to consult with Chinese officials to work out a plan of action for development that will be judged on the economic benefits it will bring to both countries (Shiu 2020).[15]

There may be some truth to Chinese statements that its government has and will continue to approach all nations that join its BRI in generally the same way—that is, by consulting with their leaders on the kinds of development projects that will result in mutual benefits while, at the same time, ignoring participant nations' internal affairs, especially those aspects that relate to human rights. The same cannot be said for how Beijing has approached US allies and other advanced nations throughout the globe, and this is particularly true for the United States' two East Asian allies, South Korea and Japan. Aside from its rhetoric of treating all nations equally, Beijing has targeted these two US allies in East Asia for very different treatment because of how they fit differently into China's vision for a new order in the Asia Pacific.

The Impact of China's Rise on South Korea and Japan

As shown above, China's levels of trade and economic engagement with South Korea and Japan have increased dramatically throughout the last two to three decades, and both Seoul and Tokyo now stand among China's most important trading partners. Despite this, these two US allies will play very different roles in the alternative international order Chinese leaders are endeavoring to realize (Kim 2019). Chinese leaders view Japan as a regional competitor, something that is true, a fortiori, because of Tokyo's ever-closer relationship with Washington. Because leaders in Beijing have grudgingly accepted Japan's closer connections to the United States, and even with the uncertainties brought to this bilateral alliance by the Trump administration,[16] their approach to Tokyo involves limiting its influence in the Asia-Pacific region and around the globe (Tokuchi 2021).

The Chinese approach to South Korea, on the other hand, is quite different because Beijing's goals with respect to Seoul involve luring it away from the United States and bringing it more into its own orbit of influence. This does not mean that China has been applying constant pressure on South Korea to leave its long-established alliance with the United States because Beijing's diplomacy toward this longtime US ally has involved both positive soft-power diplomacy and aggressively negative sanctions-based actions. China has employed the soft-power approach to build closer and closer relations with South Korea at the government, business, and citizen levels. China's more negative actions, on the other hand, have been employed either to prevent or overturn South Korean actions that move it away from Beijing to much closer relations with the United States and Japan, especially in the area of military affairs.

Clearly, Chinese efforts have not reached their ultimate goal, as South Korea's alliance with the United States remains firmly intact. Acknowledging this, however, is not the same as saying that China's carrot-and-stick approach has netted no benefits; both its soft- and hard-power approaches have been partner to many successes. Consider Beijing's softer approaches to encourage greater levels of engagement with South Korea, not just with the government in Seoul but also with South Korean businesses and the South Korean people. As data provided above have shown, Sino–South Korean trade has revealed dramatic growth in the last two decades. At the same time, Chinese leaders have been successful in growing China's ties with South Korea, especially at the citizen level, as cultural and educational exchanges have increased substantially. These efforts have made Seoul closer to Beijing than at any time since the end of the Korean War, and evidence for this is witnessed in the fact that South Korea has sent more students to study in China than any other nation has (Shambaugh 2005). Consider that, in 2003, South Korea sent over thirty-five thousand students to study in China but that, in 2017, this number grew to over seventy thousand students.[17]

In addition to its success with employing a positive, soft-power approach, Chinese leaders have also been successful at preventing Seoul from cooperating more closely with the US and Japanese militaries by using negative, sanctions-based tactics. A notable case of Chinese success in this area involves Beijing employing strong economic countermeasures when South Korea agreed to join with other US allies in installing a THAAD (Terminal High-Altitude Area Defense) missile defense system. Initial talks with the United States began with President Park Geun-Hye, who agreed to join this defensive effort, and they continued with her successor, Moon Jae-In, who agreed to maintain South Korea's membership in it. Even though the United States and South Korea assured Beijing that the system's deployment was designed only to counter short- and medium-range missiles from North Korea, which had been engaging in provocative behavior, Chinese leaders remained unconvinced and adamantly opposed to South Korea becoming part of this defense initiative.

Indeed, when South Korea agreed to join the THAAD system defense pact, China's reaction was swift and damaging. Beijing expressed concerns with the THAAD system's radar capabilities, which it feared would interfere with its own defense efforts in the region. To get South Korea to reverse its decision to join this defense pact, China began a campaign of economic sanctions that included cutting back on cultural and entertainment exchanges as well as imposing new restrictions on South Korean firms operating inside China.[18] South Korea under Moon Jae-In maintained its participation in the THAAD system but did partially acquiesce in China's demands by limiting improvements to the systems that had been installed in South Korea. When he campaigned for the South Korean presidency, Moon did note his opposition to this missile defense system, but with Pyongyang's ongoing nuclear testing, he concluded that THAAD was necessary for South Korea's defense and recently did agree to significant upgrades to already-installed THAAD systems.

These cases indicate not simply that the relationship between South Korea and China is much closer than it has been in the past but also that Seoul is more susceptible to pressure from Beijing, revealing some success in China's efforts to achieve its goals in the region. Evidence of Beijing's success is also witnessed with respect to Japan, despite the fact that Tokyo, like South Korea, remains firmly committed to its alliance with the United States. Chinese efforts to limit the influence of Japan in the Asia Pacific are evident in Japan's ongoing dispute with China over a group of islands known as the Senkaku Islands or, in Chinese, the Diaoyu Islands. These islands are currently uninhabited and were administered by the United States after the end of the Pacific War as part of the Ryukyu Island chain that included Okinawa.

These islands were given back to Japan when the United States, after occupying them during the Pacific War, returned Okinawa to Japanese sovereignty. When this transfer of sovereignty had been completed, however, both China and Taiwan protested, asserting that they had been taken from China after the first Sino-Japanese War in 1895 and that, since they were illegally arrogated by imperial Japan, they needed to be returned to China. Sovereignty over these islands remains in dispute, and ongoing tensions are fueled by the fact that both China and Japan want to maintain the ability to exploit their resource potential, which includes deposits of crude oil and natural gas. China is also motivated to control these islands because doing so would represent its successful rollback of Japan's influence in the region, particularly because sovereignty was transferred to Tokyo by the United States. To this end, China has sent naval and coast guard vessels into the area around these islands, and Japan has responded in kind to maintain its sovereignty over them.

Satisfied with neither the status quo nor with China's behavior toward this island territory, the Japanese government in September 2012 purchased the Senkaku Islands from their private owner, announcing Tokyo's ownership of this disputed area. Chinese leaders protested this action and a year later responded with an announcement that they were erecting the East China Sea Air Defense Identification Zone. This defense zone requires that any aircraft entering a very large area encompassing that body of water must prefile a flight plan with the appropriate Chinese authorities and possess the required equipment to maintain communication with Chinese officials while flying in this zone. Japan responded to this announcement by sending units of the Air Self-Defense Forces to the Senkakus, which initially heightened tensions. Shortly thereafter, however, officials in Tokyo worked to de-escalate tensions and maintain a stable but unsatisfactory status quo.

These several cases tell us that China's intentions toward South Korea and Japan are different, and they also suggest that the responses of Seoul and Tokyo to growing Chinese pressure reflect patterns that are distinctive, the fact that both South Korea and Japan maintain their separate alliances with the United States notwithstanding. Specifically, Japan has voiced its concerns about the increasing influence of China in the region, and it has also resisted Chinese pressure when it has been directed specifically at Japanese interests. Moreover, Tokyo has moved closer to the United States to help it continue to resist Chinese efforts to limit Japanese influence in the Asia Pacific.[19] South Korea, as noted above, has definitely moved closer to Beijing both in terms of its trading and economic relations and with respect to cultural and educational exchanges.

These differential responses indicate some success on the part of Chinese strategy to treat these US allies differently, but they also suggest the limits Chinese leaders have encountered because, regardless of the extent to which it has extended its economic and military influence in the Asia Pacific up to now, the East Asian alliance system continues with solid bilateral alliances between the United States and South Korea and the United States and Japan. This does not mean that all is well with this long-standing alliance system: China's successes are also witnessed in how it has from time to time weakened the informal partnership that exists between Seoul and Tokyo.

China's Rise and the South Korea–Japan Partnership

As the discussions provided above have revealed, there have been many changes in the set of triangular relations that define the East Asian alliance system, but the fundamental logic of this system's endurance and long-term stability—the ongoing commitments of South Korea and Japan to their bilateral alliances with the United States—has not changed. This continuity of alliances between the United States and its two allies is of vital importance, to be sure, but given the changes that have occurred in the region, we must ask how the informal partnership between South Korea and Japan will endure in the years to come. Specifically, this means determining if it will continue to be challenged but nonetheless remain an effective base of this relationship triangle or if relations between Seoul and Tokyo will decline in their robustness as China exploits this partnership's weaknesses, hurting the East Asian alliance system's ability to maintain the decades-long peace and stability in the region has experienced.

The differential responses of South Korea and Japan to Beijing's growing regional influence naturally make it difficult for leaders in Seoul and Tokyo to agree on a common response to challenges presented by China's rise, and this problem is exacerbated when unresolved historical issues become salient and demand the attention of South Korean and Japanese officials if they are to keep their bilateral partnership from experiencing a significant rise in tension. The underlying problem is not simply that leaders in Seoul and Tokyo have been unable to provide any long-term solutions to their outstanding issues, rendering it well-nigh impossible for them to agree on a common response to the challenges posed by Beijing. This problem is exacerbated by US presidential administrations manifesting inconsistent levels of commitment to the East Asian alliance system and also by Beijing leaders exploiting the problem of history to undermine South Korea–Japan relations as part of a larger strategy to weaken the East Asian alliance system and undermine US leadership in the region.

Specifically, leaders in Beijing exploit the historical issues that separate Seoul and Tokyo to increase the diplomatic distance that exists between these two US allies. They do so because, when South Korean and Japanese officials have to devote time and resources to managing the fallout attendant to some official action or statement that raises the salience of one or more unresolved historical issues, their work to reduce the negative impacts of such developments actually assists Chinese leaders in their efforts to realize their strategic goals in the region. Troubles in South Korea–Japan relations render a united response to China's growing influence much more difficult to mount, which in turn offers less resistance to China's advancement of its power and security interests in the Asia Pacific. Such an assessment then raises the question of exactly how leaders in Beijing exploit the problem of history in South Korea–Japan relations, employing unresolved historical issues as assets to promote their interests in the region and facilitate the realization of their alternative to the current international order.

The specific unresolved issues that combine to form the problem of history in South Korea–Japan relations tend to become salient areas of contention when Japanese officials either take policy actions or make statements that understate their nation's responsibility for the trauma and abuses the military of imperial Japan heaped upon the Korean and other peoples living in territories occupied by the Japanese army before and during the Pacific War. These issues also become salient when statements from Japanese politicians or official policy actions suggest that Japan is moving in an authoritarian or militaristic direction.[20] Officials in South Korea, China, Taiwan, and other former Japanese colonies react very quickly to such statements and behavior, and when these unresolved historical issues become salient, tensions between Seoul and Tokyo rise, impairing their abilities to perform the respective roles they play in the East Asian alliance system.[21]

When we say that Chinese officials exploit the problem of history in South Korea–Japan relations, we are not suggesting that Chinese protests against certain Japanese policies and proclamations are not justified. Rather, our point is that there is much more going on when leaders in Beijing issue declamations against certain statements and actions that have been made by Japanese leaders at different points in time. The behavior of China's leaders, media, and citizens, in response to the provocations of Japanese leaders, extend the length of time that such historical issues remain salient in South Korea–Japanese relations. China's responses to Japanese provocations are then either tacitly or overtly supported by the central government, or, when Chinese reactions lead to violence and property damage, they are simply ignored or even encouraged by leaders in Beijing.

Consider the Chinese government's lukewarm response to the anti-Japanese demonstrations that occurred in China in 2005. These widespread mass demonstrations were officially touched off by Japan's history-textbook revisions of that year, and they resulted in a significant amount of property damage to Japanese businesses in China. While the evidence is not entirely clear that the Chinese government played a direct role in the start of these destructive actions, it is clear that the Chinese government did not move quickly enough to protect Japanese property, nor did it discourage such actions in any convincing manner. Moreover, given the government's control of the Chinese media, one can conclude that it is at the center of, if not responsible for, all responses to these kinds of undesirable Japanese actions and statements, which end up sustaining them as a challenge to productive South Korea–Japan relations.

Further evidence for this conclusion rests with the idea that Chinese responses to Japanese provocations appear to be well out of proportion with the seriousness of the Japanese transgressions against which they were leveled. Indeed, China's official response to the 2005 textbook revisions was to suggest that Tokyo was returning to the East Asia Co-Prosperity Sphere of the war years, which was by any estimation hyperbolic and not based on current political realities in Japan. Moreover, the Chinese government surely knew that this kind of response to Japan's textbook revisions, which would be used in only a very small number of schools, would most likely produce a reaction that not only stiffened the Japanese government's commitment to government-sanctioned textbooks but also provided support to nationalistic elements in Japanese society. Consequently, such Chinese responses were very likely counterproductive, but given that South Koreans were also offended by the same Japanese statements and actions, they indirectly serve China's larger purpose. Specifically, Chinese responses aggravated the challenges that already existed in Japan's relations with South Korea, and they also increased the diplomatic distance that existed between Seoul and Tokyo, assisting Beijing in its efforts to weaken the US-led international order in the Asia Pacific.

While instances of Japanese leaders supporting policies or making statements that suggest a whitewashing of history or supporting a more militarist posture for their country have provided a perfect opportunity for Chinese leaders to play the problem-of-history card, in other instances Beijing has employed this approach even when there were no immediate Japanese provocations. Consider the meeting that occurred between Japanese prime minister Koizumi Junichiro and US president George W. Bush in the United States in 2005. During this meeting, the Bush administration announced that, in addition to making US-Japan relations closer, they were reaffirming their mutual desire to reform the UN Security Council in a way that benefited Japan, which meant US support for Japan obtaining a permanent seat on the council. China vehemently opposed such an action and tried to thwart these efforts by, again, raising the problem of history in South Korea–Japan relations. In their response to the announcement, Chinese leaders noted that the United States was abandoning its "One-China"

66 Strengthening South Korea–Japan Relations

policy and encouraging the rise of militarism in Japan, which naturally raised suspicions in Seoul, leading South Korean officials to note their concerns about such actions.[22]

These events illustrate clearly how strategic benefits redound to China when it exploits the problem of unresolved historical issues in South Korea–Japan relations, but they also tell us that the benefits China accrues go beyond the increase in diplomatic distance between Seoul and Tokyo. Indeed, employing this strategy provides direct assistance to China in its efforts to undermine the bilateral partnership between South Korea and Japan and also the international reputation of Japan, as evidenced in the failure of US efforts to help Japan obtain a permanent seat on the UN Security Council. In a larger sense, even though fewer incidences of provocative behavior on the part of Japanese officials would certainly lower the number of history-related problems that disrupt Japan's relationship with its South Korean partner, not only are the payoffs associated with China's strategic use of the problem of history high but the levels of risk are low. As a result, Chinese leaders will continue to employ this strategy to halt any development they view as being contrary to their interests, such as increasing military cooperation between Seoul and Tokyo.

A more recent example of Chinese leaders following such a course occurred when South Korean and Japanese leaders got together to mount a coordinated response to the increasingly provocative behavior on the part of the regime in Pyongyang. North Korea has engaged in ongoing provocative actions that disrupt the peace and stability of the Asia Pacific, such as Pyongyang's decision to withdraw from the Nonproliferation Treaty (NPT) and then develop not simply its nuclear weapons capability but also the delivery systems that could take these weapons to stated enemies throughout the region and the globe. Beginning in 2006 and 2009, North Korea conducted nuclear tests, which the United States and Japan interpreted as "reckless." These increasingly successful nuclear tests continue to the present day, and with the ascension of Kim Jong Un, they have progressed from the Unha-3 rocket, launched in February 2012, which illustrated the great advances it made in its delivery-system technology, to the Hwasong-12, which was first launched in 2017 and is continually being evolved into an intercontinental ballistic missile.[23]

These nuclear developments were naturally threatening to South Korea and Japan, but in the recent past North Korea has taken other actions against its southern neighbor that created even more concern for both of these US allies. A notable example is the sinking of the corvette-class South

Korean naval vessel *Cheonan* by a torpedo fired by a North Korean midget submarine and the shelling of Yeonpyeong Island, which set buildings on fire, forced the evacuation of civilians, and killed two South Korean soldiers and two citizens. While this island has been a point of rising tension between North and South Korea before, this particular North Korean action was quite disturbing for several reasons. First, Yeonpyeong Island lies below the Northern Limit Line, which means it is formally off-limits to this kind of military aggression. In addition to this, Pyongyang announced that it was backing out of the Armistice of 1953 and ending any cooperative efforts it had with Seoul, including the Kaesong Industrial Complex. In closing this living symbol of North-South economic cooperation, Kim Jong Un expelled all South Korean business advisers and kept North Korean workers from the much-improved economic opportunities this complex provided.

While it is true that China does not approve of all North Korean actions and opposes its possession of nuclear weapons, its response to those events did little to rein in Pyongyang. In many ways, Beijing's reaction to these events may have even exacerbated the situation. Consider that China formally rejected as unreliable the official American and South Korean version of events surrounding the sinking of the naval vessel *Cheonan*. Such Chinese behavior naturally suggested that it was fully supportive of North Korea, but its position on this event also provided Japan and South Korea with incentives to coordinate their responses to this destabilizing behavior. Although they did not act in accordance with a promulgated treaty, and although these two US allies have very different interests with respect to North Korea, South Korea, and Japan did find ways to engage in more security cooperation. This has been particularly true since the mid-1990s, when South Korea and Japan held meetings among their defense ministers and other security officials to discuss opportunities for such cooperation.

Such meetings have continued intermittently to the present day, but they have not allowed Seoul and Tokyo to hammer out a formal arrangement for official security cooperation. This does not mean that there has been no progress; since 2010, South Korean and Japanese naval forces have engaged in mutual observations of each other's drills, and both countries tried to negotiate a formal agreement for cooperation by completing the General Security of Military Information Agreement. This agreement would have been the first formal cooperation agreement between the two countries since the end of Japan's occupation of the peninsula, and it would have provided a legal framework for the two countries to exchange intelligence on North Korea's and China's military actions. Unfortunately, this agreement was to be signed in June 2012, but the official ceremony was canceled by the South Korean government because of growing pressure from China and strong domestic opposition to any military cooperation with Japan.

Again, the culprit was the rising salience of the problem of history, which fueled intense domestic opposition in South Korea. The specific incident at this time involved Japan's territorial dispute with China over the Senkaku Islands, during which Japan's previous prime minister, Abe Shinzo, purchased smaller islets within this area of dispute. As discussed above, Chinese leaders reacted strongly, but in addition to creating the East China Sea Air Defense Identification Zone, Chinese leaders also reminded South Koreans that they too have territorial disputes with Japan, specifically, Takeshima or Dokdo, which Japanese leaders might handle in a similar manner. This naturally increased the salience of this unresolved problem between South Korea and Japan, which in turn generated enough domestic concern among South Koreans that the agreement for security cooperation had to be scrapped. This turn of events resulted in not only Japan and South Korea's inability to mount a coordinated response to the destabilizing provocations of North Korea but also the end—albeit temporary—of any progress that leaders in Seoul and Tokyo had been making on security cooperation. Taken together, these two results provided Chinese leaders with a more unencumbered environment within which to pursue their interests in the region.

These examples show clearly that exploiting the problem of history has resulted in many successes for China by increasing the level of tension that exists in South Korea–Japan relations, behooving leaders in Seoul and Tokyo to spend more time on finding ways to keep their partnership functioning as the base of the East Asian alliance system. China's successes, however, have been limited up to this point because South Korea and Japan remain committed to maintaining their individual alliances with the United States and preventing their own bilateral partnership from fracturing to a point where it becomes debilitated and ineffective. This state of affairs raises the question of the extent to which China's continued efforts are likely to achieve its overall goal of creating a permanent rupture between South Korea and Japan, drawing Seoul more securely into its orbit and providing itself with more freedom ultimately to displace the United States as the region's apex power.

The answer to this question depends on several factors, but the most important are the South Korean and Japanese evaluations of the United States versus China as the region's apex power in the Asia Pacific and their perception of efforts by their respective leaders not simply to repair their bilateral relationship but more importantly to address those unresolved problems of history that have intermittently disrupted the smooth functioning of the East Asian alliance system. We address these questions in the following four chapters.

4

South Korean and Japanese Views of China and the United States

How successful Chinese leaders will be at realizing their vision for a new international order, particularly in the Asia Pacific, will depend in part on how robust the East Asian alliance system remains in the face of Beijing's efforts to weaken its triangular relations. The likelihood that the alliance system will become so weak that it cannot thwart Chinese pressure rests with the willingness of leaders in Seoul and Tokyo to solve problems in their bilateral relations and also their view of China versus the United States as the apex power in the region. Given South Korea's and Japan's repeated statements that they remain committed to their respective alliances with the United States, it does not appear that China has the level of acceptance from Seoul and Tokyo necessary to replace the United States as the region's dominant power. This does not mean that Chinese efforts have accrued no progress toward facilitating its rise as the primary challenger to the United States and the East Asian alliance system; as discussed above, there have been successes, particularly with respect to undermining the alliance-based partnership between Seoul and Tokyo. Nonetheless, to understand these dynamics more deeply requires that we examine data that allow us to map public attitudes in South Korea and Japan with respect to the United States and China as well as their own bilateral partnership.

Data from surveys taken in South Korea and Japan will provide direct indicators of these attitudes. Using public opinion data from surveys taken in these countries will also provide insight into how leaders in Japan and South Korea are likely to respond to the growing influence of China in the Asia-Pacific region and how these responses will affect each's role in the East Asian alliance system and, particularly, their own set of bilateral relations. Their response to China's growing power and influence, and the actions they take to manage their own bilateral relations, will be the result of political decisions made by leaders in Seoul and Tokyo. The phrase *political decisions* is used intentionally here because exactly how leaders in Seoul and Tokyo respond to the challenges they face will be conditioned by how their respective publics view such actions. These views may serve as either constraint against or incentive for leaders taking certain foreign policy actions in the region.

Naturally, leaders in Tokyo and Seoul will consult with their respective countries' foreign policy and international security elites, who will provide elected leaders with substantive advice as they evaluate how different foreign policy actions with respect to the United States versus China will affect their nations' essential interests.[1] In spite of this, there are reasons to conclude that domestic political forces will play a more important role in South Korean and Japanese foreign policy decisions.[2] Indeed, more and more scholars are recognizing that how Seoul and Tokyo respond to the challenges of China's growing competition with the United States and what actions they will consider with respect to managing their own bilateral relations will necessarily involve an electoral calculus. This means that any strategic decisions on these matters will not be purely bureaucratic but rather will take into consideration how any actions taken will correspond to how their respective publics are likely to view such actions.[3]

The domestic politics that factor into the foreign policy decisions made in South Korea and Japan have been given increased weight in scholarly work that focuses on the strategic choices that leaders in Seoul and Tokyo face with respect to China's growing power. For example, one scholar noted that, in Sino–South Korean relations from the late-1990s to the present, relations between these two nations, particularly how South Koreans view their increasingly powerful neighbor, have been strongly influenced, inter alia, by a bottom-up process "where ordinary citizens actively engage in foreign policy making through their respective domestic political system" (Ye 2017, 10). With respect to relations between China and Japan, another scholar stated that the lack of attention to domestic political forces has come at a cost because it led scholars to miss instances where Japanese bureaucratic and political elites have been unable to take certain actions with respect to China for "domestic reasons" (Smith 2015, 23).

We will focus on South Korean and Japanese attitudes toward the United States and China, and we will present data in a longitudinal fashion so they can reveal any trends in the manner in which South Koreans and

Japanese have viewed these two powerful countries. The overall purpose of providing this mapping is to identify any changes that have occurred in how the South Korean and Japanese publics evaluate these two countries as the top powers in the Asia Pacific and also to note if and how preferences have changed in favor of China as the new apex power in the Asia Pacific. This process will also involve us examining any specific developments that have occurred in South Korea's and Japan's relations with China and the United States and other international and domestic events they may be related to any changes we uncover in the public opinion patterns we map. Examples of such developments will include changes of administration following the US presidential elections and any relevant events in which either the United States or China is involved. We will also identify any changes that have occurred in the Chinese leadership as well as any pronouncements made by China's premiers, or Japanese and South Korean chief executives, that have an impact on how the South Korean and Japanese publics may view the United States or China as the Asia Pacific's dominant powers.

Accomplishing this will require the use of data from multiple sources, and most of the data we examine will be from public opinion surveys conducted in Japan and South Korea by different survey research organizations in those two countries. The primary source of data for the analysis of public opinion trends in Japan will be the annual public opinion surveys taken by the Cabinet Secretariat of the Prime Minister's Office. The Japanese Prime Minister's Office conducts numerous national surveys on a wide variety of topics, but its annual surveys on diplomacy and security relations will be one of our principal sources. Japanese public opinion data are extensive, with some questions dating back to the late 1970s, but available data for mapping public attitudes in South Korea are more limited, particularly in terms of the number of years covered by available public opinion surveys. Nonetheless, there are several South Korean sources that will allow us to map over-time trends that are comparable to those we employ for Japan.

One of these is the annual public opinion surveys taken by the Asan Institute for Policy Studies, and a second is the less regularly taken surveys conducted by the East Asia Institute. The latter institute's polls are known as the Genron NPO surveys, and the benefit of these surveys is that, from time to time, they were taken simultaneously in both South Korea and Japan, and that allows us to make comparisons across the two countries on similar questions. We will also use data from the South Korean General Social Survey, which are available from 2003 to 2016. The final source of public opinion data we employ in our analysis of South Korean attitudes comes from the Pew Research Center, an American organization that polled respondents on related issues in the United States and China.[4]

Japanese Views of China and the United States

As stated briefly above, the Prime Minister's Office has been polling members of the Japanese public with respect to how they feel about different nations around the world since 1978. While some of the countries that Japanese respondents were asked to evaluate were added in later years of these surveys, respondents were asked about China and the United States from the very first survey in 1978.[5] These surveys have probed the attitudes of Japanese by using two questions, one of which involves a longer time series than the other. The question with a more limited time series asks simply if relations between the United States or China and Japan are friendly, and responses are divided into the following four categories: friendly, generally friendly, somewhat unfriendly, and unfriendly.[6] The other question asks respondents if they have a feeling of closeness to a selected country, and responses also involve four gradations, where affirmative answers are divided into strong and weak, as are the negative answers. Since the latter question contains consistent responses over the forty-year period mentioned above, we will evaluate the attitudes of Japanese respondents toward China and the United States using that question.

Data on the Japanese public's feelings toward China are presented in figure 4.1, and they indicate that there has been a dramatic shift in whether Japanese respondents have a close or distant feeling toward China throughout the forty-year period that these polls have been taken. Specifically, Japan and the People's Republic of China had strained relations until the early 1970s, when American president Richard Nixon initiated a normalization of relations between Beijing and Washington. Official diplomatic relations between China and Japan began in February 1973, and five years later, the Prime Minister's Office began taking the surveys we are using for the analysis we conduct herein, a time that also corresponds to the promulgation of a peace treaty between Japan and the People's Republic of China. We see from the data in the figure that, after relations between Tokyo and Beijing were restarted, a significant plurality of Japanese respondents had feelings of closeness to China. Respondents who shared this feeling of

South Korean and Japanese Views of China and the United States 75

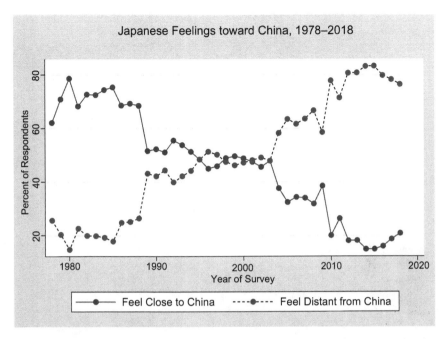

Figure 4.1. Source: Prime Minister's Office, Japan, Annual Foreign Affairs Surveys.

closeness remained steady from the late 1970s to the late 1980s, when the proportion of these respondents underwent a significant drop.

We also see from the figure that, in the 1990s, the proportion of respondents who possessed feelings of closeness had dropped by just over twenty percentage points. The size of this shift in Japanese attitudes is more notable when we subtract the percentage of respondents with distant feelings toward China from those who stated they feel close to their giant neighbor. These data are presented in table 4.1, and we see that those with close versus distant feelings changed by over forty percentage points throughout the 1990s. These two sets of respondents, those with close versus distant feelings, remained relatively balanced until the beginning to middle of the first decade of the twenty-first century, although those with negative feelings toward China were slightly more numerous than their positive-feeling counterparts. After that time, respondents with negative perceptions grew dramatically.

We see from the data in table 4.1 that, in the 1980s,[7] Japanese respondents with a positive feeling toward China were nearly 50 percentage points more numerous than those with a negative view. This changed over the

76 *Strengthening South Korea–Japan Relations*

Table 4.1. A Decadal Analysis of Japanese Feelings of Closeness to China and the United States*

Decade	China	United States
1980s	49.6%	53.6%
1990s	4.9%	55.6%
2000s	−16.6%	54.1%
2010s	−60.4%	64.5%

* Percentages indicate the difference between the percentages of respondents who feel close to China or the United States and those that do not feel close. Negative values indicate larger percentages of respondents who do not feel close to China or the United States.
Source: Compiled by the authors from Prime Minister's Office, Cabinet Secretariat, *Gekkan Yoron Chosa* (monthly compilation of public opinion polls, various years).

next decade when a nearly 50 percent plurality dropped to barely 5 percent. We also see from the decadal analysis provided in table 4.1 that this decline in respondents with positive views of China did not cease but accelerated as we proceeded through the first and second decades of the twenty-first century. From 2000 to 2009, Japanese respondents with a negative feeling toward China were more than fifteen percentage points greater than their counterparts with positive feelings, and this plurality grew to over 60 percent in the years from 2010 to 2018. We also see from the data in figure 4.1 that it was from the beginning of the century to 2015 that respondents with close versus distant feelings toward China grew apart in a dramatic fashion, reaching a nearly seventy-percentage-point difference in 2015. While these two groups of Japanese respondents have moved closer together in the last three years, Japanese who feel distant from China are still more than fifty percentage points more numerous than those with feelings of closeness.

Many factors contributed to these trends, and these include economic trends, incidents that occurred directly between China and Japan, and events and developments that did not directly involve China and Japan but nonetheless affected interstate relations in the Asia Pacific. One set of events concerns North Korea's efforts to develop nuclear weapons and conduct nuclear explosions at its Yongbyon testing facility in 1990. At issue was not simply Japan's concerns with North Korea's nuclear tests but more importantly the appearance that Beijing remained at the sidelines while

Pyongyang carried out such tests, its overall opposition to North Korea possessing such a capability notwithstanding. North Korea's nuclear provocations occurred around the same time that there were rumors that the United States would remove the nuclear weapons it had ostensibly placed in South Korea as an incentive for the North to discontinue its testing. This action did appear to mollify Pyongyang, but it worried the Japanese, citizens and leaders alike, because they believed a significant North Korean deterrent had been removed. Moreover, Japanese fears were confirmed when, although North Korea had agreed to allow International Atomic Energy Agency officials to inspect its nuclear facilities, Pyongyang announced that it would leave the Nonproliferation Treaty after inspectors from this international body found certain inconsistencies.

Such activities on the part of North Korea have always been magnified in Japan and, thus, viewed with extreme concern. Moreover, given China's post–Cold War role as Pyongyang's principal, and until very recently only, benefactor, people in Japan have always connected the provocative behavior of North Korea with their views of ostensible Chinese approval of such provocations. The data suggest that, before this crisis, there was a rise in the proportion of Japanese possessing feelings of closeness to China, which perhaps can be explained by cooperative relations occurring between Tokyo and Beijing prior to North Korea's development of a nuclear weapons program. At the same time, the data reveal that the share of Japanese feeling distant from China started to increase in the late 1980s, and the beginning of this increase can be traced to the period of Prime Minister Nakasone Yasuhiro, the first postwar prime minister to visit Yasukuni Shrine in an official capacity. Yasukuni Shrine is dedicated to the souls of Japanese who gave their lives in combat for the nation, and as expected, this action greatly upset Chinese authorities, particularly since the official reaction of the Japanese government was simply to assert that there had been no negative intent in the visit, rejecting Chinese anger as meddling in Japan's internal affairs.

This 1980s decline in the number of Japanese with feelings of closeness to China continued throughout the next decade and accelerated throughout the first decade of the twenty-first century. The accelerated decline was sustained by the Taiwan Straits Crisis that followed in the wake of the North Korean nuclear testing row of the 1990s. The Taiwan Straits Crisis of this time traces its genesis to the visit of Taiwan president Lee Teng-Hui to his alma mater, Cornell University. The official position of Beijing

78 *Strengthening South Korea–Japan Relations*

was to vigorously oppose Washington allowing any Taiwanese president to make an official visit to the United States. While the United States initially decided not to issue a visa to President Lee, pro-Taiwan elements in the US Congress passed a resolution recommending the issuance of the visa, and Taiwan's chief executive visited Ithaca, New York.

The Chinese government's angry reaction was based on what it viewed as a policy reversal on the part of the United States, the One-China policy, but it directed its anger principally at Taipei. Specifically, the Chinese military began conducting missile tests in the waters surrounding Taiwan, and, at the same time, it also conducted military drills using live ammunition. Simultaneous with these actions, Taiwan and the United States detected some troop mobilizations in the Fujian area, which is the Chinese province closest to Taiwan. Analysts in the United States viewed these actions with a level of concern sufficient to lead the Clinton administration to order two carrier battle groups to the region, one of which was led by the USS *Nimitz*, which sailed straight through the Taiwan Straits. While such actions taken by the United States did result in a reduction of tension in the region, the entire affair led to increasing suspicion of Chinese behavior, and no place was this truer than in Japan. Evaluations of the impact of this affair noted that the Taiwan Straits Crisis at this time convinced Japanese leaders that China had the definite potential for the "use of military force in Northeast Asia" (Smith 2015, 27).

In addition to these developments, other problems in Sino-Japanese relations have risen out of their growing economic contacts. In the last three decades, economic interdependence between China and Japan has increased dramatically as the volume of trade between these two nations has grown. Indeed, there are business organizations in Japan that not only have benefited substantially from trading with China but also have served as policy advisers helping to keep Sino-Japanese relations on an even keel. What must be understood is that even though Japan began its economic interactions with China as the senior partner, at times providing substantial amounts of official development assistance and foreign direct investment, things changed as China's economy grew at consistently high rates for an extended period of time. As a result of this rapid economic development, China not only overtook Japan as the world's second-largest economy but also came to be viewed by Japanese leaders and citizens as a competitor. As a result, Japanese respondents increasingly felt that their country was unfortunately becoming more and more dependent on China and that this dependence was increasingly accruing to the benefit of Beijing.

This feeling became widespread in Japan, particularly when it was reported in January 2008 that dumplings—*gyoza* in Japanese—imported from China were contaminated with an insecticide. These contaminated dumplings resulted in numerous people getting sick, which in turn led to news reports throughout Japan that advised that any food imported from China be banned, especially food that would be served in schools (Smith 2015). In addition to this food-contamination issue, there was at the same time heightened tension over an announcement that Japan's history textbooks would be revised in a way that reduced Japan's responsibility for its aggression during the war years. As discussed briefly above, in response to this announcement, there were vigorous protests in China, and, in some cases, these protests became violent and led to the destruction of Japanese property there. Witnessing the destruction of Japanese property at the hand of Chinese protesters on television news sent shock waves throughout Japan, and, when that is coupled with the increased tension caused by the dispute over toxic food, it is understandable that the proportion of Japanese with feelings of closeness to China declined precipitously.

One other issue of contention in Sino-Japanese relations became salient during this period of time. The Senkaku Islands, also known as the Diaoyu Islands in Chinese, as stated above, are a group of uninhabited islands in the East China Sea, roughly equidistant from Okinawa to the east, Taiwan to the southwest, and mainland China to the west. These islands became an issue of contention in Sino-Japanese relations when substantial oil and natural gas resources were discovered there in 1995, complicating existing disputes about their potential as rich fishing grounds. Naturally, this combination of disputes exacerbated disagreements that already existed over the islands' sovereignty because there was no consensus over the setting of maritime boundaries and, thus, the demarcation of exclusive economic zones (EEZs).

In the immediate postwar era, these islands were part of the US-occupied Japan, which means they were administered by the United States from 1945 to 1972. The US administration of this territory ended when sovereignty over Okinawa and the surrounding territory was ceded back to Japan, which led Tokyo to claim sovereignty over this part of the East China Sea. It was also at this time that Taiwan began asserting its own claim over these islands, which it argued went back to the first Sino-Japanese War in 1894–95 when they were seized by Japan as part of the military action it took then. Shortly after Taiwan began asserting its claims of sovereignty over the Senkaku Islands, Beijing noted its support for Taipei's claim.

China emphasized that, since Taiwan was legitimately part of the People's Republic of China, these islands were then under Chinese sovereignty.

Initially, the United States supported the Japanese claim, but its support turned into neutrality as its rapprochement with China proceeded throughout the 1970s. Although the United States' withdrawal of support for the Japanese claim added confusion to these conflicting claims of sovereignty, there was still relative peace in the East China Sea. In 2000, this began to change with a rise in "Senkaku nationalism," which involved more and more private citizens visiting the islands and some even planting Japanese flags there, which led to increased visits by Japanese Coast Guard vessels (Smith 2015, 29). Such actions by Japanese citizens caused the Japanese government to increase visits by Japanese Coast Guard vessels, and these activities came to a head in September 2010 when a Chinese fishing boat rammed a Japanese Coast Guard vessel, leading to the arrest of the Chinese boat's captain. To be sure, this incident led to increased tension in Sino-Japanese relations, but the situation deteriorated when the Japanese government, under Noda Yoshihiko, purchased the islands from its private owner for just over ¥2 billion. This action inflamed the Chinese leadership, which asserted that Japan had stolen the islands from China. In response, China redoubled its efforts to enhance its military presence in the region and in the South China and Yellow Seas.

As the data we have presented thus far have shown, the Japanese public's views of China have undergone a dramatic change and have remained at a low point for a number of years. By way of contrast, the Japanese public's views of the United States are just the opposite: they have remained positive and stable over the same period of time. Specifically, as the data in figure 4.2 indicate, Japanese views of the United States have undergone very little change at all throughout the four decades for which we have data. Indeed, they have remained remarkably stable, even though the small movements we have witnessed do reflect certain developments in the US-Japanese relationship as well as the changing dynamics of interstate relations in the Asia-Pacific region. We see from the figure that Japanese respondents with positive feelings toward the United States have dramatically outnumbered those with negative feelings, and we also see that, since the latter part of the first decade of the twenty-first century, this gap has widened.

When we say that Japanese views of the United States have been stable, we do not mean that there has been no change whatsoever or that the data we present reveal no notable shifts. To identify the changes that have

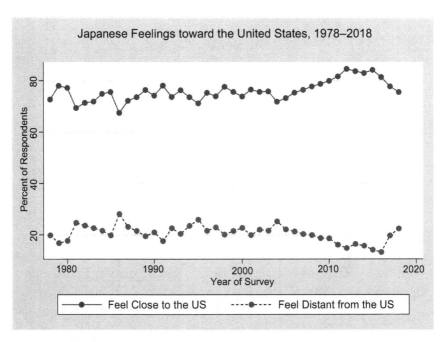

Figure 4.2. Source: Prime Minister's Office, Japan, Annual Foreign Affairs Surveys.

occurred, we present the decadal averages of Japanese who feel distant from the United States minus those shares of respondents who have expressed feelings of closeness. These decadal averages, presented on the right side of table 4.1, indicate that, despite the overall stability that has characterized Japanese views of the United States, there has been a more recent increase in those expressing feelings of closeness to the United States. During the 1980s, particularly the latter half of the decade, the distance between those with feelings of closeness versus feelings of distance was narrowest, in spite of the fact that the difference was fifty percentage points. This decade represented a difficult time in US-Japan relations because of the structural adjustment occurring in the US economy and the fact that Japan had become one of the world's most notable high-tech, manufacturing powerhouses, outproducing and outcompeting the United States in many specific industries. Less competitive sectors in the United States witnessed a significant loss of jobs, which led to deleterious impacts in a number of communities characterized by a predominance of blue-collar workers.

Moreover, there was a concomitant rise in social pathologies in the communities that experienced manufacturing employment declinations, and those socioeconomic changes helped create a negative reaction toward

Japan and its products. These negative reactions sometimes came in the form of a significant amount of Japan bashing in the United States and concerns in Tokyo that the US trade and economic policies were becoming anti-Japanese. Understandably, these years represent the time when Japanese respondents with feelings of closeness to the United States were at their lowest level for the period we examine. In spite of this, Japanese respondents with positive feelings toward the United States were still more than fifty percentage points higher than those with negative feelings. For the next two decades, the data in table 4.1 correspond to the data in figure 4.2 for the same twenty-year period. Specifically, the Japanese public's perceptions of the United States, specifically the balance between those with positive versus negative views, remained very stable, with those respondents having positive feelings being slightly higher. In the last decade of the series, we see that there was a rather notable change in that Japanese respondents with positive views of the United States expanded by nearly ten percentage points. This change, among other things, reflected the growing concern with China on the part of the Japanese public and the fact that leaders in Japan, particularly previous prime minister Abe Shinzo, worked to bring their country closer to the United States, even with the negative policies and dramatic unpredictability of the Trump administration.

South Korean Views of the United States and China

Japanese views toward China became more negative, while their views of the United States became generally more positive, particularly in the last decade and a half. South Korean views toward the United States and China, on the other hand, reveal more complicated patterns than those of Japanese respondents. Our initial mapping of South Korean attitudes toward the United States and China are from the South Korean General Social Survey, which was conducted annually throughout the country from 2003 to 2016 inclusive. This number of years represents a much shorter period of time than the data we had available for public attitudes in Japan. In addition to the South Korean public opinion series covering a shorter period of time, the questions South Korean respondents were asked concerning their attitudes toward the two largest and most powerful countries in the region were constructed differently than they were in the case of Japanese respondents. Specifically, in the South Korean General Social Survey, respondents were given a list of countries and asked to select the nation to which they felt closest.[8]

The percentages of respondents who selected either the United States or China as their first choice are provided in table 4.2, which also contains the differences in the percentages of respondents who selected one of the Asia Pacific's two most powerful countries. We immediately notice from the data in the table that the percentage of respondents selecting the United States has long been much larger than the percentage of those who selected China. We also see from these data that these percentages did change over the fourteen-year period for which the South Korean General Social Survey data are available, and the amounts by which the preferences of respondents changed were different for those who selected the United States versus China.

We see from the table that the share of South Korean respondents who selected the United States as the country to which they felt closest grew dramatically, and this growth was by as much as thirty percentage points. This is an interesting trend because, as discussed above, South Korea and China have become much more involved with each other during the period covered by this data series. This is true in an economic sense as the Chinese and South Korean economies became much more intertwined, and this naturally involved trade but also official development assistance, which grew by well over 1,000 percent throughout this period of time. Moreover, as stated above, South Korea has become much closer to China

Table 4.2. South Koreans Who Selected Either the United States or China as the Country to Which They Feel Closest

Year	United States	China	Difference
2003	45.2%	9.6%	35.6%
2004	42.9%	12.3%	30.6%
2005	45.8%	11.7%	34.1%
2006	50.6%	10.8%	39.8%
2007	50.2%	7.8%	42.4%
2008	52.0%	8.7%	43.3%
2009	62.9%	6.4%	56.5%
2010	71.6%	4.3%	67.3%
2011	68.9%	4.7%	64.2%
2012	68.3%	5.2%	63.1%
2013	73.3%	8.0%	65.3%
2014	74.1%	10.8%	63.3%
2015	72.7%	10.6%	62.1%
2016	70.2%	10.5%	59.7%

Source: Compiled by the authors from the Korean General Social Survey (various years).

84 Strengthening South Korea–Japan Relations

in terms of educational and cultural ties (Ye 2017, appendix B). Also, in the eleven-year period between 2004 and 2014 inclusive, South Korea established well over twenty Confucius Institutes and Classrooms throughout the country, adding seven in 2007 alone (Ye 2017, appendix C).

Despite such official efforts to increase formal economic and noneconomic contacts, South Koreans have not felt particularly close to China. Indeed, the South Korean General Social Survey data in table 4.2 indicate that only a small percentage of South Korean respondents selected China as the country to which they felt closest. Specifically, in the first few years, respondents selecting China grew slightly but then underwent a multiyear drop until the mid-2010s, after which this proportion of respondents recovered to make up slightly over 10 percent of all respondents. The point is that significant economic and educational developments have drawn Seoul and Beijing closer together, but other developments have enervated this closing of diplomatic distance between Seoul and Beijing. Specifically, there have been "soft clashes" in Sino–South Korean relations, and these have involved economic and territorial disputes as well as significant disagreements over Beijing's relations with Pyongyang (Ye 2017). What makes these clashes so important is that their rise in salience in Sino–South Korean relations has helped push down the percentage of South Korean respondents choosing China as the country to which they feel closest.

In the area of trade, South Korean officials were worried that their nation was becoming overly dependent on certain Chinese imports, and such concerns became highly salient and almost sensationalized in what became known as the garlic and kimchi wars. The former began in June 2000 when the South Korean government, under significant pressure from farmers who were suffering from cheaper garlic imports from China, raised tariffs on this essential food ingredient. Beijing's response was swift and severe as it banned select South Korean manufactured goods from being imported, including cell phones. This Chinese embargo of certain manufactured products resulted in significant losses to South Korean companies, and these impacts forced the government to reconsider the tariffs against Chinese garlic. In response to Chinese retaliation, South Korea considered going so far as opening its market completely to Chinese garlic (Snyder 2009).

Although the government in Seoul reacted in a generally conciliatory manner, the South Korean public's reaction was quite different. Specifically, South Koreans were dismayed by China's aggressive response to their government's efforts to provide import relief to its distressed garlic farmers.

This public dismay continued and became more intense a few years later when it was discovered that there were parasitic eggs, possibly from human waste used as fertilizer, in kimchi that was imported from China. South Korea's food and drug agency made this discovery in 2005, and the government took immediate steps to suspend kimchi imports from China. The Chinese reaction was the same as it had been in the row over garlic imports, so South Korea's action held the potential to escalate tensions into a full-blown trade war when the Chinese government threatened to ban imports of ten food items from South Korea.

Given the importance of kimchi in South Korea's culinary culture, it is understandable that the people in this country would manifest increasing suspicion toward China when the South Korean government banned imports of the product after it was found to contain parasites. Moreover, it would also be expected that this affair would lead to a decline in the proportion of respondents who expressed feelings of closeness to China. Indeed, feelings of suspicion toward China were also encouraged by other "soft clashes" that occurred throughout this same period of time. One of these involved the repatriation of refugees back to North Korea by China, the numbers of which increased dramatically between 2001 and 2009 inclusive (Ye 2017, 75). Another clash involved growing tension over disputed territory, which was exacerbated because of the inability of Seoul and Beijing to agree on the boundaries of each's EEZs. The disputed territory is a rather small land formation known as Socotra Rock and is actually submerged beneath the surface of the Yellow Sea. Nonetheless, between 2000 and 2010, there was a significant increase in Chinese fishing boats in this area, and the increased Chinese traffic led to further suspicions on the part of South Koreans with respect to Chinese actions in the region (Ye 2017, 78).

To reveal more clearly how these soft clashes helped lower the percentage of South Korean respondents with positive views of China versus the United States, we examine the results of another set of public opinion polls taken in South Korea: data collected by the Pew Research Center, which conducted surveys in South Korea from 2002 through 2018. These surveys were not taken consistently in every year, and, as a result, they do not provide a set of South Korean attitudes that can be mapped consistently across this entire period of time. Nonetheless, we do have enough data points to track the changes in South Korean attitudes toward the United States and China throughout this time period. Moreover, these Pew data are also derived from questions that are similar to those that were asked in Japan's Prime Minister's Office surveys that were reported above. Specifically, the Pew surveys asked South Korean respondents if they had feelings of closeness to the United States and China, which allows us to distinguish between those who reported having feelings of closeness and those who did not.

The data points presented in figure 4.3 represent the difference between those respondents who noted that they have feelings of closeness to the United States and China versus those who do not. The negative values represent a plurality of respondents who have negative feelings, whereas positive values represent the opposite. We see from the figure that those possessing negative views of the United States were similar in size toward the beginning of the first decade of the twenty-first century, but those who viewed the United States positively increased through the years until 2010, significantly outnumbering those with negative views in the last several surveys. We also see from the data that the trends for China were generally in the opposite direction, as those who had negative feelings toward the region's newly rising power became more than twenty percentage points larger than those who held positive views in the last several years of the surveys.

These trends in the Pew Research Center's surveys are paralleled by the data in the rightmost column of table 4.2, which presents the differences between South Korean respondents who selected China as the nation with which they felt closest subtracted from those who selected the United States. While South Korean respondents have much preferred the United States to China, the extent to which this is true has increased dramatically over the period of time for which we have data from the South Korean General Social Survey. We see from the table that respondents favoring the United States were thirty percentage points higher in 2004, but six years later, the gap between respondents choosing the United States over China had more than doubled to nearly sixty-eight percentage points. Variations in the size of this gap reflect the fact that South Koreans have not always held predominantly positive feelings toward the United States. Nonetheless, given more recent developments in Seoul's relationship with Beijing, the number of South Korean respondents choosing the United States over Beijing in this set of surveys has grown, remaining an average of sixty percentage points higher than those selecting China.

There is little doubt that Sino–South Korean relations have become more intertwined in terms of trade and other economic interactions but also with respect to educational and cultural exchanges. This tightening of relations between Beijing and Seoul has led many scholars and policy

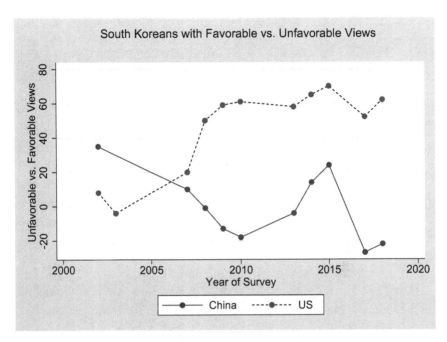

Figure 4.3. Source: Genron NPO Opinion Polls (various years).

analysts to consider that South Korea's relationship with the United States, and the East Asian alliance system overall, may be becoming less important than it was before the tightening of relations between Seoul and Beijing. This consideration has sometimes been made indirectly, as in one case analysis where the strategic choices South Korea faces include Seoul's decision to withdraw from the East Asian alliance system and move decidedly more into China's orbit (Snyder 2018). Other assessments point to Park Geun-Hye's visit to Beijing in 2013 and Xi's visit to South Korea in the following year as the beginning of a move on the part of Seoul to distance itself from Washington, possibly putting South Korea on the path ultimately to abandoning the East Asian alliance system altogether.

The data presented above, however, reveal that Sino–South Korean relations are perhaps not becoming as intimate as many have suggested, and our interpretation of relevant data tell us that the current state of Sino–South Korean relations is best described as closeness without intimacy. This was demonstrated in the multidimensional analysis of relations between South Korea and China (Ye 2017), and it was aptly demonstrated in another analysis that showed that a plurality of South Koreans viewed

China as a competitor that needs to be approached with ongoing caution (Chung and Kim 2016). Also, increased economic and cultural contacts are not tantamount to the diplomatic closeness between nations (Ye 2017), as an overwhelming majority of South Koreans viewed China's economic rise as a threat to South Korea's economic interests (Chung and Kim 2016). This is a dramatic and ongoing change in South Koreans' perceptions of China because prior to 2006, most South Koreans did not view China's rapid economic growth as being negative for their own country's economic interests.

This characterization of Sino–South Korean relations as "closeness without intimacy" also makes sense when we examine how South Koreans feel about reunification with North Korea and the role that China has been playing—and most likely will continue to play—in that process (Ye 2017). Reunification is one of the three principal goals of South Korean foreign policy, with the other two involving the ongoing expansion of trade and economic growth and the maintenance of peace and security in the region and around the globe (Chung and Kim 2016). The overwhelming majority of South Koreans believe that China will be a necessary participant in these processes, but, at the same time, they believe that China favors the interests of Pyongyang over those of Seoul and will behave in accordance with this bias in whatever role it has played and will continue to play in inter-Korean relations.

This is not a new understanding on the part of South Koreans with respect to how an increasingly powerful China has behaved in the region and how its behavior has affected the foreign policy interests in South Korea. Rather, this belief has long been sustained by South Korea's past experience with China, especially with respect to North Korea, including such Chinese actions as returning refugees back to North Korea. Moreover, this belief about the biases of China vis-à-vis North Korea persists in spite of South Korea and China having moved closer together in the last two decades. Given the overall evolution of Sino–South Korean relations, it is most likely that Seoul's policy of building closer ties with Beijing without abandoning its relationship with the United States, as well as its commitment to the East Asian alliance system overall, will continue to be the best approach leaders in Seoul can take to maintaining the regional environment of peace and security that has facilitated its economic development and international rise throughout the post-Armistice period.

Showing that solid bilateral ties between Seoul and Washington are not likely to be usurped by an increasingly assertive and powerful China any time soon does portend well for the East Asian alliance system, at least that portion of it represented by ties between the United States and South Korea. In combination with Japan's maintaining close relations with the United States, this would appear to be sufficient evidence to conclude that the East Asian alliance system will remain robust in the face of an increasingly powerful and assertive China. There is, however, one more part of the triangle of relations that form the East Asian alliance system that must be assessed before such a conclusion can be rendered with confidence. The strength of this alliance system also depends on a base consisting of bilateral relations between Seoul and Tokyo and the amount of stability and cooperation these two US allies will offer each other in the face of the growing pressure exerted by China. Given the importance of this bilateral relationship, in the next chapter we turn to South Korea–Japan relations and the ways in which the Japanese and South Korean publics' perceptions of each other and this bilateral relationship will help shape their quality and direction.

5

Public Attitudes and Relations between South Korea and Japan

The bilateral relationship between South Korea and Japan is vitally important because its overall health is essential to the proper functioning of the East Asian alliance system. As stated above, this alliance system helped provide an environment of peace and security in the Asia Pacific throughout the postwar period, and this supportive environment then facilitated both South Korea's and Japan's rapid economic growth, which in turn helped increase the prosperity of the Japanese and South Korean publics and ultimately led to both countries' rise to international influence. To be sure, these developments have given South Korea and Japan a strong incentive to maintain their respective relationships with the United States, which has been the region's apex power for many decades. However, the question remains whether leaders in Seoul and Tokyo view their own bilateral partnership with the same level of importance. To what extent do leaders and citizens in both countries see the need to work harder to overcome the challenges their nations face in their bilateral relations?

To be sure, these are difficult challenges because of the troubled history shared by South Korea and Japan, but they have been complicated by both the damaging pressure attendant to China's growing influence and the evolution of this alliance system's triangular relations throughout the last several decades. Concerning the former, we explained above that the rising power and influence of China in the region has challenged the underlying architecture of the East Asian alliance system, particularly by China exploiting the difficulties that exist in South Korea–Japan relations to increase the diplomatic distance between these two US allies. Moreover, we also mentioned that South Korea and Japan have not responded uniformly to China's rise and that this differential response has been facilitated by changes in the set of triangular relations that form this alliance system's

92 Strengthening South Korea–Japan Relations

underlying architecture. The reference here is specifically to the last few decades' decline in the asymmetry that long existed in South Korea–Japan relations, and in the East Asian alliance system overall (Cha 1999; Kim 2017).

To understand the importance of this decline, we must recall that, at the end of the Korean War, Japan's economy was much larger than South Korea's, and over the next few decades it remained a more prosperous and internationally influential country. This made South Korea the weakest and most dependent member of the East Asian alliance system, and South Korea's leaders were essentially forced to give appropriate weight to the foreign policy preferences of their two alliance partners, sometimes at the expense of their own preferences and interests. In other words, South Korea's leaders had to be careful that their country's foreign policy actions did not undermine Seoul's close relations with the United States or interfere with efforts to overcome any challenges that would threaten its bilateral partnership with Japan. Because South Korea's foreign policy actions were generally conducted in this manner, the roles played by the United and Japan in their respective alliance positions remained intact, and the East Asian alliance system continued to maintain the region's peace and stability and ensure Seoul's security in the face of a hostile regime to the north.

The alliance system's original asymmetries helped keep the bilateral alliances that these two allies shared with the United States intact and in a generally robust condition, and they also helped keep South Korea–Japan relations relatively stable. However, these asymmetries declined as South Korea's level of economic and military development rose dramatically, and this change began altering the strategic calculus that leaders in Seoul and Tokyo faced, particularly with respect to how they would respond to the growing power and influence of China. As stated above, both South Korea and Japan remain committed to their separate bilateral alliances with the United States, and they also remain committed to the East Asian alliance system overall. However, the declining asymmetry in their own bilateral relationship—and in the alliance system's triangular relations overall—has certainly affected how South Korea and Japan relate to each other and, by extension, how their publics view each other and the importance of this bilateral partnership.

The growing parity between South Korea and Japan means that South Korea is no longer the dependent nation that it once was, which in turn means that it can be less concerned about the reactions its foreign policy decisions will elicit from Tokyo and to a lesser extent the United States. Indeed, South Korea's foreign policy behavior is more independent today than it was in the past, which will most likely make working with Japan to solve challenges in their bilateral partnership somewhat more complicated. These complications have rendered the perceptions that their respective publics have of each other and their bilateral relationship increasingly important. To keep their partnership operating smoothly, leaders in Seoul and Tokyo will be required to craft what are essentially political solutions—that is, solutions that require agreement by elected officials who hold their legislative positions because of the support they receive from members of the South Korean and Japanese publics. As a result, examining public perceptions is an essential task to which we turn in the remainder of this chapter.

This effort will involve mapping how the Japanese public views its country's relations with South Korea and then how the South Korean public views its country's relations with Japan. In this effort, we will identify trends that exist in the Japanese and South Korean publics' views of the other and the ways these trends have been affected by specific issues in their bilateral relations, combined with significant regional developments. Throughout the post-Armistice period, several unresolved historical issues have elevated tensions between South Korea and Japan, and among the more notable are, first, those that involve Japanese leaders engaging in behavior or making pronouncements that either reduce Japan's responsibilities for the hardships that occurred during its occupation of the Korean Peninsula or understate the levels of death and destruction attendant to Japan's military actions during the Pacific War. These challenges also include visits on the part of Japan's elected leaders to Yasukuni Shrine, the resting place for the souls of Japan's war dead, which leaders in Seoul—and elsewhere throughout Asia, for that matter—find not just disrespectful but indicative of Japanese officialdom not being sincerely committed to remaining on the peaceful path the Allied Occupation put that country on in the wake of the Pacific War.

In addition to historical issues that are rendered salient by this kind of Japanese behavior, there are also ongoing territorial disputes between Japan and South Korea as well as prominent human rights issues that have elevated tensions between Seoul and Tokyo. The former involves the dispute over the contested island of Takeshima in Japanese or Dokdo in Korean, while the latter involves imperial Japan forcing Koreans into labor that supported the war effort and using Korean, Chinese, and women of other nationalities as forced sex slaves during the Pacific War.[1] We are examining such events and the challenges they pose for South Korea–Japan relations to assess their impact on public attitudes in both countries. This is important because public opinion in South Korea and Japan will act either as a constraint, impeding leaders from taking certain policy actions, or as an incentive, encouraging leaders in Seoul and Tokyo to follow certain paths that can help deal with the challenges that such issues pose for their bilateral relations.

Conducting this kind of analysis will help us better understand the specific influences that have pushed Seoul and Tokyo farther apart, as well as those that can help to bring them closer together, improving their bilateral partnership and strengthening the base of the triangle of relations that form the East Asian alliance system. Conducting this analysis is also intended to make clear the problems that leaders in Seoul and Tokyo will have to address if they are to strengthen their bilateral relations and, thus, help keep the East Asian alliance system robust and functioning as the Asia Pacific's ongoing source of peace and stability.

Japanese Views of South Korea

To determine how Japanese respondents have evaluated South Korea, we use the same Japanese Prime Minister's Office surveys we employed in the previous chapter for our mapping of the Japanese attitudes toward the United States and China. These attitudes are presented in figure 5.1, and the data, beginning in 1978 and ending forty years later in 2018, include Japanese respondents who stated that they had feelings of closeness to South Korea as well as respondents who expressed feelings of distance. We see immediately from the data in figure 5.1 that Japanese feelings toward South Korea have undergone some major shifts throughout the forty-year period covered by the series, revealing some interesting dynamics. These changes suggest some complicated patterns in Japanese views of South Korea, and we can identify three periods that are characterized by distinct patterns in these views.

The first of these periods, witnessed in the initial eighteen years of the data series (1978–96), are characterized by a plurality of Japanese respondents who reported feelings of distance from South Korea. This is particularly true for the initial years and the second half of this eighteen-year

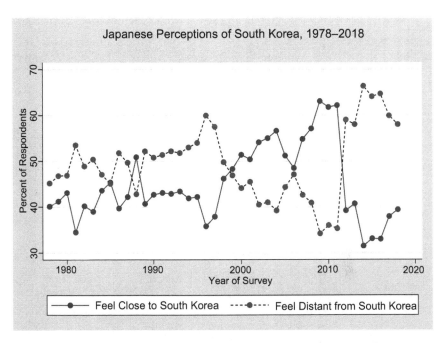

Figure 5.1. Source: Prime Minister's Office, Japan, Annual Foreign Affairs Surveys.

period, when respondents who reported feeling distant from South Korea were clearly more numerous than those who expressed feelings of closeness. The distance between respondents with positive versus negative feelings reached a high point in 1996, but after that, a dramatic change began to take place. In the 1996 survey, Japanese feeling distant from South Korea were nearly twenty-five percentage points more numerous than those expressing feelings of closeness, but, over the next eight years, these two groups of Japanese respondents reversed themselves completely. Specifically, from 1997 to 1999, respondents feeling distant and those feeling close converged, and, over the next five years, those registering feelings of closeness to South Korea began to outnumber those who registered feelings of distance. In 2004, Japanese respondents expressing feelings of closeness were nearly twenty percentage points more numerous.

This was a dramatic change to be sure, but the plurality of respondents expressing feelings of closeness to South Korea did not remain unchanged. Over the next two survey years, these two groups of Japanese respondents converged, and then the gap between them widened again, reaching a high point in 2009, when respondents expressing feelings of closeness

96   *Strengthening South Korea–Japan Relations*

were almost thirty percentage points more numerous. Respondents who expressed feelings of closeness remained more numerous over the next two years, but then the positions underwent a dramatic reversal whereby respondents with feelings of distance became more numerous by anywhere from seventeen to thirty-five percentage points. This most recent change is more clearly reflected in the data presented in table 5.1, which have been constructed by collapsing the annual percentages reported in figure 5.1 into larger time aggregates of one- and two-decade averages. Collapsing the data across decades and then calculating decadal averages provides a reinforced perspective on the significant dynamics in the Japanese attitudes toward South Korea.

We see from the data in table 5.1 that, in the 1980s, Japanese respondents who felt close to South Korea were outnumbered by those feeling distant by an average of just under seven percentage points. The data indicate that this gap increased to over ten percentage points in the next decade, but we also see from the data that the first decade of the twenty-first century represented a reversal. Specifically, over the next ten to fifteen years, Japanese respondents feeling close to South Korea became the larger group. Indeed, throughout that decade, the number of Japanese feeling close to South Korea was larger on average by more than twelve percentage points, and, when the first few years of the 2010s are included, this plurality increases to nearly fifteen percentage points. We also see from table 5.1 that there was another dramatic reversal from 2010 to 2018, when

Table 5.1. A Decadal Analysis of Japanese Respondents' Feelings of Closeness to or Distance from South Korea

	Closeness	Distance	Difference
1980s	41.7%	48.4%	−6.7%
1990s	42.4%	52.7%	−10.3%
1980s & 1990s	42.0%	50.4%	−8.4%
2000s	54.2%	41.9%	+12.3%
2000–2012	55.5%	40.9%	+14.6%
2010s	36.5%	61.4%	−24.9%

Source: Compiled by the authors from Prime Minister's Office surveys (various years).

Japanese respondents with feelings of distance from South Korea began to outnumber their counterparts with feelings of closeness. This change occurred over a short period of time, and, as the data in the table indicate, the gap produced by this change has grown to an average of nearly twenty-five percentage points.

There is no single explanation for the changing patterns in Japanese respondents' views of South Korea throughout the decades for which we have data. These notable changes in the Japanese public's perceptions of South Korea ostensibly correspond to the theoretical perspective that focused on Japan's entrapment versus South Korea's abandonment concerns (Cha 1999). Throughout the 1980s and 1990s, the United States was governed by the two Republican administrations of Ronald Reagan and George H. W. Bush and by the democratic administration of Bill Clinton. As a result, this was a period when Japan's entrapment concerns were relatively high, which then accounts for the general negativity of the Japanese public's views of South Korea. It is also true that the power dynamics of the Asia-Pacific region began changing significantly at the end of the 1990s, when China began employing its growing economic wherewithal to increase military and economic presence in the region while at the same time becoming more aggressive in the promotion of its regional interests. This is particularly true with respect to Taiwan and to China's advancement of its naval interests in nearby bodies of water, particularly the East and South China Seas.

Developments in Northeast Asia at this time are particularly relevant in that they continued to evolve after the United States experienced the tragedy of the 9/11 attacks, which led it to direct more of its foreign policy and military resources to conducting a war on terror, particularly in the Middle East and Central and South Asia. Among the implications of this shift in focus was a growth in the costs of the United States' international efforts, especially in the context of its military actions in Iraq and Afghanistan. This growth in costs led to renewed US efforts to get its allies in Seoul and Tokyo to contribute more not just to the United States' international efforts but also to their own security in the region. In Tokyo, this increased pressure certainly led its leaders to experience higher levels of concern about US abandonment, helping to encourage more positive views of South Korea as its partner in the East Asian alliance system.

This combination of regional development and the shift in US focus to other parts of the globe are important to be sure, but there were other developments in the Asia-Pacific region that provided Japan's leaders with additional incentives to be more cooperative with its partner regime in Seoul. First, North Korea began engaging in increasingly dangerous provocations, which heightened concerns throughout the entire Asia Pacific. At the same time, North Korea's benefactor nation, an increasingly powerful and aggressive China, did not appear to do much about Pyongyang's provocative actions. Consequently, with the United States ensconced in other parts of the globe, the Japanese, both leaders and citizens alike, increasingly came to realize how important South Korea was to their own security and to the ongoing peace and stability in the Asia Pacific. As a result, we see that these exogenous developments led to a period of time when more Japanese respondents expressed feelings of closeness to South Korea. Unfortunately, we also see from the data that this period of positive perceptions did not last but started turning negative right after 2012.

This increase in the share of Japanese respondents who said they felt distant from South Korea can be traced to the beginning of the Obama administration's second term in office. This was close to the time when President Obama announced his "pivot to Asia" policy, where his administration began refocusing American attention on the Asia-Pacific region. Obama's purpose in implementing this "pivot to Asia" was first to counter the past years of relative neglect given the previous administration's focus on the Middle East and Central and South Asia. It was also intended to give the United States more of a regional presence, particularly in response to China's growing power and influence. The return of the United States as a more engaged regional power helped reduce concerns in Tokyo about US abandonment, even in the context of North Korea's provocations and China's increasing regional influence, and this led to Japanese respondents' lower level of concern over the importance of Japan's relationship with South Korea. In other words, with the United States expressing a renewed commitment to the region, a rise in the share of Japanese respondents who would express feelings of distance toward South Korea was expected (Cha 1999).

Two other aspects of the South Korea, Japan, and United States triangular relations help account for this recent negative turn in the Japanese public's view of South Korea. We discussed above that, in the last decade and a half, South Korea experienced high levels of economic growth and significant advances in technological development, and this resulted in it beginning to close the developmental gap between itself and Japan. For example,

South Korea's economy has become the world's twelfth largest, and its economic presence throughout the globe has grown significantly. By way of illustration, consider that, in 2017, South Korea's largest company, Samsung, overtook Japan's largest corporation, Toyota, in Interbrand's ranking of the world's Best Global Brands.[2] South Korea has developed enough economic wherewithal to no longer be dependent on Japan—or any nation, for that matter—and, thus, it possesses the economic strength and diplomatic influence to begin evolving a more independent foreign policy. This is a relatively new dynamic in South Korea–Japan relations, one where Seoul is much less deferential to Tokyo than it was decades ago, and these developments have contributed to the decline in feelings of closeness that many in the Japanese public expressed toward their partner in the East Asian alliance system.

We also discussed above the fact that South Korea moved closer to Beijing and that this was quite evident during the presidency of Park Geun-Hye, who managed to build closer relations with China. During the Park presidency, several reciprocal visits by the two countries' leaders were completed, where South Korean president Park visited Beijing and Chinese leader Xi Jinping reciprocated with visits to Seoul. These visits were viewed quite negatively in Japan as leaders in Tokyo were disturbed by the tightening of relations between Seoul and Beijing, and while the growing closeness of relations between South Korea and Japan helped account for the shift that occurred in Japanese respondents' views of their partner country

Table 5.2. Countries Most Favored by South Koreans

Year	United States	Japan	North Korea	China	Russia	Don't Know	Total
2003	45.2%	10.0%	25.9%	9.6%	0.7%	8.6%	100%
2004	42.9%	9.1%	28.6%	12.3%	1.3%	5.9%	100%
2005	45.8%	6.3%	27.9%	11.7%	1.2%	7.1%	100%
2006	50.6%	6.2%	26.7%	10.8%	1.6%	4.0%	100%
2007	50.2%	9.1%	27.0%	7.8%	1.6%	4.3%	100%
2008	52.0%	10.2%	21.7%	8.7%	2.5%	4.9%	100%
2009	62.9%	10.1%	15.3%	6.4%	1.1%	4.3%	100%
2010	71.6%	7.2%	12.2%	4.3%	0.7%	3.9%	100%
2011	68.9%	8.5%	11.2%	4.7%	0.9%	5.9%	100%
2012	68.3%	7.1%	14.4%	5.2%	0.5%	4.4%	100%

Source: Compiled by the authors from the Korean General Social Survey.

in the alliance system, it is also true that increasing closeness between Seoul and Beijing was not without its own ongoing troubles (Ye 2017).

Returning to the data in figure 5.1, particularly the last several data points presented, we see that there is the beginning of a positive turn in Japanese attitudes toward South Korea. This change was expected given that the regional developments we highlighted above have continued to affect the region and also because the Trump administration's approach to the Asia Pacific, both adversaries and allies alike, engendered higher levels of uncertainty, particularly because its policy shifts raised questions over the reliability of the United States' long-term commitment. Moreover, when we combine these developments with the replacement of the Park presidency with the more left-leaning administration of Moon Jae-In, particularly Moon's engagement-based approach to North Korea, we can see that fears of abandonment on the Japanese side would grow, encouraging more positive feelings on the part of the Japanese respondents toward their South Korean alliance system partner.

Despite this positive movement in the attitudes of Japanese respondents toward South Korea, a significant gap remains between respondents who expressed feelings of closeness and those who expressed feelings of distance, and, as we explain below, we expect this gap to remain until leaders in Seoul and Tokyo, with encouragement and support from the United States, succeed in reducing the deleterious impacts associated with the unresolved historical issues that have challenged South Korea–Japan relations for many decades.

South Korean Views of Japan

Our assessment of the South Korean public's perceptions of Japan begins with a discussion of the different sources of public opinion data that we will use for mapping these perceptions. We note first that, while the extensive time series we used to map public opinion in Japan is not available for public attitudes in South Korea, there are adequate data available to reveal how South Koreans view Japan and their country's bilateral relationship with Tokyo. The first source is the South Korean General Social Survey (GSS), where respondents were asked to select the country for which they had the most favorable view. We presented some of these data in the previous chapter when we examined the South Korean public's view of the United States and China, but in this chapter, we expand our presentation in table 5.2 to include all nations that South Korean respondents selected as their most favored country. In addition to the United States and China, countries selected by South Korean respondents included Japan, Russia, and North Korea. By presenting all of the countries reported in the South Korean GSS, we can compare how South Koreans felt about the favorability of Japan compared to the four other countries that they also selected.

Even a cursory scan of the percentages in the table leads us to conclude that Japan is not a country that many South Koreans highly favored in the past. Naturally, part of the reason for this is that the United States figures so prominently in the measure of country favorability. Indeed, South Korean respondents who selected the United States as their most favored country averaged more than 50 percent of all respondents in most of the Korean GSS surveys reported in the table, but they grew to over two-thirds of respondents in the last three years for which the data were available. In addition to this, Japan's unpopularity is rendered even more notable in that, for many years, more than twice as many South Koreans chose North Korea as their most favorable country over Japan. Although these data end in 2012, such a lack of favorability, even if only for the ten years this particular series covers, does not portend well for South Koreans being strongly supportive of a tightening of relations with Tokyo. In spite of this, other patterns in these and other public opinion data suggest that there is hope for better relations than the Korean GSS data would suggest.

After the United States, North Korea is the country most often selected by South Koreans in the GSS as the nation they favor most. In spite of North Korea being in this position, we see that respondents selecting South Korea's adversary to the north declined by nearly one-half over the ten-year period for which these data exist, and we also see that the same is true for South Korean respondents selecting China as the country that is most favorable to them. These trends are made clear in the data presented in table 5.2, which also tell us that virtually no South Koreans had feelings of favorability toward Russia. This would be expected given the history of trouble between the two countries and tragic events like the shooting down of a Korean airliner (Korean Air Lines Flight 007) by a Russian military aircraft (Dallin 1985).

Moreover, while South Koreans with favorable views of Japan remained low throughout the entirety of the Korean GSS data series, there is a positive trend that comes into relief when we compare respondents favoring Japan versus China, particularly in surveys taken after 2009, as we see from

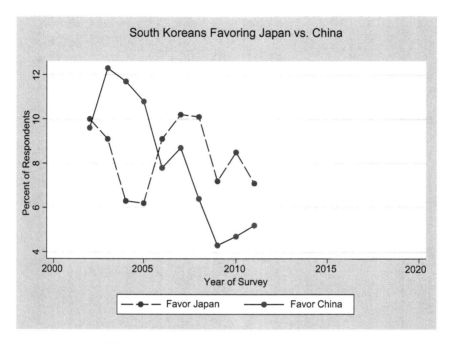

Figure 5.2. Source: Korean General Social Survey (GSS).

the data in figure 5.2. Even though respondents selecting these two countries experienced fluctuations throughout the entirety of the series, variations in respondents who selected Japan varied around an average of 8.5 percent, while fluctuation in respondents who selected China as the nation they most favored revealed a higher level of variance and a notable decline. This is an important finding given that China remains the principal challenger to the United States in the region and to the triangular relations that form the architecture of the East Asian alliance system.

We examined two other sources of data for our general mapping of how South Korean respondents have viewed Japan and South Korea–Japan relations. The first of these comes from the Asan Institute of Policy Studies in Seoul, which has been polling the South Korean public on their views of selected domestic and international issues for a number of years. Among the poll data are what the institute refers to as country favorability studies, where respondents were asked to rank the United States, China, North Korea, Russia, and Japan on a favorability scale ranging from 0 to 10, with 10 being the most favorable rating. These favorability rankings are available from 2010 and involve as many as twelve surveys in one year.[3] From 2010 to 2013, the favorability of Japan declined among South Korean respondents from 4.3 to 2.6 out of 10, where it remained for the next two years. However, from 2015 to 2019, the favorability of Japan began to rise, albeit slowly, to 3.6, particularly in 2018 and 2019.

The other source of public opinion data with which we can map South Korean views of Japan is the joint surveys taken in South Korea and Japan by the Genron NPO in Tokyo in cooperation with the East Asian Institute in Seoul. The Genron NPO is a Japanese nonprofit founded in 2001 with the mission of strengthening democracy in Japan, promoting peace and stability in East Asia, and developing solutions for pressing global issues.[4] This organization began taking joint public opinion polls in South Korea and Japan in 2013, and these studies do include questions about how the publics in Japan and South Korea feel about the other country. To provide a clearer illustration of the proportion of South Korean respondents having a favorable view of Japan, compared to those with negative perceptions, we used the Genron NPO polls and plotted these two groups of respondents in figure 5.3.

We see from the figure that the percentages of South Korean respondents with negative views of Japan are consistently higher than those with positive views. Despite this imbalance, there have been notable changes that were likely prompted by the rise in North Korean provocations and an increasingly powerful China that has become more assertive in the region. From 2013 to 2019, the distance between South Koreans with positive views and those holding negative perceptions of Japan narrowed significantly, from over sixty percentage points to just under twenty. We see that a rise in tensions occurred over the next two years, but we also see that this increase in distance appears to have narrowed again, which gives us some optimism that leaders in Seoul and Tokyo will find ways to more effectively manage the challenges in their bilateral relations and, ultimately, build a stronger and more effective partnership.

Given that, overall, South Korean and Japanese respondents view each other in a generally negative fashion, our next task is to explore existing data more deeply to identify the sources of these negative feelings. Moreover, given that we have witnessed some optimistic trends in public attitudes, we also need to examine available data more deeply to determine what issue areas involve some degree of common understanding and, thus, offer opportunities for South Korean and Japanese leaders to improve their bilateral relations. Naturally, this examination of available data will need to connect sources of division in this essential bilateral partnership with areas of common understanding—that is, where the publics in Japan and

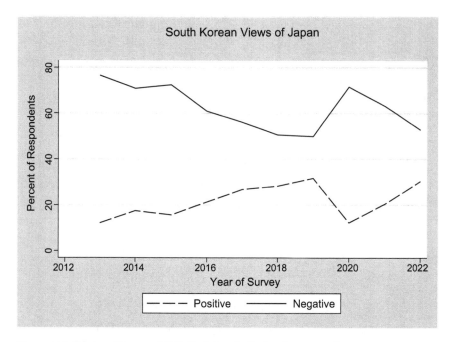

Figure 5.3. Source: Genron NPO Opinion Polls (various years).

South Korea will support efforts on the part of their respective leaderships to begin solving these problems, ultimately putting their bilateral relationship on a more solid footing.

Sources of Distrust and Common Understanding in South Korea–Japan Relations

Although the proportions of the Japanese and South Korean publics that registered negative impressions of the other country have declined in recent years, the data presented above tell us that bilateral relations between Seoul and Tokyo are generally perceived to be negative. This means that any effort to improve this bilateral partnership and strengthen the East Asian alliance system overall will be a challenge for leaders in Seoul and Tokyo. This is not lost on members of the Japanese and South Korean publics who recognize that bilateral relations between their two countries are not in the best of shape.

We see from the data in figure 5.4 that the proportions of Japanese and South Koreans who view the state of their respective nations' bilateral relations as being either somewhat or very bad have been quite similar, at least until recently. There is also a similarity in that the proportions of respondents in both countries who assess their countries' bilateral relations negatively are on average much larger than the proportions who say that bilateral relations are good or neither bad nor good. We see from the data in this figure that proportions in both countries varied in similar ways, particularly in the first six years the surveys asked this question. However, in spite of similar patterns of variation, the proportion of South Korean respondents viewing bilateral relations negatively jumped dramatically from 2018 to 2020, and this increase was much higher than what occurred with Japanese respondents. Fortunately, as stated briefly above, these proportions of respondents in both Japan and South Korea have declined in the last two years, suggesting that recent problems in this bilateral partnership may have begun to abate.

There are many reasons that bilateral relations between South Korea and Japan are challenged and that majorities in both countries see them in a negative way, recent improvements notwithstanding. Most of these reasons, as we will discuss in detail below, involve substantive problems that leaders in both countries will need to address and for which they must ultimately offer solutions that are satisfactory to both sides, something that can happen only if leaders in Seoul and Tokyo can garner a significant amount of political will. However, even with leaders who have the will to improve South Korea–Japan relations, the problems that separate Seoul and Tokyo involve significant divisions of opinion and, thus, do not lend themselves to quick and easy solutions.

As the data in table 5.3 indicate, only small minorities in both South Korea and Japan have viewed past chief executives of the other country in a positive fashion.[5] For Japanese, fewer than 10 percent of respondents in these Genron NPO polls viewed the South Korean president, be it Park Geun-Hye or Moon Jae-In, in a positive manner. However, Japanese views of South Korea's most recent president, Yoon Suk-Yeol, have revealed a dramatic shift. While representing only a single data point, we see that Japanese respondents have given President Yoon a favorable rating overall. At the same time, we also see that those giving the current South Korean president an unfavorable rating are the smallest they have been across these surveys.

We also see similar movements in how South Korean respondents have rated Japan's current prime minister, Kishida Fumio. South Koreans held quite negative views of former Japanese prime minister Abe Shinzo.

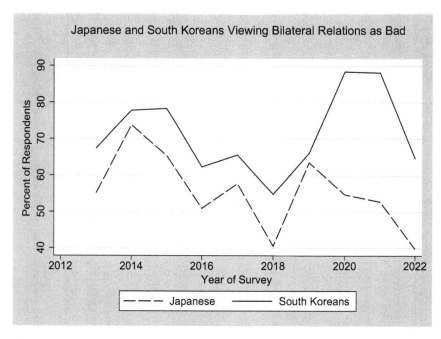

Figure 5.4. Source: Genron NPO Opinion Polls (various years).

Indeed, on average, fewer than 5 percent of South Korean respondents had a positive view of Prime Minister Abe, while those who viewed him negatively were consistently around 80 percent. For the current prime minister, however, South Korean respondents have given Kishida Fumio the highest rating in all of the years that these surveys have been taken. While this favorable rating is still rather low, it is nevertheless a notable data point because, at the same time, South Korean respondents who give the current prime minister an unfavorable rating are at the lowest level registered in these Genron NPO polls.

While the overall negativity manifested in these public opinion data clearly presents a challenge in South Korea–Japan relations, the most recent data may provide a reason for optimism. This is particularly important since it is the current South Korean president and Japanese prime minister who will be primarily responsible for taking the necessary action to reduce tensions, solve outstanding problems, and bring these two nations closer together. Moreover, the more positively and less negatively respondents in both countries view each other's leaders, the

Table 5.3. South Korean and Japanese Views of Each Other's Leaders

	Good	Bad	Neither
The Japanese Public's View of South Korea's Presidents			
Park Geun-Hye			
2015	5.2%	48.3%	25.8%
2016	6.7%	36.6%	32.9%
Moon Jae-In			
2017	5.2%	17.9%	31.9%
2018	10.2%	24.5%	31.6%
2019	2.8%	50.8%	17.3%
Yoon Suk-Yeol			
2021	2.0%	47.6%	13.0%
2022	20.1%	4.6%	22.3%
The South Korean Public's Views of Japan's Prime Ministers			
Abe Shinzo			
2015	2.1%	80.5%	8.8%
2016	4.1%	79.9%	10.8%
2017	2.6%	80.3%	12.4%
2018	2.0%	79.6%	13.2%
2019	3.0%	79.3%	11.7%
Kishida Fumio			
2021	3.1%	56.1%	21.5%
2022	6.6%	21.8%	42.7%

Source: Compiled by the authors from Genron NPO, Japan–Korea Opinion Polls, 2015–19.

fewer constraints they will have to face when taking any compromising action necessary to address very difficult problems with solutions that are not just acceptable to publics in both countries but more importantly trusted sufficiently to be welcomed as helping to produce better relations between Seoul and Tokyo.

This means that there is a reason for optimism that current leaders will improve South Korea–Japan relations, and this is reinforced by the fact that both South Koreans and Japanese have positive feelings about their countries' future relations. In polls taken in both countries from 2015 to 2019 inclusive, strong majorities of South Korean and Japanese respondents stated that bilateral relations between their two countries would either improve or remain unchanged and, thus, not get worse (table 5.4). We must note here that the proportions of respondents with positive and neutral views did decline between 2018 and 2019, by more than twenty percentage points in the case of Japanese respondents and just over nine percentage points in the case of South Korean respondents. These declinations reflect an emerging row between the two countries that began with President Moon essentially abrogating the agreement made by his predecessor on the comfort women problem and with a South Korean court requiring Japanese companies to provide compensation for forced wartime labor. In response, the Abe administration imposed trade restrictions against South Korea by removing the country from Japan's "white list of special trading partners."[6]

Despite the negative turn in the data for the most recent poll, which contains data up to 2022, results at the bottom of table 5.4 suggest that there is still hope that South Korea–Japan relations will not continue to deteriorate and that leaders will do what is necessary to prevent a threat to their essential integrity. These results are from questions posed to Japanese and South Korean respondents about the importance of bilateral relations between Seoul and Tokyo. Specifically, the percentages in the columns are the sum of respondents who said that South Korea–Japan bilateral relations are either very important or somewhat important, and we see from the data that strong majorities in both countries see this relationship as being important. South Korean respondents overwhelmingly recognize the importance of their country's relationship with Japan at averages amounting to well over 80 percent of respondents. Japanese respondents also recognize the importance of their relationship with South Korea, albeit less so, as respondents note that the bilateral relationship with South Korea is important averaged just under 60 percent for the eight-year period covered by available data.

While certain patterns in the distribution of public attitudes in South Korea and Japan support an optimistic view for the future of their relationship, improvements will require that leaders in Seoul and Tokyo work together to address the challenges that exist in their bilateral relations. Exactly what these challenges are can be gleaned from the Genron NPO surveys taken in Japan and South Korea at several points in time. Specifically, in the data presented in table 5.5,[7] we see what South Korean and Japanese respondents view as the principal reasons that each country's publics possess negative views of the other. While these reasons do touch on certain thematic areas, unresolved historical issues in particular, they

Public Attitudes and Relations between South Korea and Japan   109

Table 5.4. The State and Importance of South Korea–Japan Bilateral Relations

	Japan	South Korea
Respondents Who Said South Korean–Japanese Bilateral Relations Will Either Improve or Stay the Same		
2015	63.3%	64.9%
2016	71.7%	74.5%
2017	64.1%	77.5%
2018	66.1%	82.3%
2019	44.3%	73.4%
Respondents Who See South Korea–Japan Bilateral Relations as Very or Somewhat Important		
2015	65.3%	87.4%
2016	62.7%	86.9%
2017	64.3%	89.9%
2018	56.3%	82.4%
2019	50.9%	84.4%
2020	48.1%	82.2%
2021	46.6%	71.9%
2022	56.5%	82.6%

Source: Compiled by the authors from Genron NPO, Japan–Korea Opinion Polls, 2015–19.

do not quite reflect a common understanding as to why these issues persist as challenges to a better bilateral relationship.

Results in the upper portion of the table are from Genron NPO surveys taken in Japan, and we notice immediately that some reasons for the Japanese public's negative views of South Korea involve well-defined, tangible problems in the bilateral relationship, while other reasons are intangible and are not tied to identifiable real-world problems. The latter category involves what are generally emotional judgments that Japanese have made about South Koreans as a people. Two problems in particular capture the latter category: Japanese believing that South Koreans are overly patriotic and are essentially too emotional about Japan. These reasons cannot simply be relegated to a category of irrelevance, since they represent the views of over 35 percent and 40 percent of Japanese respondents in the two time periods reported. In addition to this, while these problems are not representative of a specific challenge that can be tackled by both countries'

110   *Strengthening South Korea–Japan Relations*

leaders, they are strongly connected to the number one reason that Japanese respondents reported having negative views of South Korea.

Most Japanese hold negative views of South Korea because of their dislike of the continued criticism that emanates from that country over historical issues. This is a complicated issue in South Korea–Japan relations that is very definitely tied to the actions of certain Japanese leaders who have made official visits to Yasukuni Shrine or announced revisions to history textbooks that gloss over the tragic years of the occupation of the Korean Peninsula and the Pacific War. They also include the utterances of Japanese politicians that downplayed or denied Japan's past military aggression. These kinds of behaviors do indeed elicit a negative reaction on the part of the South Korean government and lead members of the South Korean public to see Japan and its leaders in a very negative light. On the other hand, it is not just the undesired behavior of Japanese leaders that raises the salience of this historical problem; China also suffered at the hand of Japan's past military aggression and, as we discuss in more detail in the following chapter, is only too quick to use this problem to try to move South Korea further apart from Japan.

What is most interesting about the reasons Japanese respondents give for their negative perceptions of South Korea is that the overwhelming majority are tied together around the problem of unresolved historical issues and the reaction of South Koreans to anything related to these ongoing problems. Japanese respondents did offer other reasons for their negative perceptions of South Korea, like the territorial conflict over Takeshima/Dokdo, recognized by one-third of the Japanese public early on in the reported data and then one-fourth in the more recent polls. Moreover, there is a growing, albeit small, concern on the part of the Japanese public over South Korea's increasing closeness to China, but at the same time, a shrinking share of Japanese respondents viewed their negative perceptions as tracing back to the actions of South Korean leaders. In spite of this, most Japanese see the unfair criticism of their country over unresolved historical issues and the overly emotional or patriotic responses of South Koreans as being the principal causes of their negative views of South Korea.

It is interesting that South Koreans also see the problem of unresolved historical issues as the principal cause of their negative perceptions of Japan, a result that is clearly revealed in the bottom portion of table 5.5. More than any other reason, the lack of remorse from Japan over its past

Public Attitudes and Relations between South Korea and Japan 111

Table 5.5. Reasons for Japanese and South Korean Negative Views of Each Other

	2015–16	2018–19
Japanese Reasons		
Continued Criticism over History Issues	74.9%	60.7%
Territorial Conflict (Takeshima/Dokdo)	38.2%	26.7%
Incomprehensible South Korean Patriotism	14.6%	19.2%
South Koreans Are Too Emotional	20.9%	21.3%
SK Is Too Close to China	1.8%	7.6%
Disapprove of SK's Politicians' Actions	23.0%	10.8%
South Korean Reasons		
Lack of Remorse for Historical Actions	75.2%	73.1%
Territorial Dispute (Takeshima/Dokdo)	69.7%	61.4%
Discrimination against Japanese-Koreans	7.2%	6.0%
Disapprove of JPN's Politicians' Actions	19.7%	17.4%
Actions Do Not Reflect True Feelings	20.5%	17.8%
Japan Aiming to Be a Military Power	1.6%	3.2%
Comfort Women Issue	18.2%*	18.7%

* Includes 2016 data only.
Source: Compiled by the authors from Genron NPO, Japan–Korea Opinion Polls, 2015–19.

militaristic behavior was selected by an average of three-fourths of South Koreans in the polls conducted by Genron NPO. This problem of history as a source of negativity becomes even more prevalent when one considers that 20 percent (2015–16) and 18 percent (2018–19) of South Korean respondents noted that their negative feelings stem from Japan's corrective actions not reflecting their true feelings, something that is interpretative and, thus, something that is not quite a solvable problem. In addition to this, 20 percent (2015–16) and 18 percent (2018–19) of South Koreans indicated that they simply disapprove of the actions taken by Japanese politicians.

South Korean respondents cited other causes for their negative views of Japan, and these additional reasons are distinct from those cited by their Japanese counterparts. Perhaps the most notable contrast rests with the 70 percent and 61 percent of South Koreans noting that the territorial dispute over Takeshima/Dokdo was the principal source of their negative feelings toward Japan. This represented a significant departure from Japanese respondents, whose proportions were more than thirty percentage points lower in the 2015–16 surveys and more than forty percentage points lower

112 Strengthening South Korea–Japan Relations

in the 2018–19 surveys. In addition to this, South Korean respondents cited three other reasons for their negative impressions of Japan, and two of these involved rather small proportions of respondents, while one involved a somewhat larger proportion. Small proportions said their source of negative feelings rested with Japan's goal of becoming a military power and its discriminatory treatment of Koreans living in Japan. More notable than these was that almost 20 percent of South Koreans said that their negative impressions of Japan stemmed from the comfort women issue.

This is significant because no Japanese cited this issue as a source of negative feelings toward South Korea, but this should not be unexpected because it is not something that Japanese can specifically hold against South Korea save for the excessive criticism it generates among South Koreans. Moreover, for many Japanese, the comfort women problem was largely resolved when President Park Geun-Hye and Prime Minister Abe brokered an agreement that appeared to provide a path forward to solve this divisive issue. Unfortunately, the succeeding administration of Moon Jae-In put this agreement's implementation on hold. While we will discuss this problem in more detail in the following chapters, what is important here is that the combination of this issue and the others identified by the publics in these two countries makes it clear that leaders in Seoul and Tokyo have a difficult path ahead. This leaves us with the question of how leaders in these two US allies should proceed.

In the Genron NPO data provided above, we see how Japanese and South Korean respondents prioritized the importance of the issues that separate their two nations. The responses are provided in table 5.6, and they suggest that leaders should focus on the general problem of unresolved historical issues but should also address, or at least reduce the saliency of, the territorial dispute over Takeshima/Dokdo and the comfort women problem. While these were among the top three problems selected by both the Japanese and South Korean respondents in Genron NPO polls, the proportions of respondents selecting these three items were not the same across the two US allies.

Specifically, while more Japanese want to solve the issue of history than any other issue, the proportion citing this as the primary issue to address was an average of just over 40 percent for Japanese, whereas more than two-thirds of South Korean respondents favored this focus. This support-level disparity also characterized differences between Japanese and South Korean respondents with respect to the territorial dispute and the comfort

Public Attitudes and Relations between South Korea and Japan   113

Table 5.6. South Korean and Japanese Opinions on Actions Needed to Improve Bilateral Relations

	Japan	South Korea
Resolve Historical Disputes		
2016	46.5%	74.9%
2019	39.8%	64.0%
Resolve Territorial Dispute		
2016	39.0%	81.1%
2019	41.3%	75.6%
Resolve Comfort Women Issue		
2016	29.6%	75.7%
2019	53.7%	84.5%
Increase Cooperation on North Korea		
2016	19.0%	7.0%
2019	22.4%	3.6%

Source: Compiled by the authors from Genron NPO, Japan–Korea Opinion Polls, 2015–19.

women problem. We see from the data in table 5.6 that, in 2016, more than twice as many South Koreans as Japanese—a difference of more than forty percentage points—wanted to focus on solving the territorial dispute over Takeshima/Dokdo, but this difference dropped to just over thirty percentage points in 2019. An even greater difference existed in 2016 with respect to the problem of comfort women, as South Koreans who wanted to focus on solving this issue were more than forty-five percentage points higher than Japanese who agreed. This difference narrowed significantly in 2019, as Japanese wanting leaders to focus on this problem grew by more than twenty percentage points. Specifically, in 2019, the percentage of Japanese respondents wanting to focus on the comfort women problem grew to nearly 54 percent, while the South Korean proportion grew almost ten percentage points to 84 percent.

While some of the issue-preference gaps narrowed between 2016 and 2019 inclusive, there is one more notable difference in the problem-solving preferences of Japanese and South Korean respondents. Japanese are not unlike South Koreans in that they recognize that the three more important problems separating their two countries are the unresolved problems of history, the Dokdo/Takeshima territorial dispute, and the comfort women problem, but Japanese respondents were also rather strongly in favor of working to reduce the negative impacts of North Korean provocations. Unfortunately, this is not likely to happen because, while the positive feelings that many South Koreans had toward their northern neighbor have declined over time, there is little support among South Koreans to cooperate with their Japanese counterparts on taking joint action to deter the provocative behavior of their adversary north of the thirty-eighth parallel.

Leaders in South Korea and Japan clearly have their work cut out for them if they are to solve the problems that face them in their bilateral relations. The issues that separate these two US allies are difficult if not well-nigh intractable, and they will require courageous, politically difficult efforts on the part of each country's leadership to have any hope of resolution. Nonetheless, the question remains as to what the prospects are that the necessary effort will be undertaken and what solutions can be approved by both sides. This is the topic that we take up in the next chapter of this volume, and in addition to providing background on the principal unresolved historical issues that divide South Korean and Japan, we will also examine the latest rise in negativity in South Korea–Japan bilateral relations as well as the role that the United States can play to help its allies in Seoul and Tokyo make closer relations between them a reality.

6

Territorial Disputes, Human Rights, and Court Case Challenges in South Korea–Japan Relations

The preceding analysis has shown that the challenges that exist in South Korea–Japan relations not only contribute to the negative perceptions that the publics in each country have of the other but more importantly stand in the way of leaders in Seoul and Tokyo addressing extant challenges in their bilateral relations and doing what is necessary to strengthen the East Asian alliance system overall. These challenges stem from the larger problem of unresolved historical issues that elevate tensions between South Korea and Japan not simply because they are unresolved but also because they are exploited by Beijing, making it even more difficult for South Korea's and Japan's leaders to keep their partnership functioning smoothly as the base of the alliance system's set of triangular relations. To be sure, these historical problems have encompassed many aspects of how leaders in Seoul and Tokyo interact with each other, but a number of specific disputes are important for understanding the challenges faced by these two US allies in their efforts to find long-term solutions to tensions that exist in their bilateral partnership.

What is most important to understand is that unresolved problems of history are high-politics issues in both South Korea and Japan, and they not only touch directly on both the interests and emotions of leaders and citizens in both countries but also have been taken up by numerous pressure groups that are deeply vested in promoting certain aspects of these problems in South Korea–Japan relations (Bukh 2020; Huth, Kim, and Roehrig 2021). The issues referenced here concern the Takeshima/Dokdo territorial dispute, the human rights problem of South Korean "comfort

116 *Strengthening South Korea–Japan Relations*

women," who were forced to work as sex slaves during the Pacific War, and a recent row that began when a South Korean court ruled that Japanese companies must compensate South Korean workers who were forced into labor during the Pacific War.

As we stated above, these unresolved problems of history have been a divisive force in the South Korea–Japan partnership, particularly in the last several years, and to reduce their disruptive potential, leaders in both countries will need sufficient political will to move against the tide of public opinion and counter the preferences of many influential organized interests. This is a tall order, to be sure, and it leads to this chapter's focus on the rise and impacts of these unresolved historical problems with an eye toward how leaders in Seoul and Tokyo can work together to reduce the tensions they cause and to ensure that their bilateral relations can continue to function effectively as the base of the East Asian alliance system's set of triangular relations.

Our effort to accomplish these goals will begin with acknowledging that these outstanding problems in South Korea–Japan relations were never adequately dealt with at the end of the Pacific War, neither at the Tokyo War Crimes Trials nor with the signing of the San Francisco Treaty that ended the US occupation of Japan. Despite this, it is important to note here that the problems of the Dokdo/Takeshima territorial dispute, the South Korean comfort women, and other unresolved problems of history did not prevent South Korea–Japan relations from being conducted in a relatively smooth manner throughout the entire Cold War period.[1] This does not mean that there were no challenges; tensions did arise throughout this period, but what disruptions did occur were generally not at the level that these unresolved historical problems have led to recently. For a number of reasons, South Korea–Japan relations became more troubled after the fall of the Berlin Wall.

We note first that there was little reason to expect that unresolved problems of history in South Korea–Japan relations would remain permanently dormant. Indeed, in 1962, one observer writing about early negotiations between Seoul and Tokyo to reach an agreement that would pave the way for a treaty of reconciliation, Donald Hellman (1962, 19), noted that the substantive issues leaders in South Korea and Japan were addressing at the time would likely form "both basic and continuing international problems of this area of the world." Both countries have gone through dramatic transformations since this time, as have other actors in the region,

Territorial Disputes, Human Rights, and Court Case Challenges   117

which influenced the manner in which they interact with each other. Taken together, the combination of declining hierarchy in the alliance system's triangular relations, an inconsistent level of commitment on the part of the United States, and the impact of a rising China on relations among the alliance system's members provide an environment wherein more independent foreign policy action on the part of Seoul and Tokyo was incentivized.

We will investigate the growing salience of these unresolved problems of history in South Korea–Japan relations with a focus on sketching out what a path leading to the amelioration of their destructive influences will need to look like, but even reducing the tensions these divisive issues cause will most likely not result in a complete resolution of the ongoing problems. Rather, significant progress will be characterized by the adoption of confidence-building measures built around agreements that address some aspects of these unresolved problems of history in South Korea–Japan relations but do not eliminate them completely. Implementing narrower, more directed agreements will help reduce the disruptive aspects of these unresolved historical issues so that leaders in Seoul and Tokyo can do what is necessary to keep their essential partnership intact and operating effectively as the base of the triangle of relations that forms the East Asian alliance system.

The Dokdo/Takeshima Territorial Dispute

Despite his actions being domestically unpopular, it was the diplomacy of South Korean president Park Chung-Hee that paved the way for the formation of the South Korea–Japan partnership, which began in earnest with the Reconciliation Treaty between South Korea and Japan that was put into effect in 1965.[2] Despite a very troubled past and the persistence of unresolved issues between the two nations, this treaty has gone a long way toward improving relations between Seoul and Tokyo, and, indeed, it even helped establish a multidecade period of somewhat smoothly operating relations between South Korea and Japan. In spite of the many years of relatively good relations between these two US allies, President Park and his Japanese counterpart, Prime Minister Sato Eisaku, did not in fact resolve all outstanding issues that separated South Korea from Japan, and, ultimately, these have reemerged as challenges in South Korea–Japan relations.

As emphasized above, the specific issues that were left unresolved all revolved around the historical problems that remain at the heart of relations between Seoul and Tokyo, but past and current attempts to address these unresolved issues have been and will continue to be complicated by the fact that Tokyo and Seoul do not interpret the Reconciliation Treaty in the same manner. Specifically, this treaty notes that all of South Korea's claims against Japan would be resolved upon its promulgation. The South Korean interpretation is that, while claims between the two countries are settled, the settlement does not include individual human rights claims. Leaders in Japan do not agree with this interpretation, but despite this disagreement, relations between Seoul and Tokyo throughout the Cold War were generally smooth in operation. This period of relatively stable relations may have lulled some officials in both nations into believing that such problems as the Dokdo/Takeshima territorial dispute and other human rights problems would no longer have a negative impact on relations between these two US allies. This was not to be; as stated above, they have recently become increasingly problematic and disruptive in South Korea–Japan relations.

Concerning the Dokdo/Takeshima dispute, at the end of the Pacific War, South Korean president Rhee Syngman remained deeply concerned about the territorial integrity and overall sovereignty of South Korea, and this in turn led him to oppose vehemently any attempt on the part of Japanese leaders to extend their country's claim of sovereignty over what he saw as his country's territorial waters. The South Korean president's concerns were heightened by certain provisions of the San Francisco Treaty—specifically, the provision that removed previously sanctioned prohibitions against Japan extending its territorial waters and, thus, its sovereignty over areas simultaneously claimed by South Korea. These prohibitions had been put in place during the Pacific War, and, in reaction to their removal in accordance with the San Francisco Treaty, South Korean president Rhee Syngman announced the establishment of what he referred to as the "peace line." This "peace line" not only barred Japanese fishing vessels from entering waters closer than sixty miles from the South Korean coast but also placed the Dokdo/Takeshima Island territory under South Korean sovereignty.

Japanese leaders protested the establishment of this "peace line," but they did not receive support from the United States, which not only allowed the dispute to continue but also took a very ambiguous position regarding who had sovereignty over this territory. Because the United States did not provide any guidance to either of its East Asian allies as to how to proceed toward a resolution, this territorial dispute led to increased problems in

Territorial Disputes, Human Rights, and Court Case Challenges   119

South Korea–Japan relations. Early in the post-Armistice period, tensions between South Korea and Japan continued to increase, and they reached a dangerous point when the South Korean Coast Guard seized Japanese fishing vessels and the Japanese responded by sending their own Coast Guard ships to the area. This combination of actions ultimately escalated into incidents where the South Korean Coast Guard fired on one of its Japanese counterparts.

Although the United States did not provide guidance on how to resolve this territorial dispute, Washington did make known its desire to see reduced tensions in Seoul's relations with Tokyo. For this reason, the United States encouraged leaders in South Korea and Japan to negotiate a reconciliation agreement, and these efforts ultimately resulted in the promulgation of the 1965 Reconciliation Treaty. This treaty was approved by both the South Korean and the Japanese governments, and it dealt with many issues that separated these two countries. Unfortunately, it did not end the problems surrounding the disputed islands of Dokdo/Takeshima, which were not mentioned in this document. Rather, the treaty was accompanied by another agreement, a fishing agreement, that did address but did not resolve this territorial dispute.

This fishing agreement was approved by the governments in Seoul and Tokyo at the same time they sanctioned the Reconciliation Treaty. While the fishing agreement did help reduce tensions, it, unfortunately, did not really end the dispute between South Korea and Japan over which country had sovereignty over the islets of Dokdo/Takeshima. This is because the 1965 fishing agreement noted that a permanent solution would have to be left to future negotiations and that, in the meantime, it would be acceptable for one side to announce its own claim of sovereignty and the other side to respond with an equivalent counterclaim. Moreover, while both sides were allowed to use this disputed territory, South Korea would occupy these islands, but neither Japan nor South Korea was to take any action that would increase its police presence or install any new facilities.

What followed the Reconciliation Treaty was a period defined by an uneasy but relatively peaceful equilibrium, and, to help maintain this period of relative quiescence in South Korea–Japan relations, the US Board on Geographic Names changed the official name of Dokdo/Takeshima to Liancourt Rock. Initially, US officials hoped that this neutral name would incentivize both sides to uphold the terms of the 1965 fishing agreement, but neither side was satisfied with the territory's status. Nonetheless, this period of relative stability endured until two to three decades ago, when tensions over this disputed territory began to grow in salience and, ultimately, became a challenge in South Korea–Japan relations. The principal reason that tensions increased over the Dokdo/Takeshima territory concerned the changed behavior of leaders in Seoul and Tokyo, which upset the uneasy status quo that had defined this dispute since the fishing agreement was put into place.

Leaders in both countries sometimes engaged in behavior that rendered this unresolved territorial dispute salient, forcing the other side into a response that escalated tensions between these two US allies. Unfortunately, this behavior has often been motivated by a domestic political calculus—that is, by attempts to elevate lagging popular support for incumbent politicians by stimulating nationalist enthusiasm. There are several examples of such behavior, which perhaps began with the politically unpopular but first democratically elected president of South Korea, Roh Tae-Woo, who declared a "diplomatic war" on Japan when newly issued textbooks announced that the islets of Dokdo/Takeshima were under Japanese sovereignty in addition to omitting any discussion of aggression during the occupation of the Korean Peninsula.

While disputes over Japanese history textbooks continued, tensions over Dokdo/Takeshima did not escalate again until 1996, when Japanese leaders announced that they would commence building a wharf on the disputed islets (Ku 2018), which would be a manifest violation of the 1965 fishing agreement that prohibited the expansion of any facilities on Dokdo/Takeshima. In response, South Korean president Kim Young-Sam responded by stating that he would deal "sternly" with his Japanese counterpart, elevating nationalist fervor in South Korea. It is interesting that Kim's announcement corresponded to a period when his support levels had precipitously dropped. Nonetheless, President Kim's announcement led to another rise in tensions in South Korea–Japan relations, which again subsided after a short period of time, only to increase again more than a decade later when South Korean president Lee Myung-Bak reacted to a South Korean court ruling. The ruling said that Japan had not done enough to address the issue of his country's comfort women, and President Lee responded to this by unexpectedly taking a trip to the disputed territory of Dokdo/Takeshima. President Lee's visit was not simply a protest against Japan's lack of adequate action on unresolved historical issues but was also an event intended to inflame South Korean nationalist passions and boost his falling support levels (Ku 2018).

Incidents like these confirm the high-politics aspects of this territorial dispute in South Korea–Japan relations, suggesting strongly that a first step toward reducing its disruptive tendencies would need to involve each side refraining from provocative behavior that renders the dispute salient. This is extremely important because, when tensions are high in each country over this territorial dispute, public attitudes act like constraints on leaders in both countries, rendering it more difficult for them to pursue any form of compromise that could help reduce tensions. This does not mean that, without disruptions attendant to this kind of provocative behavior, leaders in Seoul and Tokyo would be better able to broker a solution that reduces tension over this unresolved territorial dispute, because, as we and others have argued, there really is no compromise that would satisfy both sides.

The underlying difficulty of South Korea's and Japan's claims of sovereignty over Dokdo/Takeshima is that the opportunity costs of continuing this dispute are not that great for either side, making it unrealistic that leaders in Seoul and Tokyo would simply ignore the disputed territory (Huth, Kim, and Roehrig 2021). This is true particularly from the South Korean point of view because, when asked why South Korean respondents hold negative views of Japan, two issues were mentioned most often. As we see from the data in table 6.1, South Korean respondents attribute their negative views of Japan to it not being fully cognizant of its historical burden with respect to its occupation of the Korean Peninsula. Nearly three-quarters of respondents in South Korea cited this issue in both 2018 and 2019, but a close second in the view of South Korean respondents was the territorial dispute over the islets of Dokdo/Takeshima. Nearly 58 percent of respondents mentioned this issue in 2019, and while this was down from nearly two-thirds in 2018, it was still well over half of all South Korean respondents. The importance of these two issues is manifest in these data: the next most cited issue was that of South Korean comfort women, which is an important issue in relations between Seoul and Tokyo but was more than thirty-five percentage points lower than the territorial dispute issue in 2019.

Compared to their South Korean counterparts, Japanese respondents did not see this territorial dispute as having that much weight as a problem in its relations with South Korea. Evidence for this is clear in the data contained in table 6.1, which indicates that in both 2018 and 2019 only about one-quarter of Japanese respondents viewed the Dokdo/Takeshima dispute as a true problem in South Korea–Japan relations. In fact, in both years, more Japanese than South Korean respondents viewed the comfort

122   *Strengthening South Korea–Japan Relations*

Table 6.1. Most Important Reasons South Koreans and Japanese Hold Negative Views of Each Other

South Korean Respondents	2018	2019
Because Japan Has Not Properly Reflected on Its History of Invading South Korea	70.0%	76.1%
Because There Is a Territorial Dispute over Takeshima/Dokdo	65.3%	57.5%
Because of the Comfort Women Issue	17.2%	20.1%
Japanese Respondents	**2018**	**2019**
Because South Korea Continues to Criticize Japan in Historical Issues	69.3%	52.1%
Because of the Comfort Women Issue	30.5%	23.8%
Because There Is a Territorial Dispute over Takeshima/Dokdo	27.6%	25.7%

Source: Compiled by the authors from Genron NPO (2019).

women issue as a source of negative perceptions between the two countries. However, in spite of the fact that more Japanese respondents heavily weighted the comfort women issue than did their South Korea counterparts, it was still not the most important source of their negative views of South Koreans. The number one reason can be traced to the Japanese respondents seeing the problem of history differently from South Korean respondents. Specifically, Japanese view the problem of history as a tool utilized by South Koreans to continue to criticize Japan, and they also reported believing that this criticism should stop because, contrary to the South Korean view, these issues were resolved by the Reconciliation Treaty and fishing agreement of 1965.

This is a difficult challenge in South Korea–Japan relations because, while South Koreans want their government to continue its efforts to resolve this territorial issue, Japanese respondents do not see it as a pressing problem in their relations with South Korea. Again, this will make any satisfactory resolution of this territorial dispute very difficult, especially given that South Koreans have a very high standard for what they would consider an acceptable solution. For example, when former president Park Geun-Hye was pressing for a summit with Japanese prime minister Abe Shinzo

Territorial Disputes, Human Rights, and Court Case Challenges   123

to address this territorial problem—as well as other outstanding issues—South Koreans were overwhelmingly dissatisfied with their president's accomplishments because they said she was not sufficiently tough with respect to Japan's position on the Dokdo/Takeshima dispute. Moreover, at one point in the planning of this summit, the Japanese prime minister proposed having the International Court of Justice adjudicate competing claims of sovereignty over this territory. President Park opposed the proposal, but her opposition was viewed as inadequate by South Koreans who believed their president should have prevented the idea from being raised at all (Genron NPO 2019).

The point is that neither South Koreans nor Japanese will be satisfied with anything short of having complete sovereignty over these disputed islets, and for Japanese respondents, this territory should involve no dispute at all because they believe it was resolved with the promulgation of the fishing agreement that was partner to the 1965 Reconciliation Treaty. This helps explain why the percentages of Japanese respondents who view this territorial dispute as a source of negativity are so much lower than those of South Korean respondents. Indeed, the higher shares of South Koreans who want a resolution to this dispute suggests not simply that leaders in Seoul will continue to advance their preferred solution but also, as stated above, that the South Korean public will have very high standards for an acceptable solution.

Indeed, when we compare what South Koreans, in contrast to their Japanese counterparts, see as an acceptable solution, any resolution seems impossible.[3] According to surveys taken by the Japanese Prime Minister's Office, more than three-quarters of Japanese believe that Takeshima is plain and simple Japanese territory, and, at the same time, slightly less than two-thirds of Japanese respondents believe that South Korea's claims are not legal. In addition to this, more than 60 percent of Japanese respondents stated that Takeshima was within Japan's territorial limits and, specifically, that it is part of Shimane Prefecture. Consequently, as we discuss in more detail later in this volume, the best interim strategy for leaders in Seoul and Tokyo to contain the disruptive potential attendant to this territorial disagreement is to be certain that no provocative actions are taken by either citizens or leaders with respect to Dokdo/Takeshima. Clearly, this will not solve this difficult problem, but it will keep the dispute from functioning as a wedge between these two US allies, further straining their bilateral relations.

The Problem of South Korean Comfort Women

If the Dokdo/Takeshima dispute is an intractable problem in South Korea–Japan relations, the unresolved human rights issue of comfort women is not; it represents a problem for which leaders in Seoul and Tokyo could coordinate their efforts and broker an acceptable solution. This does not mean that this issue is simple or that it does not cause divisions in the relationship between South Korea and Japan. Indeed, it is intermittently a source of high-level tension in South Korea–Japan relations that has stood in the way of leaders in Seoul and Tokyo improving their bilateral partnership. This unresolved problem traces its origins to a tragic series of events that violated the human rights of hundreds of thousands of young women who were forced into sexual slavery by the Imperial Japanese Army during its occupation of numerous Asian countries throughout the Pacific War. This issue is known euphemistically as the "comfort women" problem, and while it is presently unresolved, this is not due to a lack of effort on the part of leaders in South Korea and Japan to work toward a solution.

While reports on the actual number of women who were forced into sexual slavery vary, there is little disagreement that, from the late 1930s to the surrender of Japan in 1945, more than two hundred thousand women of Chinese, Korean, Philippine, Dutch, and other ethnicities were forced to work in brothels set up by the Imperial Japanese Army across the expanse of its empire. The treatment of these women was inhumane, and high percentages of these sex slaves suffered permanent physical damage and psychological trauma, not to mention death. As a result, reports of the suffering of these women came out at the Tokyo War Crimes Trial, and, beginning in the early 1950s, negotiations were held between Japan and South Korea over how and at what levels to compensate not just individual survivors for the human rights violations they suffered but also the families who lost female members to this inhumane practice. The *Chosun Ilbo* reported that, leading up to the 1965 treaty, South Korea demanded $364,000 from Japan for survivors, especially those who suffered injuries, as well as comfort women who perished as a result of the treatment to which they were subjected. This was agreed to by Japan, which considered the matter closed once the Reconciliation Treaty was signed and promulgated.

While the Japanese position on this human rights problem has been clear since 1965, South Korea's leadership has been guided by a different interpretation of what the Reconciliation Treaty meant for Korean comfort women. This was particularly important for the surviving comfort women in South Korea, who were subjected to wartime abuses. In fact, all along, surviving comfort women noted that their principal claim was not so much compensation but rather a formal statement from the Japanese government that it was legally responsible for the human rights violations they had suffered. Moreover, despite South Koreans and Japanese having different views as to whether or not this problem was actually resolved, efforts to broker an agreement and find a resolution did continue between South Korea and Japan. Among the more notable was the 1994 establishment of the Asian Women's Fund, set up by Socialist prime minister Murayama Tomiichi, who also issued a direct apology to the survivors for the physical and psychological suffering they had endured.

More recently, former South Korean president Park Geun-Hye and Japanese prime minister Abe Shinzo hammered out an agreement to resolve the comfort women issue even though Abe had been known in the past to offend the South Korean people greatly with statements about comfort women that were, to say the least, historically inaccurate.[4] In December 2015, these two leaders agreed that Japan would set up a fund for survivors in the amount of ¥1 billion, and the South Korean government agreed that in the future it would refrain from criticizing Japan about this particular issue.

While the agreement had the potential to reduce the tensions caused by this unresolved historical issue, it suffered from the same problem as all past efforts on the part of South Korea and Japan to come to an understanding of this tragic problem of South Korean comfort women. Specifically, not only did leaders in both countries perhaps move too quickly to get it negotiated and approved but the parties with the greatest stake in this agreement were not consulted about the contents worked out by President Park and Prime Minister Abe. As a result, several comfort women noted that it was not acceptable, and twelve of them even filed lawsuits in a South Korean court, which ruled that the agreement did not deal with the Japanese government's legal responsibilities in a clear and definitive manner and, moreover, did not consider the legal rights of the survivors.

The result was that, despite this earnest attempt on the part of President Park and Prime Minister Abe, the difficult and tragic problem was not resolved, and public opinion in Japan and South Korea reflect such a recognition, albeit more so among South Koreans than among Japanese.

The 2016 Genron NPO poll reported that only 28 percent of South Koreans felt that this agreement addressed the problem "significantly," compared to 65 percent who did not. Moreover, 48 percent of Japanese noted that this agreement addressed the problem in a "significant" manner, while 45 percent stated that it did not. In addition to this, a 2017 Genron NPO poll taken in both countries noted that only 21 percent of South Koreans approved of the agreement and 56 percent did not, while 45 percent and 48 percent of Japanese did and did not approve of the agreement. These data indicate that even Japanese respondents have not been solidly convinced that the agreement between President Park and Prime Minister Abe solved the issue of comfort women, and this was verified in the same 2017 poll. Specifically, 75 percent of South Korean respondents noted that the issue was not resolved, and a majority (54%) of Japanese respondents answered the question in exactly the same way.

Such similarities are also witnessed in how Japanese and South Korean respondents view the impacts associated with solving the comfort women problem. Specifically, data in table 6.2 indicate that over 40 percent of Japanese respondents stated that resolving the comfort women problem would help build better bilateral relations, while more than three-quarters of South Korean respondents shared this view. This is not a small difference, and it suggests more urgency on the part of South Korean respondents, but it is rendered less dramatic when we also note that an average of 50 percent of Japan's respondents noted that a resolution of unresolved historic disputes between South Korea and Japan would go a long way toward improving bilateral relations between these two US allies. In other words, respondents in both countries believe that solving the problem of comfort women, and other unresolved historic issues, would help improve their bilateral relations, but this similarity does not exist when South Korean and Japanese respondents are pushed to specify how they would solve these problems, particularly the problem of South Korean comfort women.

When asked what exactly should be done to address the unresolved human rights problem of comfort women, a plurality of Japanese respondents (34%) in 2018 noted that the 2015 Park-Abe agreement should stand as it is and not be changed. In the same poll, only 13 percent of Japanese respondents felt that either a revision or an addendum would be appropriate to resolve the comfort women problem. South Korean respondents, on the other hand, stated that the agreement should be revised (48%) or

Territorial Disputes, Human Rights, and Court Case Challenges 127

Table 6.2. Comfort Women and Building Better South Korean–Japanese Relations

South Korean Respondents	2017	2018
Resolve Comfort Women Problem	75.8%	76.1%
Resolve Dokdo/Takeshima Dispute	82.1%	82.1%
Resolve Historical Disputes	75.8%	78.1%
Build State-Level Trust and Communication	18.9%	20.4%
Resolve North Korea's Nuclear Issues	10.9%	5.6%
Japanese Respondents	**2017**	**2018**
Resolve Comfort Women Problem	42.6%	42.2%
Resolve Dokdo/Takeshima Dispute	39.2%	38.7%
Resolve Historical Disputes	49.0%	54.7%
Build State-Level Trust and Communication	29.8%	32.1%
Resolve North Korea's Nuclear Issues	21.2%	18.8%

Source: Compiled by the authors from Genron NPO (2018).

that additional measures should be appended (39%). Public opinions on solving this tragic problem in South Korea–Japan bilateral relations reveal views that are distributed very differently, but respondents in both countries are in relative accord with respect to the difficulties that will be associated with addressing these problems of unresolved historical issues.

The data contained in table 6.3 are from five surveys taken in South Korea and Japan from 2015 to 2019 inclusive, and they suggest that public views related to addressing unresolved historic issues and improving bilateral relations have remained relatively consistent over this five-year period. While an average of 7 percent more Japanese respondents stated that historical issues would be difficult to solve even if bilateral relations improved, an average of 8 percent more South Korean respondents stated that historical issues would gradually be resolved as bilateral relations between these two US allies improved. That these positions were taken only by one-quarter to one-third of respondents in each country is less encouraging than if they involved majorities of each country's publics. Nonetheless, they still indicate relative accord in how South Koreans and Japanese view the connection between their two countries and solutions to unresolved historical issues.

Where there is less accord between these two countries' publics rests with whether they believe that bilateral relations will remain in a challenged

128 *Strengthening South Korea–Japan Relations*

Table 6.3. Japanese and South Korean Perceptions of Historical Issues and Bilateral Relations

	Japan	South Korea
Historical Issues Will Be Difficult to Improve Even If Bilateral Relations Improve		
2015	35.1%	24.8%
2016	28.1%	22.6%
2017	29.3%	25.0%
2018	35.2%	27.4%
2019	32.6%	25.0%
Historical Issues Will Gradually Be Resolved as Bilateral Relations Improve		
2015	19.3%	20.9%
2016	20.2%	32.9%
2017	26.2%	31.9%
2018	21.9%	35.8%
2019	20.4%	30.8%
Bilateral Relations Will Not Improve Unless Historical Issues Are Resolved		
2015	27.1%	52.5%
2016	21.9%	42.8%
2017	25.5%	39.5%
2018	22.6%	33.5%
2019	23.6%	39.1%

Source: Compiled by the authors from Genron NPO, Japan–South Korea Public Polls, 2015–19.

state if there is no progress in solving outstanding historical issues. In each of the surveys taken over these five years, an average of 17 percent more South Koreans said that bilateral relations would not improve unless there was progress on resolving outstanding historical issues, and this difference was as high as 25 percent in 2015 but as low as 11 percent in 2018. Unlike the previous questions, for which South Korean and Japanese responses were relatively stable across the five surveys, responses to whether or not bilateral relations could improve without progress on unresolved historical issues did fluctuate throughout the five-year period.

Again, these fluctuations indicate that the view of the South Korean and Japanese publics have responded to external developments in South Korea–Japan relations. This is particularly evident when we examine the attitudes of South Korean and Japanese respondents on another issue, one that directly affected efforts by South Korean and Japanese leaders to make progress on unresolved historical issues. This issue was not the result of political leaders engaging in provocative behavior or even leaders in Beijing exploiting these unresolved historical issues to promote their own interests in the region. Rather, it was the result of a judicial decision rendered by a court in South Korea.

Court Cases and Forced Wartime Labor

There is no way to overstate the importance of South Korean and Japanese leaders avoiding the kind of provocative behavior that renders these and other unresolved problems of history salient and, thus, elevates tensions between their two countries. Unfortunately, as noted above, it is also true that unresolved issues of historical significance sometimes become salient and raise tensions in South Korea–Japan relations without leaders in either nation acting in the provocative ways described above. This happened in the later months of 2018 when the South Korean Supreme Court issued a decision over forced wartime labor, another unresolved issue of historical significance in South Korea–Japan relations. This decision then led to a series of responses and counterresponses that resulted in a significant rift in South Korea–Japan relations, which began to recede only recently.

The South Korean Supreme Court decision and the row it caused made it more difficult for leaders in Seoul and Tokyo to engage in a more cooperative and productive dialogue, and it also led to an escalation of tension that increased the diplomatic distance between these US allies, reducing the small amount of fragile trust that had been built up between them in recent years. Moreover, it has added additional baggage to South Korea–Japan bilateral relations that must be cleared away before any sincere negotiations can take place not simply to reduce tensions between Seoul and Tokyo over unresolved historic issues but also to create the conditions necessary for the two countries to build a more cooperative partnership within the East Asian alliance system.

As stated briefly above, the row began late in 2018 when the South Korean Supreme Court decided that Nippon Steel and Sumitomo Metals would have to pay $87,000 in compensation to four workers who were forced into labor during the Pacific War. This demand for compensation was then extended to Mitsubishi Heavy Industries, which also used forced

130   *Strengthening South Korea–Japan Relations*

labor during the war. The Japanese response was swift and expected: it noted that all such claims for compensation were resolved once and for all when the two nations signed the 1965 Reconciliation Treaty. This has always been the Japanese government's position even though it did agree in a separate accord to compensation measures designed to resolve the comfort women problem, which was regarded as a violation of so many women's civil rights. The Japanese response was clearly expected, and it led South Korean leaders to issue a swift and clear response stating that, although the 1965 Reconciliation Treaty did settle all financial compensation matters between the two countries, it did not prohibit individuals from acting on their rights to seek damages for the mental anguish and physical harm they had suffered as forced laborers during the Pacific War.

That the South Korean and Japanese reactions to this Supreme Court decision were dramatically different is made clear in the data contained in figure 6.1. The population shares represented by the two sets of bars in the graph indicate that only 7 percent of Japanese respondents registered support for this court decision, while nearly 60 percent said they did not. South Korean respondents, on the other hand, were much more supportive. Indeed, more than 75 percent of South Korean respondents registered support for the Supreme Court decision, while barely over 5 percent said they did not. These differences are expected because this decision touched directly on how differently South Koreans and Japanese view the unresolved historical issues that separate their two nations and challenge their bilateral relations.

As stated above, members of the Japanese public noted feeling that South Koreans continually make unfair demands on Japan for historical issues that, in their view, have already been resolved by agreements accepted by leaders in both countries. This understanding is reflected in the response of Japan's leadership to this Supreme Court decision, which made clear that, since this problem of wartime labor was settled, the South Korean Supreme Court decision was not legitimate. While this was the official response, Japanese leaders did make a side proposal to have this particular dispute arbitrated by three representatives, one from South Korea, one from Japan, and the last from a third country agreed to by both sides. President Moon did not respond to this proposal, and South Korean officials continued to press those Japanese companies named in the court decision for compensation. The Japanese arbitration proposal came with a deadline, and when this time passed with no response from the South

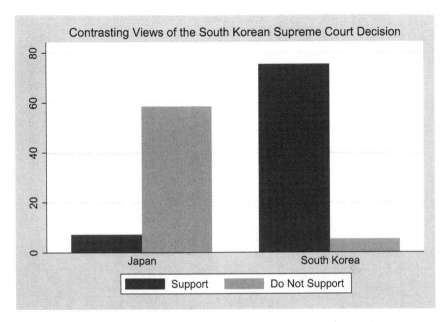

Figure 6.1. Source: Genron NPO Opinion Polls (2019).

Korean president, Prime Minister Abe noted that he would take the matter to the International Court of Justice. The Japanese prime minister also took one more action that escalated this dispute to a higher level of tension, beginning a dangerous game of brinkmanship.

Japan had placed South Korea on a "white list" of preferred trading countries, but Prime Minister Abe not only imposed export restrictions on a number of important items used by South Korea's high-tech companies but also decided to remove South Korea from this list of preferential trading partners. Japan's official justification for these actions emphasized that they had no connection to the Supreme Court ruling or to President Moon's nonresponse to Japan's proposal for arbitration on this matter. South Koreans, on the other hand, were not moved by this explanation but instead focused on the fact that Japan's actions created export restrictions that required a much longer process of permit granting and licensing that was not previously required. The products subjected to such restrictions included over eight hundred items that are critical to South Korean high-tech manufacturing processes, and these restrictions carried the potential to disrupt trade in finished high-tech goods. Many finished products that contain high-technology components, like cell phones and other consumer products, are sourced globally—that is, put together in multiple countries—which means that the restrictions Japan imposed affected not just South Korea but also China, the United States, and a number of other countries.

Naturally, the South Korean president launched a protest in response to the Japanese prime minister's action, but he did not stop there, instead taking action that escalated tensions further. President Moon, in retaliation against Prime Minister Abe's restrictions on Japanese exports to South Korea, engaged in a tit-for-tat move that removed Japan from its "white list" of preferred trading nations. This pair of actions naturally resulted in a state of heightened concern between South Korea and Japan on matters of their trading relations, and while trade is not typically one of those issues that generates strong public reactions—like those attendant to problems over unresolved issues of historical significance—the use of trade as a tactic in this South Korean Supreme Court decision row did affect the manner in which the publics in each country viewed the benefits and liabilities of their two nations trading with each other.

As the data in table 6.4 indicate, South Korean and Japanese respondents have generally held rather different views with respect to who benefits from South Korea–Japan bilateral trade. Overall, South Koreans have traditionally been nearly equally divided over whether bilateral trade benefits both sides or is an economic threat to their country. On the other hand, Japanese who see bilateral trade as beneficial to both countries have traditionally been more than double those respondents who see bilateral trade as a threat to their country. The trade restrictions that each government imposed on the other did affect these shares, rendering each side more suspicious of the benefits of bilateral trade than before. From 2015 to 2017, more South Korean respondents said that trade with Japan benefits both nations, but in 2018 and 2019, these proportions were reversed as respondents who felt that trade with Japan was a threat to South Korea became the plurality category. Japanese respondents were clearly of the view that trade benefits both countries, but this share had declined throughout the five years for which we have data from these joint surveys. Specifically, in 2016 and 2017, 33 percent and 35 percent more respondents said trade with South Korea benefits both countries. By 2019, however, this excess share of respondents had dropped to just over 20 percent, its lowest value in the five surveys.

Table 6.4. How South Koreans and Japanese View Trade with Each Other

South Korean Views of Trade with Japan	Benefits Both Countries	Threat to South Korea
2015	46.6%	37.0%
2016	44.6%	37.6%
2017	42.3%	39.9%
2018	40.0%	47.6%
2019	41.6%	42.6%
Japanese Views of Trade with South Korea	Benefits Both Countries	Threat to Japan
2015	49.2%	22.6%
2016	52.4%	17.2%
2017	51.1%	17.3%
2018	47.6%	17.8%
2019	42.6%	19.7%

Source: Compiled by the authors from Genron NPO, Japan–Korea Opinion Polls, 2015–19.

These trade actions carried negative consequences that were felt almost immediately by businesses not just in South Korea and Japan but also throughout the region and even in China and the United States. Leaders in both countries were undoubtedly aware of these negative consequences, but instead of initiating a dialogue that could halt escalating tensions, begin to reestablish confidence levels, and build goodwill between South Korea and Japan, a member of Japan's ruling Liberal Democratic Party (LDP) rendered this matter worse. LDP politician Hagiuda Koichi stated that Japan's recent move to require more extensive permitting and licensing for certain of its critical exports to South Korea were entirely justified because of Japanese fears that these vitally important items might reach North Korea. This was an insulting statement to South Koreans, leaders and citizens alike, because allowing components important for the manufacture of high-technology goods to fall into the hands of Pyongyang would be utterly contrary to South Korea's own interests. Thus, any suggestion that this would happen, either accidentally or intentionally, could only be interpreted as an affront to the competence and sincerity of the South Korean government in its relations with its adversary in Pyongyang.

This statement from a Japanese politician elicited a bitter declamation from Seoul, and, in combination, these statements resulted in a continued escalation of tensions between South Korea and Japan, which made the decline in trust between the two governments likely to continue. This decline in trust, combined with another important incident that occurred in December 2018, put a halt to one area where Seoul and Tokyo had made notable progress in building confidence through coordination: security cooperation, specifically, South Korea's participation with Japan in the General Security of Military Information Agreement (GSOMIA), which began in November 2016. Although in operation for only a short time, the GSOMIA did provide valuable security information to both sides. In November 2019, President Moon Jae-In informed Japanese leaders that South Korea would not continue its participation in the GSOMIA, which was unfortunate because leaders on both sides had expended much domestic political capital to hammer out this formal security cooperation agreement in the first place.

Indeed, this agreement had a rocky beginning, but after years of fits and starts, in late 2016, leaders in South Korea and Japan worked out a formula for cooperation that both countries could sign and implement. South Korea had expressed an interest in sharing intelligence with Japan as early as the 1980s, and leaders in Seoul noted that they were particularly interested in intelligence that was available from satellite data. In the late 1980s, South Korea's intelligence capabilities in this area were not well developed, but, since this time, it has acquired advanced satellite technology, which enhanced its own intelligence-gathering capabilities while, at the same time, reducing its incentives to pursue cooperation with Japan for this kind of information. Nonetheless, with North Korea engaging in provocative behavior and China leading an evolution in Northeast Asia's power dynamics, efforts to reconsider intelligence sharing between Seoul and Tokyo began.

In 2012, during the presidency of Lee Myung-Bak, a cooperation agreement was drafted and reviewed, and a signed agreement appeared to be in the offing. Unfortunately, with opposition from the South Korean National Assembly, the effort was scrapped. Two years later, however, President Park Geun-Hye signed a Memorandum of Understanding (MOU) with her counterpart in Japan, pledging to share information on North Korean missile development between the two sides. The MOU led to a limited agreement, but, with encouragement from US president Obama as part of his "pivot to Asia" policy shift, the GSOMIA between Seoul and Tokyo was signed and promulgated. Clearly, many factors went into the South Korean president's decision to cease participation in the GSOMIA, including Seoul's continued development of its own capabilities, but another incident, the radar lock-on incident, challenged South Korea–Japan relations even further.

In December 2018, the South Korean Navy and Coast Guard were coordinating a rescue mission in response to a distress signal sent out by a North Korean fishing vessel. A Japanese maritime patrol aircraft in the area reported being subjected to fire-control radar from a South Korean destroyer, and the following day the Japanese Ministry of Defense reported that this was a dangerous and provocative act that violated the Code for Unplanned Encounters at Sea (CUES).[5] In response to this Japanese report, South Korea asserted that it had not used that kind of fire-control radar in the rescue effort and that it had not intended to aim the surveillance and tracking radar it was using for the rescue mission at the Japanese patrol aircraft. This response was not accepted, and the Japanese foreign minister pressed Seoul for an explanation. South Korean officials responded with their original message but added that the Japanese maritime patrol aircraft had been flying low and in a threatening manner. This process of assertion and counterassertion repeated itself for many months without producing any satisfactory explanation for Japanese officials.

In June 2019, the Japanese minister of defense decided to suspend negotiations with South Korea, and as stated above, six months later President Moon said he would pull South Korea out of the GSOMIA, ending the sharing of military information. This announcement resulted in the suspension of progress in an area of cooperation that not only had worked well for both sides but had also been generally supported by the publics in both countries. Between May and June 2019, respondents in both countries were asked if they thought Japan and South Korea should pursue defense cooperation, and 53 percent of Japanese respondents answered in the affirmative, while 65 percent of South Koreans agreed. It is also important here that only one-third of these supporters noted that cooperation on security issues should simply move forward under current conditions, while two-thirds of supportive respondents noted that defense authorities in both countries should improve their communication before pursuing specific areas of security cooperation.

To be sure, improving bilateral communication to help build closer security ties will be a great challenge for South Korean and Japanese leaders, especially in light of the mistrust that the December 2018 radar lock-on incident generated on both sides. This is not just because efforts to negotiate an understanding of the incident that was acceptable to both sides failed but also more importantly because this failure was well-nigh preordained given the fact that neither side trusted the other's position on the incident. In 2019 Genron NPO polls, respondents in both countries were asked which country's version of the incident was legitimate. Of Japanese respondents, 0 percent said South Korea's version was legitimate and 62.9 percent said they believed their own government's version. Of South Korean respondents, a similar percentage, 61.9 percent, noted that their government's version was legitimate, whereas only 3.1 percent said the Japanese version had legitimacy.

These dramatic differences tell us that communication to achieve security cooperation will continue to be a problem. Although the South Korean and Japanese publics support closer ties in this area—especially in light of North Korean provocations and their mistrust of the growing power and influence of China—such communication will be difficult at best. If this division were not enough of a challenge, there is also the problem of South Koreans and Japanese not seeing eye to eye on all issues with respect to increasing their military and security cooperation. Specifically, South Koreans are not in favor of security arrangements that in any way increase the military power of Japan. While South Koreans support increased cooperation with Japan, they do not support an increase in Japan's actual military role. In a 2015 Asan Institute poll, 50 percent of South Korean respondents noted that they did not support an increased security role for Japan, and this response was related to their strong feelings that there should be no increases in the amount of military power Japan already possesses.

Two reasons help explain this concern in South Korea. The first is that increases in Japanese military power may include the acquisition of nuclear weapons, a possibility to which South Koreans have long been and continue to be strongly opposed. This is not an issue for which there is conflict with Japan because the publics in both countries are in sync with respect to Japan not acquiring nuclear weapons. Genron NPO polls taken in 2016 and 2017 asked both Japanese and South Korean respondents about the advisability of Japan acquiring nuclear weapons, and the proportions of respondents who were opposed were nearly identical in both countries. Averaging the two polls over the 2016 and 2017 results, the data indicate that 78 percent of Japanese and 79 percent of South Koreans agreed that Japan should not acquire nuclear weapons.[6]

The other reason that South Koreans are against Japan acquiring any increased military strength has to do with the manner in which publics in both countries assess military threats to their respective countries. In some instances, there is a very close accord between the Japanese and South Korean publics on this threat assessment, and this is particularly true for North Korea; 80 percent or more respondents in both Japan and South Korea listed Pyongyang as a military threat. Publics in both countries were also fairly close to China being a military threat, with an average of 60 percent of Japanese respondents viewing China as a military threat but somewhat less than 45 percent of South Koreans agreeing. Although these proportions are different with respect to China, Beijing still registered fairly high on the threat scale for South Koreans. There was, however, a significant difference in how publics in Japan and South Korea assessed Russia as a military threat: very few South Koreans saw Russia in this manner, while around 30 percent of Japanese did.

There were also significant differences in how South Koreans and Japanese viewed the potential military threats that each represented to the other. To illustrate such differences more clearly, the data in table 6.5 cover five polls taken by the Genron NPO organization from 2015 to 2019 inclusive, and the columns contain the percentages of South Korean and Japanese respondents who view the other country as a potential military threat. While there has been a decline of greater than twenty percentage points in the proportion of South Korean respondents who view Japan as a military threat since the 2015 poll, the data indicate that more than one-third of South Koreans still view it as a threat. This is quite different from the results obtained by polling Japanese respondents, as the proportions of respondents who view South Korea as a military threat to them fluctuated five to six percentage points from survey to survey, but a much smaller average of 12 percent of Japanese possessed this view.

These differences in perceptions of Japan and South Korea as military threats to each other are most likely related to lingering historical issues rather than any actual potential for war between the two, but they are nonetheless related to how South Korean and Japanese respondents understood the likelihood of actual conflict breaking out between their two countries. Our expectation is that respondents who saw the outbreak of war as likely in a "few years" or "eventually" should match the proportions of respondents who see the other as a military threat, and the data confirm this, with 8 percent of Japanese respondents viewing conflict with South Korea as likely in the future and with just over 30 percent of South Koreans seeing such a conflict with Japan as likely.[7] The only positive side

Table 6.5. South Korea and Japan as Military Threats to Each Other

Percentages of South Koreans Who View Japan as a Military Threat		Percentages of Japanese Who View South Korea as a Military Threat	
2015	58.1	2015	11.2
2016	37.7	2016	16.9
2017	36.0	2017	10.5
2018	33.6	2018	7.0
2019	38.3	2019	12.3

Source: Compiled by the authors from Genron NPO, Japan–Korea Opinion Polls, 2015–19.

we can see in responses to these questions is that an average of 70 percent of South Koreans either were not sure if the conflict would occur or were convinced it would not happen. The Japanese average for the same two responses was over 90 percent.

These and other data presented above are strong indicators of the amount of work that leaders in both nations have to undertake to improve their bilateral relations. Accomplishing this goal will have to involve leaders taking some kind of joint action to reduce tensions attendant to the punctuated salience of unresolved historical issues, but the data provided above also indicate that South Koreans and Japanese do not always agree on how best to define the kind of joint action that can accomplish this goal. This problem is aptly illustrated with respect to the South Korean Supreme Court decision over forced wartime labor.

The data in table 6.6 provide the proportions of respondents in each country who supported different solutions to the forced labor problem, and it is immediately noticeable that there is a dominant response for South Koreans but not for Japanese respondents, whose modal answer was "Do Not Know." In fact, Japanese respondents are fairly evenly divided over whether an arbitration panel of third-country members should be established so the case can be heard by the International Court of Justice or whether the South Korean government should simply compensate these individuals who were forced into wartime labor. These two responses were just over 20 percent each, both of which were lower than the 30 percent of respondents who simply said that they did not know if there is a way to solve this problem. South Korean respondents, on the other hand, were strongly supportive (60%) of the idea that Japanese firms should simply compensate those individuals they forced into wartime labor.

Territorial Disputes, Human Rights, and Court Case Challenges   139

Table 6.6. How South Korea and Japan Should Respond to the South Korea Supreme Court Decision Requiring Compensation for Forced Labor

Japanese Preferences	South Korean Preferences
22.2%: Establish an Arbitration Board Made Up of Third-Country Commissioners or Bring the Case to the International Court of Justice	58.1%: Japanese Firms Should Compensate Laborers in Accordance with the Supreme Court Decision
20.5%: The South Korean Government Should Compensate Former Wartime Laborers	13.7%: South Korean Government Should Establish a Foundation to Compensate Laborers and Their Families and Ask for Voluntary Donations from South Korean and Japanese Firms
16.5%: It Will Be Difficult to Solve This Issue	9.4%: Former Laborers as Plaintiffs and Companies as Defendants Should Talk and Seek Solutions
6.4%: Former Laborers as Plaintiffs and Companies as Defendants Should Talk and Seek Solutions	7.2%: It Will Be Difficult to Solve This Issue
28.4%: Do Not Know	4.4%: Do Not Know

Source: Genron NPO (2019).

These data were updated by Genron NPO with two surveys taken in 2021 and 2022 in both South Korea and Japan. What distinguishes these recent surveys from that completed in 2019 is that respondents selected their preferred responses from a fixed list provided by interviewers, which allowed for a more direct comparison of preferences across South Korean and Japanese respondents. The data reveal that there were response similarities across the two samples, but there were also some notable differences. Again, the modal answer for Japanese respondents was "Do Not Know," but the data also reflected the well-documented disagreement that survey data have manifested with respect to this problem. Specifically, about one-third of Japanese respondents said the court decision violated the 1965 Reconciliation Treaty, whereas a similar one-third of South Korean respondents said that any settlement should proceed in accordance with the ruling issued by the South Korean Supreme Court.

These findings do not portend well for the hope of solving this problem in South Korea–Japan relations any time soon. At the same time, however, the data in table 6.7 do suggest that leaders in Seoul and Tokyo might be able to build support for two potential solutions, the first of which involves establishing a third-country arbitration panel whereby the issue could eventually be adjudicated by the International Court of Justice. In addition to this, Japanese and South Korean leaders might be able to build support for some form of hybrid plan that involves both governments making contributions to compensate forced laborers and then seeking contributions from involved Japanese firms and possibly even from South Korean firms. This approach has some potential because the small pockets of respondents in both countries who share common views on how to solve this problem may allow leaders in both countries to begin to move toward a workable compromise.

The truth is that, for now, neither side will have to expend significant effort to resolve this lingering historic problem of forced wartime labor. The 2018 Supreme Court Decision in South Korea led many groups representing individuals forced into wartime labor to file lawsuits in order to receive compensation that the court said was permissible. One of the largest of these lawsuits involved over eighty victims who sued sixteen Japanese business firms for compensation. This suit—and others as well—was being heard by the Seoul Central District Court, which in January 2021 dismissed the suit. In its decision, the court ruled that the 1965 Reconciliation Agreement limited the right of individuals to sue for compensation, and, thus, it noted that it could not consider this case further without violating international law, which it stated it would not do. While this district court ruling ceased legal proceedings on matters of compensation for such cases for now, the decision did note that the possibility for a political solution was open and that through diplomacy it would be possible to find a way to compensate victims who were forced into labor during the Pacific War.

With the Seoul Central District Court decision halting legal proceedings on this matter, there is now a possibility that trade restrictions imposed by both countries on each other in the wake of the South Korean Supreme Court decision can begin to be loosened in the hope of reducing the increased tensions and economic hardships created by these trade actions. Getting to such a point, however, would require that both sides make some tangible effort to reduce the negative implications of the trade decisions that leaders in Tokyo and Seoul made as part of this row. This

Territorial Disputes, Human Rights, and Court Case Challenges 141

Table 6.7. Contrasting South Korean and Japanese Views on the Forced Labor Issue

	South Koreans 2021 2022	Japanese 2021 2022
Carry Out a Settlement in Accordance with the South Korean Supreme Court Decision	32.6% 36.5%	2.9% 3.6%
No Compliance Needed Because the South Korean Supreme Court Decision Violates the 1965 Treaty	13.1% 15.1%	32.8% 30.6%
The South Korean Government Should Compensate Former Forced Laborers	12.1% 13.5%	5.4% 7.1%
The South Korean Government Should Make a "Subrogation Payment," and Then Japanese and Korean Companies Should Make Subsequent Payments to the Foundation	N/A 10.6%	N/A 3.2%
Establish an Arbitration Panel by a Third-Party Country or Take the Case to the International Court of Justice	20.1% 14.8%	14.5% 15.2%
Do Not Know	13.6% 9.5%	40.2% 39.5%

Source: Genron NPO (2022).

would not be a simple process under current conditions, but to explore in more detail how this approach might work, we will first need to have a clearer understanding of how South Koreans and Japanese view each other and other nations in terms of their overall economic importance.

The data in table 6.8 are from polls taken from 2016 to 2019 inclusive, and they contain shares of South Korean and Japanese respondents expressing which countries or blocs of countries are of economic importance to their own country. In terms of recent economic problems between South Korea and Japan, neither country's respondents see the other as being their country's most important trading partner, but they nonetheless recognize that trade with each other is very important. This is particularly true for South Koreans, where more than one-third of respondents in

Table 6.8. South Korean and Japanese Views of Countries of Economic Importance

Japanese Views		South Korean Views	
South Korea		Japan	
2016	32.2%	2016	36.9%
2017	23.3%	2017	35.7%
2018	22.9%	2018	33.4%
2019	21.2%	2019	46.5%
China		China	
2016	63.0%	2016	81.1%
2017	49.5%	2017	78.4%
2018	47.5%	2018	76.3%
2019	49.9%	2019	83.9%
United States		United States	
2016	77.3%	2016	68.3%
2017	73.6%	2017	69.8%
2018	70.0%	2018	74.5%
2019	72.1%	2019	72.6%
European Union		European Union	
2016	32.2%	2016	12.3%
2017	26.1%	2017	17.5%
2018	24.5%	2018	15.3%
2019	22.9%	2019	20.0%
ASEAN Nations		ASEAN Nations	
2016	34.8%	2016	6.4%
2017	32.5%	2017	9.9%
2018	28.7%	2018	13.7%
2019	26.5%	2019	12.9%

Source: Compiled by the authors from Genron NPO, Japan–Korea Opinion Polls, 2016–19.

polls conducted between 2016 and 2018 inclusive saw Japan as an important trading partner, a proportion that was more than twelve percentage points higher in the latest survey of 2019. While fewer Japanese saw South Korea as a very important trading partner, still more than one-fifth of Japanese respondents viewed South Korea as being important when it comes to international trade.

Respondents in both South Korea and Japan also noted that the United States is an extremely important country economically, but as pointed out above, they differed on how they see the economic importance of China. As expected, more South Koreans viewed China as the most economically important country, with shares averaging around 80 percent of all respondents. Shares of Japanese respondents, on the other hand, averaged just less than 50 percent for the surveys from 2017 to 2019 inclusive. These data reinforce how much closer South Korea has become to China in recent years compared to Japan, but this does not mean that the United States' economic importance to South Korea has declined. In fact, percentages of South Korean respondents who see the United States as economically important revealed moderate increases over the years covered by these national polls, and in the latest polls, over 70 percent of South Koreans see the United States as a very economically important country. This is nearly equivalent to the proportions of Japanese who feel the same, which means that reducing tensions in the partnership between Seoul and Tokyo and ultimately reinvigorating the East Asian alliance system will require renewed leadership from the United States.

As we reveal in the next chapter, the two US allies in East Asia are desirous of a deeper, more unwavering US commitment to the region and, more importantly, to the East Asian alliance system, which they would like to see reformed to reflect the current economic and power dynamics of the region. Indeed, US leadership is much desired, especially as that leadership can function as an essential balance to the increasing influence of a rising China. This does not mean, however, that leaders in Seoul and Tokyo want a return to the past, because the alliance system's old hierarchy will not be effective, especially in light of the changes that have occurred, not just among members of the East Asian alliance system but also throughout the entirety of the Asia Pacific. Indeed, neither South Korea nor Japan wants the renewal of US engagement to force them to make a choice between Washington and Beijing, because both US allies are looking for a reformed pattern of triangular relations that will allow them the flexibility they need to manage their economic and political relations with an increasingly powerful and assertive Beijing. Only with these kinds of reforms can the East Asian alliance system continue to offer the security and stability that it has consistently provided since the end of the Pacific and Korean Wars.

7

US Leadership and the Evolution of Interstate Relations in the Asia Pacific

Introduction: A Tale of Two Speeches

On November 10, 2011, a day before ministers from Asia-Pacific Economic Cooperation member nations were to begin their meeting in Honolulu, Hawaii, then secretary of state Hillary Clinton gave a speech at the East-West Center to a distinguished audience of domestic leaders and foreign dignitaries. Shortly after recognizing members of her audience, Secretary Clinton (2011) stated emphatically that the twenty-first century would be "America's Pacific Century," which would be characterized by a "period of unprecedented outreach and partnership in this dynamic, complex, and consequential region." Clinton noted that making this century America's Pacific Century would require that the United States increase its commitment to the region and, more importantly, realize the objectives embedded in the Obama administration's "pivot to Asia" policy by implementing a strategy of "forward-deployed diplomacy." The secretary of state then explained that there were six "key lines of action" implied by this regionally engaged and active diplomatic approach, and they included "strengthening . . . bilateral security alliances, deepening . . . working relationships with emerging powers, engaging with regional multilateral institutions, expanding trade and investment, forging a broad-based military presence, and advancing democracy and human rights" (Clinton 2011).

There is little doubt that the secretary's words affirming the United States' commitment to the region and describing how it would elevate its leadership role there were heartening to US allies and partners throughout East and Southeast Asia. However, despite this reassurance, the question remains as to whether or not Secretary Clinton's assertion that the twenty-first century would be America's Pacific Century has proved to be accurate and, if so, will continue to be accurate as the century continues to unfold. Before exploring the evidence provided by regional developments thus far in the twenty-first century, we first fast-forward eight years to Beijing, where Chinese leader Xi Jinping delivered an important speech in honor of the seventieth birthday of the People's Republic of China.

In his speech, Xi talked about all the progress China had made throughout the last seven decades under the leadership of the Chinese Communist Party (CCP), emphasizing that the country's future would be best safeguarded by the CCP continuing in its current position of unchallenged leadership, which it has held since 1949. Clearly, the Chinese leader had a point, because to say that China in its seventieth year is a stronger and more prosperous country than it was when it was founded by Mao Zedong in the wake of the Nationalist Government's defeat and abdication is simply to state the obvious. It is more important here that the Chinese leader made clear that the profound changes China had experienced since it was founded have included not just a complete economic transformation, highlighted by many decades of high-level economic growth, but also a continuation on a path that elevates the country as an increasingly powerful and important global leader that can shape international affairs to serve China's interests. Xi's speech was over three hours long, and its contents complicate the question of the twenty-first century being America's Pacific Century, requiring that both the words of Secretary Clinton and those of the Chinese leader be evaluated against actual developments in the Asia Pacific thus far in the twenty-first century. This begins with asking what impact the Obama administration's "pivot to Asia" had on the East Asian alliance system, particularly in the context of China's ongoing rise in influence.

We know that since the Obama administration announced its "pivot to Asia," China's rise in influence has not slowed. In fact, in addition to enhancing his own power as well as that of the CCP, Xi has also imposed tighter restrictions on foreign firms and their investments in China and has reduced the presence in China of the World Wide Web and foreign-owned social media companies. These and other actions combine to form what has been called China's third revolution, which is designed to solidify the power of both Xi and the CCP so that the Chinese leadership can be certain that all domestic resources support government efforts to facilitate China's global rise and mold the international order's institutions and rules to better serve essential Chinese interests (Economy 2018a, 2018b).

These developments suggest that, although the twenty-first century began as America's Pacific Century, China's growing economic and military influence in the region—and around the globe—may be making this designation less and less true. Indeed, despite the United States reinvigorated forward-deployed diplomacy in service of its growing commitment to its allies and other partner nations in the Asia-Pacific region, Beijing has succeeded in projecting its own power throughout the entirety of the South China Sea as well as in other nearby bodies of water, such as the East China Sea. Moreover, outside of the Asia Pacific, China has extended its influence through its Belt and Road Initiative as well as other programs and institutions, such as the Asian Infrastructure Investment Bank. This extension of Chinese influence is not just economic but also military, and it occurs in a Chinese pattern that is best described by the idea that where Chinese economic influence goes, so does a Chinese military presence. As of 2018, Chinese state-owned enterprises (SOEs) were involved in the running of over seventy-five ports and terminals in thirty-four countries throughout the world, and in many of these cases "Chinese investments in ports have been followed by high-profile visits from Chinese naval vessels" (Economy 2018b, 66).

These advances in China's economic and military power in the Asia Pacific and around the globe did not occur because of a lack of engagement on the part of the Obama administration. This administration's "pivot to Asia" helped improve bilateral relations between the United States and its allies in Seoul and Tokyo as US diplomatic, military, and economic engagement in the region deepened. Moreover, the United States' renewed emphasis on the Asia Pacific stood to benefit a reinvigorated US-led effort to build stronger and more expansive economic and trading relationships throughout the region. Movement toward achieving this goal would have been advanced even more significantly with the implementation of the Trans-Pacific Partnership (TPP), which would have remade the region's economic order under rules and institutions guided by US leadership. Unfortunately, the TPP was not to be; although this pathbreaking trade and economic development accord had the full support of the Obama administration, the forty-fourth president's successor, Donald Trump, pulled the United States out of the partnership as one of his administration's first executive actions.

US Leadership in the Asia Pacific

Different presidential administrations often approach US allies and other partner nations in different ways, and although sometimes these differences are minor, at other times they are dramatic. Presidential administrations generally provide justification for their distinctive approaches, but changes in approach should always be balanced against the potential damage that can be attendant to inconsistencies in the United States' commitments to its allies and partners. We noted above that the Trump administration quickly pulled the United States out of the TPP, but this abrupt action was not the only foreign policy change his administration implemented that affected the United States' commitment to the region as the Asia Pacific's apex power.[1] This is important because any US effort to strengthen the East Asian alliance system and enervate the growing influence of an increasingly assertive China in the region—and around the globe—rests with the United States and its engagement with its allies as essential partners in the process of maintaining the international order that helped establish and preserve the peace and stability of the Asia-Pacific region for many decades.

To clarify the changes in the United States' levels of commitment to its allies, specifically South Korea and Japan as essential members of the East Asian alliance system, we examine how the Trump administration departed from the renewed level of US engagement in this region that followed the Obama administration's "pivot to Asia" policy. We must recall that the "pivot to Asia" was intended not just to check China's growing economic and military influence in the region but also to strengthen the East Asian alliance system itself. Indeed, President Obama, in addition to increasing US engagement in the region, also wanted to help keep tensions between South Korea and Japan from negatively affecting the base of the alliance system's set of triangular relations so that the East Asian alliance system could remain as strong and solid as possible. Moreover, acting as a check on China's rapidly rising economic and military influence did not necessarily mean a more confrontational approach toward Beijing, nor did it mean getting Japan and South Korea to abandon the economic and diplomatic relationships each had evolved with Beijing. It did mean that US leaders viewed reestablishing its leadership in the region, particularly as the honest broker it had traditionally been, as necessary to help adjudicate the real differences that existed between its allies in Seoul and Tokyo.

We are not trying to suggest that the foreign policy changes that occurred under the Trump administration were the start of US inconsistencies in its approach to its East Asian allies because the United States has long displayed inconsistencies in its engagement with its allies and partners in this region. Consider the administration of George W. Bush and the first term of Barack Obama, a period of time that coincides with the growing economic and military influence of China in the region and a US foreign policy that was more focused on the Middle East than the Asia Pacific. The Obama administration's "pivot to Asia" was not simply seen as overdue; it also represented the US endeavor to return to a higher and more consistent level of engagement in the Asia-Pacific region. Obama's pivot did result in some positive outcomes, including partial success in brokering an agreement between Japan's prime minister Abe Shinzo and South Korean president Park Geun-Hye over the problem of Korean women being forced into sexual slavery during the war years and also fostering more cooperation on security matters between Seoul and Tokyo.

We know that uncertainty will be attendant to any presidential transition in the United States, but that which occurred in the transfer of power from Obama to Trump was much more notable because it became very clear early in his administration that Donald Trump's approach to all of the United States' alliances throughout the globe would be very different from that of his predecessor. As stated above, the Trump administration's approach is best captured in his "America First" policy, which elevated the salience of economic issues to a position of primacy over all other factors that have influenced US foreign policy decision-making. Trump's emphasis on economic issues included applying diplomatic pressure to accomplish two economic goals in particular. The first of these involved the administration's demand that all allies stop taking advantage of the United States, contribute more to their own security, and reduce US costs. The second of these involved the Trump administration asking its trading partners to reduce their bilateral trade surpluses with the United States.

To accomplish these goals, the Trump administration turned up the heat on both ally and adversary, even raising tariffs on selected exports from allied nations to induce cooperation and reduce the United States' bilateral trade deficits with them. In addition to creating a more uncertain atmosphere in its relations with the nations he targeted, Trump's "America First" approach led to more sour feelings toward the United States among US allies. These are important developments, and their impact has been a weakening of South Korea–Japan bilateral relations as well as of the East Asian alliance system overall and an increase in the distance between the United States and its allies in Seoul and Tokyo. Moreover, the Trump administration's approach to the Asia Pacific led to increased diplomatic distance between South Korea and Japan as leaders in each country competed to curry favor with the forty-fifth president of the United States.

150 *Strengthening South Korea–Japan Relations*

Clearly it is easy to be critical of the Trump administration's approach to East Asian alliance partners—and all US alliance partners, for that matter—particularly in light of how his administration's approach to bilateral relations with US allies led to so much uncertainty about the United States maintaining its security commitments. This is witnessed particularly in the competing demands that the Trump administration heaped on its allies in what were ostensibly bullying tactics. Recent US behavior toward South Korea with respect to security burden sharing—particularly, the negotiations both countries held over the Special Measures Agreement that concern Seoul's contributions to US forces on the peninsula—is illustrative. The administration proposed that South Korea increase its current level of contribution from $890 million to $5 billion, an increase of more than 500 percent, which leaders in the Moon administration viewed as shockingly unrealistic. As stated above, the Trump administration has characterized US allies as free riders, which helps explain its requests for increased contributions from them but certainly cannot account for the exorbitant increase it requested from leaders in Seoul.

Requesting such a large jump in South Korea's security contributions created an atmosphere of confusion if not shock and suspicion in Seoul, which negatively affected these negotiations over the Special Measures Agreement. This is especially true because the administration's request for such a dramatic increase in South Korean contributions came at a time when it was also demanding that Seoul work more closely with the United States to counter China's growing economic and military influence in the region and around the globe. It is true that the requested increase in South Korean contributions may have simply been a starting point for the Trump administration's negotiating position, but such an extreme request, coupled with suggestions for South Korea to do more to assist the United States on matters relating to China's growing influence, do not signal a strong US commitment to defending its allies in East Asia or maintaining the East Asian alliance system and the peace and stability it brought to the region for so many decades.

If the Trump administration's new foreign policy approach resulted in weakened bilateral relationships between the United States and its East Asian allies, it also did nothing to strengthen the bilateral relationship that exists between South Korea and Japan. Even when the Trump administration's actions did not focus directly on South Korea or Japan, its behavior still undermined the East Asian alliance system, and Trump's actions with respect to North Korea are an apt illustration of this. The Trump administration attempted to meet and negotiate directly with the North Korean leader, Kim Jong Un, and the meetings that took place failed to achieve their principal goal of denuclearizing the Korean Peninsula. In fact, they did not enervate at all the North's nuclear program development actions, and the regime in Pyongyang continues to conduct nuclear warhead and missile delivery-system tests to the present day. This does not mean that nothing positive came out of the Kim-Trump meetings: the net result was a temporary reduction in direct tensions between Pyongyang and Seoul.[2]

While this was a positive consequence of the Trump approach, his administration's actions were not welcomed by South Koreans in general,[3] and they also led to an increase in tension between Pyongyang and Tokyo. Japanese leaders viewed these summits not simply as failing to halt Pyongyang's development of its nuclear weapons capability but as essentially rewarding Pyongyang for its continued engagement in provocative behavior that threatens the peace and security of the Asia Pacific. In fact, the continued development of North Korea's nuclear capability and intermittent tests of missile delivery systems have encouraged former Japanese prime minister Abe Shinzo and his successors to move closer to the United States to improve Japan's military capabilities as well as focus on helping the country make the legal changes necessary for it to participate in collective self-defense with the United States.[4] This is not a problem for US-Japan relations, but it does carry a downside for South Korea–Japan relations because such Japanese defense behavior is generally not welcomed by South Korea, which, as shown above, remains concerned about any increase in Japanese military power.[5]

A very clear theme in the Trump campaign for the presidency was how many countries were taking advantage of the United States by running large bilateral trade deficits. Trump called out China in particular for this, and when he assumed office, he threatened China with tariffs if it did not alter such economic practices as manipulating currency and requiring joint ventures and technology transfers as necessary conditions for US companies to operate there. Trump also echoed a longtime US complaint about China's illicit efforts to acquire US technological knowledge and to keep US high-tech and social media companies from operating freely there. In response to China's refusal to compromise on any of these issues, the Trump administration imposed tariffs on many Chinese goods, not only expanding the list but also increasing the tariff amounts that had been initially imposed. In his negotiations with his Chinese counterparts, former US Treasury secretary Steven Mnuchin made progress on some trade and tariff issues, which led to some reductions, but most of the tariffs have remained in force and have not been eliminated by the Biden administration.

Unlike other Trump administration policy initiatives, the imposition of tariffs on China has not directly weakened the East Asian alliance system, but the Trump tariffs have been partner to some indirect impacts on the set of triangular relations that form the underlying architecture of this alliance system. These indirect but nonetheless negative impacts have impeded the functioning of global supply chains and thereby provoked unintended consequences that go beyond the United States and China. It is well known that global businesses will always seek not just low costs but more importantly stability in their economic interactions. Given that the net impact of the China tariffs has been higher costs and less transactional and market stability, South Korean and Japanese enterprises have endeavored to create a more predictable environment by seeking closer ties with their Chinese business partners. Consequently, the tariffs that the Trump administration imposed on China have led to closer relations between the two US allies and business partners in China, moving South Korea and Japan closer to Beijing than they had been before the tariffs were imposed.

To say that these and other developments that followed the Trump tariffs have not strengthened the East Asian alliance system does not capture the damage that has been done, and this damage becomes quite clear when the Trump administration tariffs are assessed in combination with his administration's efforts to get South Korea and Japan to agree to increased burden sharing with respect to their defense and security expenditures. The Trump administration has pressed both Japan and South Korea to provide more money and other in-kind contributions for the troops and equipment that the United States has stationed on their soil, while at the same time rendering these nations less able to provide such increases because of the way that its tariffs, particularly on steel and aluminum, have hurt these two allies economically. This means that the Trump administration effectively punished its allies while at the same time seeking higher levels of cooperation in checking China's growing power and influence. Overall, the net effect of this has redounded to the benefit of China while weakening the East Asian alliance system.

As we now know, Donald Trump was not reelected to the US presidency, and on January 20, 2021, Obama administration vice president Joseph R. Biden assumed the office of the chief executive of the United States. Biden was clear that he wanted to restore the United States to a position of leadership in the world, and he noted that this would begin with the United States reengaging with its allies in a more positive and constructive manner. Biden's desire to reestablish the United States' long-established global leadership role would begin with making the US alliances in the Asia-Pacific region a top priority, not just because these relationships had been diminished during the four years of the Trump administration but also because restoring the stable and productive relationships the United States had maintained for so many decades with Seoul and Tokyo was essential to countering the negative consequences of China's growing economic and military influence. Evidence that the Biden administration did elevate the importance of the US alliances with Japan and South Korea rests with the fact that the first and second in-person meetings he held with foreign leaders were with former Japanese prime minister Suga Yoshihide and former South Korean president Moon Jae-In.

Prime Minister Suga came to Washington in April 2021, and his discussions with President Biden were wide ranging, covering a number of global problems. Their discussions also covered issues specific to the Asia-Pacific region and US-Japan bilateral relations in particular, and these discussions led to a number of agreements on the necessity of maintaining a free and open Indo-Pacific and of dissuading China from unilaterally changing the status quo in such Asian subregions as the Taiwan Straits, the East China Sea, and the South China Sea. Most importantly, the US president and Japanese prime minister admitted that achieving these regional goals would require trilateral cooperation, which meant that improved relations between Tokyo and Seoul were imperative and also that part of encouraging improved trilateral cooperation would require more leadership from the United States. Moreover, Biden and Suga agreed that, at a minimum, Washington must manifest a more consistent commitment to the region and its allies and also be more consistent and evenhanded in the way it signals its expectations to its Japanese and South Korean allies.

A month later, President Biden held his second in-person meeting with a foreign leader, this time with former South Korean president Moon Jae-In. Because South Korea had been evolving closer relations with China as Beijing's influence grew in the region, the two leaders set a goal of reaching a mutual understanding on how not simply to strengthen US–South Korean bilateral relations and the set of triangular relationships that formed the East Asian alliance system, but more importantly to guarantee an elevated role for the United States to help keep China from continuing to undermine the international order that has been in place since the end of the Pacific and Korean Wars. Achieving this goal would be a challenge, to be sure, but the Biden administration agreed to offer South Korea more flexibility in how it would contribute to these goals while managing its own relationship with Beijing. This was reflected in the joint statement issued by the two presidents, which also echoed a theme of opening a new chapter in US–South Korean relations, whereby South Korea reiterated its commitment to US–Japanese–South Korean cooperation for solving the region's problems, strengthening the East Asian alliance system so it could continue to help maintain regional peace and security based on the rules-based international order that had been in place for many decades.

China and the Challenge of US Leadership in the Asia Pacific

President Biden's meetings with the leaders of its two East Asian allies have done much to reveal to South Koreans and Japanese how important their alliances with the United States are, and they also set the tone for members of the East Asian alliance system to begin taking action to reform this alliance system so it could be a more effective force for peace and stability in the region. This portentous beginning, however, is no guarantee that the end game will be a reinvigorated and more effectively operating set of triangular relations because many of the ingredients of success for this new effort rest with the United States committing itself to rebuilding its allies' trust and confidence as the basis for the reassertion of its leadership in the region. A sincere and consistent commitment to the region and US allies and partners there is thus essential, not just to strengthen the United States' leadership as the region's apex power but also to avoid setbacks that will require extra work to undo, undermine efforts to strengthen the East Asian alliance system, and provide an advantage to China as it increases its power and influence throughout the Asia Pacific.

Consider that the Trump administration's approach to the US alliances in the Asia Pacific was hardly welcome and actually undermined any US attempts to continue as the alliance system's top power. The negative impacts are evidenced in how the publics of South Korea and Japan viewed the Trump administration. The data presented in table 7.1 are from the Genron NPO surveys taken in both South Korea and Japan, and they indicate strongly that very few respondents in either South Korea or Japan supported the Trump administration. In fact, just under two-thirds of Japanese respondents and nearly three-fourths of South Korean respondents said they did not support the Trump administration or the way it approached their respective countries as long-term US allies. Indeed, the publics in these two countries were similar in their strong dislike of the Trump administration and its behavior in the region, but South Korean and Japanese respondents did reveal some differences in terms of why they expressed such little support for the presidency of Donald Trump.

Respondents in both South Korea and Japan expressed concerns about the security problems posed by North Korea's nuclear weapons program, although nearly 20 percent more South Koreans expressed this specific concern. This was still the principal issue for Japanese respondents, in that two-thirds mentioned nuclear weapons as their primary issue of concern. South Korean respondents also mentioned two other issues with which they held deep concerns as a result of Trump administration policies. These included questions about Trump's negative impact on the East Asian alliance system (72.7%) and concerns about trade and economic issues (70.2%). Japanese respondents also expressed reservations over Trump's negative impact on trade and economic issues (49.6%) and mentioned concerns about the weakening of the East Asian alliance system, resulting from the Trump administration's lack of commitment. Although a little more than one-third of Japanese respondents mentioned this concern, nearly three-quarters of South Korea's respondents did the same.

To be sure, negative views of the US presidents have not been exclusive to the Trump administration. Nonetheless, evaluations of this administration tended to be dramatically different from those of other US administrations, which the South Korean and Japanese publics tended to evaluate more positively. In these data, Japanese and South Korean respondents were asked how they rated the Trump administration compared to the previous Obama and Bush administrations. For Japanese respondents, the data covered fifteen years of surveys, while for South Korean respondents, we have data covering seven years. As we see from table 7.2, the lowest percentages of respondents who expressed confidence in the US president were contained in surveys during the last three years of the George W.

156 Strengthening South Korea–Japan Relations

Table 7.1. Support for and Concerns about the Trump Administration

	Japanese	South Koreans
Support the Trump Administration		
Yes	5.8%	8.7%
No	65.3%	73.1%
Not Sure	28.7%	18.2%
Concerned about Security Problems with Respect to North Korea's Nuclear Weapons	66.4%	85.7%
Concerned about Alliance Issues, Especially the United States and Japan and the United States and South Korea	35.4%	72.7%
Concerned about Economic Issues Such as Trade and Investment	49.6%	70.2%
Concerned about Environmental Problems Such as Climate Change	22.2%	25.6%
Concerned about Democracy Issues Such as Human Rights	17.3%	23.1%
Concerned about Immigration-Related Issues Such as Issuances of Visas	12.7%	14.3%

Source: Genron NPO (2018).

Bush administration and the first two years of the Trump administration. Japanese confidence in the Bush presidency averaged 31 percent for the last three years he was in office, and, for the Trump administration, the average was 27 percent. The average level of confidence for the Obama administration was 74 percent, more than forty percentage points higher than that for G. W. Bush and over forty-five percentage points higher than that for the Trump administration.

While employing a different scale, which does not permit a direct comparison across respondents, we still observe similar patterns of support for the Trump administration and its predecessor. The South Korean favorability rating was measured with data from Asan Polls and is reported in the table on a scale of 1 to 10, which is roughly equivalent to the percentages in the Japanese polls that were also reported in the table. In these data, we

Table 7.2. Favorability of and Confidence in US Presidential Administrations

Year	President	Japanese Confidence in the US President*	South Korean Favorability of the US President**
2006	Bush	32%	
2007	Bush	35%	
2008	Bush	25%	
2009	Obama	85%	
2010	Obama	76%	
2011	Obama	81%	
2012	Obama	74%	
2013	Obama	70%	6.3
2014	Obama	60%	6.3
2015	Obama	66%	6.3
2016	Obama	78%	6.4
2017	Trump	24%	3.4
2018	Trump	30%	4.5
2019	Trump		4.3

* Percentage of respondents stating that they had confidence in the US president.
Pew Research Center (various years).
** Favorability ratings of the US president from 0 to 10.
Asan Polls (2016–19).

see that the Trump administration's favorability was slightly higher among South Korean respondents compared to their Japanese counterparts; his administration's average favorability rating was 4 out of 10 for the three years for which the Asan Institute data are available. In spite of suggesting a small contrast with Japanese respondents, the data reveal a very similar pattern. Specifically, Trump's favorability ratings were much lower than those that were recorded for the Obama administration, which averaged over 6.3 out of 10 for the four years for which the Asan poll data were available.

Given that most respondents in South Korea and Japan held negative views of the Trump administration, our expectation is that a new presidential administration would be seen in a much more favorable light. The data in table 7.3 compare the views that respondents in South Korea and Japan had of US presidents and the United States itself in 2020 and 2021. Since the Biden administration began its term in January 2021, we should see a notable difference in how South Korean and Japanese respondents evaluated the United States and its chief executives in these two years. Specifically, if the Biden administration was perceived as truly reinvigorating the

158 *Strengthening South Korea–Japan Relations*

Table 7.3. South Korean and Japanese Views of the United States and US Presidents

	2020	2021	Change
Percentages of Respondents Who Have a Favorable View of the United States			
South Korean Respondents	59%	77%	+18%
Japanese Respondents	41%	71%	+30%
Percentages of Respondents Who Have a Favorable View of the US President			
South Korean Respondents	17%	67%	+50%
Japanese Respondents	25%	73%	+48%
The Difference between Those Who Have Positive versus Negative Views of the United States, 2021			
South Korean Respondents	+55%		
Japanese Respondents	+45%		
	2020 to 2021 Change		
The United States Considers the Interests of Other Nations in Its International Policy Decisions			
South Korean Respondents	+7% (From 24% to 31%)		
Japanese Respondents	+20% (From 28% to 48%)		

Source: Pew Research Center, *America's Image Abroad Rebounds with Transition from Trump to Biden* (2021).

United States' bilateral relations with Seoul and Tokyo, we should see more positive scores in 2021 than in the previous year.

We see from the data in table 7.3 that favorable views of the United States itself held by South Koreans increased by 18 percent, while this score grew by 30 percent among Japanese respondents. Differences in scores for these two years were even more dramatic when it came to how South Korean and Japanese respondents viewed the occupant of the White House. Indeed, the number of South Korean respondents with favorable views of the US president grew by fifty percentage points, and among Japanese respondents the number was similar, at an increase of forty-eight percentage points. We also see from these data that the percentages of respondents who had a positive view of the United States were larger than those with negative views by fifty-five percentage points in South Korea and by forty-five percentage points in Japan.

US Leadership and the Evolution of Interstate Relations in the Asia Pacific 159

There are undoubtedly many reasons that South Korean and Japanese respondents have moved in such a positive direction, and among them are President Biden's assertion that he intends to reestablish US leadership in the region and the fact that many in South Korea and Japan thought that the United States would be more considerate of their respective countries' interests in the US approach to the Asia Pacific. As the data at the bottom of table 7.3 indicate, South Koreans who held this view went from 24 percent to 31 percent of all respondents, while Japanese respondents with this view of the new administration grew by twenty percentage points, from 28 percent to 48 percent of all respondents.

These positive trends portend well for improved bilateral relations between the United States and each of its East Asian allies, but the problems of South Korea–Japan relations and of the East Asian alliance system overall remain unaddressed. To ensure that these positive changes are sustained by a renewed US effort to strengthen all relations that compose the East Asian alliance system, we will have to assess what steps the United States must take to remake the alliance system's set of triangular relations so that they are sufficiently robust to remain a force for the continued peace and stability of the Asia Pacific. Of particular concern is how the changes that have occurred in the Asia Pacific have altered the logic that underpinned the international order that was created in the wake of the Pacific and Korean Wars. While the South Korean and Japanese publics overwhelmingly approve of the United States as the region's apex power compared to China, especially as Beijing continues to grow its regional power and influence, this does not mean that they approve of all of the United States' actions. Consequently, it is essential for decision makers in Washington to understand what the publics in South Korea and Japan expect from US leadership in the region.

The data in table 7.4 measure the affinity that South Korean and Japanese respondents have with each other as well as with the United States versus China. The data cover three years of joint surveys, and they indicate, first, that Japanese respondents registered higher feelings of affinity with South Koreans in each of the reported surveys than South Korean respondents reported having with Japanese. Moreover, South Korean respondents reported slightly higher feelings of affinity with China in each survey than they did with Japan. Japanese respondents, on the other hand, reported having very low feelings of affinity for China, but most respondents reported not having feelings of affinity with either China or South Korea. While these data may paint a negative picture of the possibility of

160 *Strengthening South Korea–Japan Relations*

Table 7.4. South Korean and Japanese Perceptions of Affinity and Importance

	Japanese			South Koreans		
	2017	**2018**	**2019**	**2017**	**2018**	**2019**
Perceptions of Affinity						
With Each Other	31.9%	23.5%	26.9%	20.8%	20.6%	17.8%
With China	7.6%	6.7%	6.4%	27.3%	25.2%	25.9%
With Neither Country	32.2%	36.8%	35.8%	28.6%	24.2%	22.8%
Affinity with the United States versus China: Direct Comparison						
United States		59.9%	61.9%		65.8%	65.3%
China		4.7%	3.3%		5.8%	6.3%
Countries That Are Important for the Future of Each Nation						
United States	63.5%	63.4%	67.8%	45.1%	55.6%	55.5%
China	5.8%	8.6%	5.9%	42.0%	31.4%	33.3%

Source: Genron NPO (2018 and 2019).

building better triangular relations among members of the East Asian alliance system, there are two positive conclusions that can be drawn. First, we see that when asked directly to compare their feelings of affinity with the United States versus China, respondents in both South Korea and Japan feel much more affinity with the United States, and these feelings of affinity were overwhelming for both Japanese and South Korean respondents. When asked which nation was important for their future, both South Korean and Japanese respondents mentioned the United States, but Japanese respondents were much stronger in this opinion.[6]

The strength of Japanese and South Korean feelings toward the United States are definitely reflected in how these respondents see China compared to the United States as either a top ally or their most significant threat. The data at the bottom of table 7.5 indicate that very few South Korean and Japanese respondents viewed the United States as their top threat, but half of Japanese respondents and just about one-third of South Korean respondents reported that they saw China as their top threat. In terms of these two great powers' importance as alliance partners, over 60 percent of Japanese respondents and more than 70 percent of South Korean respondents see

US Leadership and the Evolution of Interstate Relations in the Asia Pacific   161

Table 7.5. Trilateral Cooperation and Perceptions of Threat and Alliance Importance

	Japanese		South Koreans	
	2018	**2019**	**2018**	**2019**
It Is Important to Strengthen Trilateral Cooperation				
Strongly Agree	7.3%	9.6%	14.5%	16.1%
Agree	28.5%	33.7%	46.4%	50.1%
Total	33.8%	43.3%	60.9%	66.2%
	Top Threat		**Top Ally**	
	United States	**China**	**United States**	**China**
South Korean/Japanese Perceptions of China and the United States as Top Ally or Top Threat, 2019 Data				
Japanese	6%	50%	63%	1%
South Koreans	13%	32%	71%	4%

Source: Genron NPO (2018 and 2019).

the United States as their number one ally, while less than 5 percent in each country see China in the same manner.

These data tell us that there is support in both South Korea and Japan to build stronger bilateral relations with each other because of the common way that South Koreans and Japanese view China's growing power and influence. Moreover, there is much support to build stronger relations with the United States because there are strong feelings of affinity for the United States to continue as the Asia Pacific's apex power. These public attitudes then lead to the question of what it will take for the United States to reform and strengthen its relationships with South Korea and Japan as well as reestablish itself as the region's leader, working closely with leaders in Seoul and Tokyo to build better relations with each other and strengthen the East Asian alliance system overall. We provide a discussion of the actions that the United States will need to take to accomplish this in the final chapter of the volume.

8

The Challenge of Maintaining the Liberal International Order in the Asia Pacific

In the last several years, the international actions of the United States and China can be thought of as a study in contrasts, if not polar opposites. On one side is China, the chief competitor to the United States on the world stage,[1] operating with apparently unwavering and "ruthless efficiency" to remake those international economic institutions that facilitated the growth of world trade and the rising prosperity of so many nations in the postwar period and to challenge the predominance of that model of democratic governance that made the United States a beacon of hope for people around the world suffering from political repression (Power 2021). These have been China's imperatives for at least the last decade and a half, and as a country directed by a Communist Party that is quick to counter any domestic or international criticism and to suppress any challenge to its own power, it will continue its efforts to change the norms and institutions of the current international order so it can more effectively serve its own long-term interests.

The contrast to this image of Chinese strength and operational efficiency is the United States: a country currently symbolized by Washington, DC, that, although the center of American power, is paralyzed by extreme partisan divisions that have taken America's governing institutions, once fueled by a vigorous can-do spirit that helped sustain the United States as a global leader, and ground them to a virtual halt. Indeed, the United States' clumsy and rather ugly withdrawal from Afghanistan and its cautious, and for many unsatisfactory, response to Russia's invasion of Ukraine are evidence that its formerly active and generally respected global leadership is

163

164   *Strengthening South Korea–Japan Relations*

not what it once was. Moreover, the extreme partisan divisions that define the American political system today have rendered reestablishing US global leadership an even more difficult challenge, not simply because evaluations of whether or not certain international actions are appropriate for the United States are informed by individuals' partisan preferences but also because current political divisions have led to rather significant swings in the levels that the United States has engaged in its long-standing alliances and the activity with which it continues its efforts at preserving the peace and stability of the liberal international order it established and maintained throughout the postwar period.[2]

Partisan-driven shifts in how deeply the United States is engaged in the Asia Pacific have led to much uncertainty among US allies in terms of its reliability as the region's leader, but more than this, the extreme partisan divisions that exist in Washington, DC, have hindered US efforts to mount an effective and coordinated response to the Asia Pacific's evolving power dynamics, something that has undoubtedly redounded to the advantage of China. In addition to this, inconsistent messages about alliance commitments have helped fuel a rise in more and more members of the US public asking whether the United States can or even should reestablish the leadership role it has long held and once again become that positive force that leads in solving the world's most pressing problems.

These domestic political challenges and foreign policy inconsistencies have not gone unnoticed internationally, as, in their public pronouncements and interactions with the leaders of other nations, Chinese officials have issued numerous declamations against the United States as the hope for future global leadership. Nonetheless, while officials in some nations have agreed with these kinds of Chinese statements and others have even expressed hope that they ultimately prove to be true, there are still many reasons that it is not a foregone conclusion that today's rising China will ultimately succeed at remaking the international order to better serve the interests of the CCP.

One reason is simply that, given China's international behavior in the last several years, the idea of the United States being replaced by China as a global leader "has not inspired a surge in faith" (Power 2021, 14). We know that this is the case for many nations around the globe, and we also know that it is particularly true for countries in the Asia Pacific, especially US allies (Economy 2022). The point is that China's interactions with other nations have not resulted in high levels of confidence with respect to the

Chinese leadership. In fact, interactions with Chinese officials have in many instances generated a backlash whereby many countries have reconsidered their relations with Beijing as their respective publics have viewed China with increasing levels of distrust (Power 2021, 14–17). Another reason for this is simply that a US commitment to leading on producing solutions to global problems by rejoining those international institutions and accords it abandoned a short time ago and reconnecting with its allies and other partners to rebuild the global trust it once had would be a very welcome development, particularly in the Asia Pacific. This was shown clearly in the public opinion data for South Korea and Japan that we examined above, but it is also a hope that is nearly universally held throughout the globe.

Reestablishing itself as a committed and active global leader is certainly an important goal for leaders in Washington, DC, and this is especially true for US leadership in the Asia Pacific because this region has been first in experiencing the direct impacts associated with China's rising power and influence. As stated above, however, the United States restoring its long-held leadership role in this region does not mean a simple return to the past. Although reestablishing once-abandoned commitments to rebuild trust in its role as the apex power in the Asia Pacific is a necessary first step, it will not be sufficient to preserve the liberal international order the United States and its allies sustained for many decades. Indeed, the United States must take other actions in the Asia Pacific to reform and rebuild the East Asian alliance system so that it is sufficiently robust to endure the pressures that China's rise has presented and, thus, to preserve the liberal international order that maintained the peace and stability of the region for so many decades.

The data and discussions provided above support two conclusions about how the United States, in partnership with its allies in Seoul and Tokyo, can reinvigorate the East Asian alliance system and secure that system's future as the principal source of peace and stability in the Asia Pacific. The first conclusion involves the fact that, whatever challenges exist in this alliance system's triangular relations, South Koreans and Japanese, both citizens and leaders alike, support the East Asian alliance system and the United States—not China—as the apex power in the Asia Pacific. The level of support for the United States in this role stands out even more when members of the South Korean and Japanese publics are asked to evaluate the United States as the region's leader compared to China as it continues to increase its power and influence. Indeed, support for the United States as the Asia Pacific's top power far exceeds that which exists for China, particularly when the publics in both of these allied nations are reminded that Beijing's long-term goal is to replace the United States as the region's predominant power and remake interstate relations in the Asia Pacific so that they can better serve Chinese interests.

The second conclusion the data and discussions presented above support refers to the current state of relations between South Korea and Japan—specifically, the idea that problems in this bilateral partnership will not lend themselves to any quick solution. This is true not simply because there is very little common ground for leaders in Seoul and Tokyo to propose solutions to the unresolved historical issues that separate them that their respective publics would accept but also because Beijing successfully exploits these issues to increase the diplomatic distance that exists between South Korea and Japan, rendering it more difficult for their leaders to respond in concert to the challenges presented by China's rise. Committed US leadership in the region will be necessary to counter the negative consequences of unresolved historical issues and their exploitation by Beijing.

Unfortunately, making this a reality will involve more than an announcement that the United States is "back," as the Biden administration made when it assumed office, and this is because of the negative impacts attendant to inconsistencies that have existed in levels of US engagement in the region and also because of how the challenges attendant to strengthening South Korea–Japan relations and the East Asian alliance system overall have changed as the region's power dynamics have evolved with China's rise in influence. The United States currently has some distance to travel if it is to succeed in its efforts to help improve bilateral relations between South Korea and Japan and its own bilateral alliances with Seoul and Tokyo and to strengthen the East Asian alliance system overall.

To be sure, this is a sobering assessment, but it does not mean that the health of South Korea–Japan relations, and the East Asian alliance system itself, must remain in a state of debility in the face of China's continued rise in influence. Indeed, as the data provided above also indicate, the publics in both South Korea and Japan recognize that there is a problem in their countries' bilateral relations and that improving this partnership is an important strategic goal. This public support to improve bilateral relations between Seoul and Tokyo is partner to another common understanding, specifically, that a more committed and consistent leadership role for the United States is necessary. These areas of common understanding offer a more optimistic outlook for the future of the international order in the Asia Pacific, in part because they have been reinforced in statements made by Japan's prime minister and South Korea's president in their face-to-face meetings with President Biden. Indeed, both President Yoon and Prime Minister Kishida have reiterated the importance of improving the South Korea–Japan relationship. This call by the leaders of two US allies portend well for improving this essential bilateral partnership, and the optimism in these statements is reinforced by the fact that strengthening this partnership can begin with South Korea and Japan finding ways to reduce the salience of unresolved historical issues and keep them from being exploited by Beijing and escalating tensions in their relations with each other.

To build a more robust and productive relationship, the United States must engage more cooperatively with leaders in Seoul and Tokyo and work to help them promote policy positions that tap into the pools of public support that exist in both countries for improving their bilateral relations. This is certainly possible given that the data presented above show that there are those among the publics of both countries who acknowledge the importance of this bilateral relationship and its continuation as the base of the alliance system that has helped keep the peace in the region and essentially allowed all the nations of the Asia Pacific to enjoy the benefits of rising prosperity levels throughout the postwar period. A deep and consistent US commitment to the region is, thus, most important not only because such a commitment is the only way Washington will be able to work with its allies to overcome their differences but also because a strong US commitment to the region is necessary to help Seoul and Tokyo expand their own contributions to the East Asian alliance system.

This does not necessarily mean that leaders in Washington will require that South Korea and Japan respond to China's growing economic and military power in exactly the same manner; the United States can accomplish the goals described above while providing its East Asian allies the expanded space they need to manage their diplomatic and economic relationships with China in their own ways. It does, however, mean that the United States, South Korea, and Japan still need to become better at coordinating their responses to China's growing regional influence so they can ensure that their combined efforts prevent Beijing's foreign policy and military actions from weakening the East Asian alliance system and allowing any undermining of the region's current liberal international order.

At the same time, such efforts from alliance system members do not require that China be confronted in a way that puts the United States and its allies on a path to war, but this recognition does not imply shying away from the understanding that what the United States and its allies face is nothing short of a great power competition, which has been called the "defining geopolitical aspect of the twenty-first century" (Denmark 2020). The guiding point here is that it will be necessary to replace past naive and ineffective policies of positive engagement in the hope of getting leaders in Beijing to embrace the current international order's institutions and rules with an approach that recognizes Beijing's intentions to mold current norms and institutions so they more directly serve its own interests. Indeed, China is very unlikely to become what some proponents of positive engagement have referred to as "a responsible stakeholder,"[3] which means that the United States can address the challenge of China by responding to the incompatibilities that this rising power represents to the US-led international order while working closely with its two principal allies in the Asia Pacific to keep the peace and maintain stability throughout the region and the globe (Brands and Gaddis 2021).

This is still a daunting challenge that will require the United States to employ all elements of its national power if it is to rebuild the triangular relationships that form the East Asian alliance system and maintain the liberal international order that the East Asian alliance system helped sustain for many decades. As a prerequisite to realizing its reinvigorated engagement with its allies in Seoul and Tokyo to reform and strengthen the East Asian alliance system, the United States must first make qualitative improvements in the diplomatic and economic aspects of its statecraft in the Asia Pacific, both of which have suffered from neglect and underinvestment in the last several years (Gates 2020). The United States will also need to make qualitative changes in how it organizes and deploys its military wherewithal to more effectively serve the goals of strengthening the East Asian alliance system and preserving the Asia Pacific's liberal international order. In addition to these changes in what the United States will need to bring to its overall commitment to the Asia Pacific, rising to the challenge of the region's evolving power dynamics will be greatly served by US leaders making progress in healing the United States' own political divisions so that it can more effectively, as George Kennan pointed out, "measure up to its best traditions and prove itself worthy of preservation as a great nation" (Brands and Gaddis 2021, 29).

The Challenge of Maintaining the Liberal International Order   169

These are the general domestic and international actions that the United States will need to complete if it is to strengthen the East Asian alliance system and effectively counter the efforts of Beijing to replace it as the Asia Pacific's apex power. However, success at keeping the liberal international order in the Asia Pacific intact will also require that the United States employ its combined diplomatic, economic, and military powers to help strengthen its own bilateral alliances with South Korea and Japan and also help improve South Korea–Japan relations. These efforts do comprehend significant reforms to the United States' bilateral relationships so that South Korea and Japan can assume greater responsibilities within the alliance system while at the same time navigating their respective connections with China. Moreover, leaders in the United States must employ its three instruments of national power directly to address the negative consequences of China's growing influence in the region, which taken together will require the addition of a communication component to the employment of its diplomatic efforts, an extended maritime component to the deployment of its military power, and a thorough reassessment of how it engages economically with its allies and other partner nations in the Asia-Pacific region and around the globe.

Reforming and Strengthening the Alliance System's Relationship Triangle

The first part of reforming and strengthening the East Asian alliance system focuses on the bilateral relationships South Korea and Japan each have with the United States and, specifically, the actions the United States needs to take to strengthen its connections with these allies while empowering leaders in Seoul and Tokyo to do more in their roles as alliance system members. Naturally, these two areas of focus imply that the United States will reestablish a more consistent level of engagement with these two long-standing allies and avoid the wide swings in its level of commitment to the region that have occurred in the past. It also means that the United States must recognize how much both Japan and South Korea have changed since the ends of the Pacific and Korean Wars and that, because these changes help explain why they have responded to the growing economic and military power of China in the region in such different manners, they will require more flexibility in how they contribute to the East Asian alliance system while managing their respective relationships with Beijing.

The changes that both South Korea and Japan have experienced since the ends of the Pacific and Korean Wars, as well as those that have been put in motion more recently by China's growing economic and military influence in the region, present a dilemma for the United States and its allies in their efforts to reform and strengthen their respective bilateral relations. The word *dilemma* is used deliberately because it captures the competing pressures that these two US allies face to become more economically connected to an increasingly powerful China while remaining increasingly dependent on the United States for their own and the region's security. This dilemma requires that alliance system members respond more effectively to China's rising influence to preserve the liberal international order that helped maintain peace and stability in the postwar Asia Pacific for so many decades. At the same time, it also requires that the United States be sensitive to the fact that each alliance member is now much more dependent on China than it was in the past, which means that South Korea and Japan must increase their contributions to make the East Asian alliance system more robust and refrain from engaging with China in a way that disrupts their economic interactions with Beijing.

Navigating such a tricky course of action will involve both continuity and change in how each alliance system member approaches this dilemma, but common to each member's efforts is the need to put in place mechanisms of cooperation so that all responses to Chinese behavior, be they military, diplomatic, or economic, not just coordinate but also involve actions that all members sanction. Naturally, clearly defined procedures for such cooperation are necessary so that the responses of alliance system members do not involve any disagreement on the types of action that should be taken and that such actions do not lead to any rise in tension between South Korea and Japan (Denmark 2020). At the same time, cooperation is necessary so that the intended benefits of their coordinated responses to Chinese behavior will be shared equally by alliance system members. As former German foreign minister Heiko Maas told an audience in Tokyo, "If we pool our strengths . . . we can become something like 'rule shapers,' who design and drive an international order that the world urgently needs" (Daalder and Lindsey 2018, 76).

In light of this, the United States, South Korea, and Japan will need to begin building mechanisms that will facilitate cooperation for the kinds of responses that can counter the deleterious impacts of China's rising influence in the region as well as North Korea's provocative behavior. However, designs for such mechanisms of cooperation must ensure that they reflect the features of interstate relations in the Asia Pacific, particularly the fact that South Korea and Japan each face different economic and security imperatives in the region, so that they can better protect the security needs of members of the East Asian alliance system while providing the flexibility that South Korea and Japan will each need to continue managing the different relationships they have evolved with China in the last several decades.

Whatever the final form such mechanisms of security cooperation take, they must be able to coordinate the responses of all East Asian alliance system members while not being negatively affected by the potentially undermining impacts of political change in the United States. The seriousness of this problem came into relief during the Trump administration when its policies negatively affected the North Atlantic Treaty Organization (NATO) and other alliances through its "America First" approach to US relations with other nations, allies and adversaries alike. Thus, to avoid the deleterious consequences associated with significant foreign policy shifts that result from the political changes that presidential elections can produce, mechanisms of cooperation must guarantee operational coordination in the Asia Pacific across such areas as defense planning and deployment among members of the East Asian alliance system regardless of changing domestic political winds in the United States. Short of this, political changes that result from national elections will continue to have the potential to result in a weakening of the cooperative efforts of the United States, South Korea, and Japan vis-à-vis an increasingly powerful China.

In addition to the need to design mechanisms that can better coordinate US, South Korean, and Japanese responses to Chinese efforts to undermine the Asia Pacific's liberal international order, one area of security cooperation demands immediate attention from alliance system members: the General Security of Military Information Agreement (GSOMIA), which began as a promising area of security information exchange between South Korea and Japan but has not yet realized its full potential as an effective instrument of security cooperation. It is time for the Biden administration to build on this agreement and do what it can to formalize its provisions so they will be less susceptible to the interruptions that are often attendant to escalating tensions in South Korea–Japan relations.

In addition to ensuring that all members of the East Asian alliance system are privy to the full spread of the most up-to-date military information, the United States will need to help its allies upgrade their military capabilities employed in defense of the East Asian alliance system. There are three areas in particular that the United States, South Korea, and Japan will have to address if they are to upgrade their military capabilities and restructure their deployments to ensure that their efforts as alliance system members have the highest likelihood of enervating the growing influence of China in the Asia Pacific and ensuring continued peace and stability in this region under the current international order. Upgraded military capabilities and restructured deployments of military assets will be necessary because of the manner in which Beijing has modernized the People's Liberation Army (PLA). What is especially concerning about the current capabilities of the PLA is Beijing's goal to "dissuade, deter, and, if necessary, defeat technologically advanced adversaries" through the use of "precision-strike ballistic and cruise missiles, offensive cyber and counterspace weapons, and coercive 'gray zone' tactics short of war" (Gill 2022, 3).

Enhancing the military readiness of the United States and its East Asian allies will first involve upgrading the missile defense capabilities of alliance system members. Specifically, the United States needs to ensure that each of its allies has missile defense capabilities that are sufficient in quantity and quality to deter aggressive action from China and North Korea and defend against an overt attack should one occur. The point is not just that China and North Korea possess significant capability with respect to their theater-level ballistic missile arsenals, which can cause significant military and civilian damage, but also that their capabilities are constantly being upgraded. Consider that reports suggest that North Korea is developing a capacity for its missile force to carry anthrax to its targets, which if successfully used in an attack would be devastating to any targeted nation (Denmark 2020, chap. 4).

This is not to suggest that, at the present time, neither South Korea nor Japan currently possess missile defense capabilities, nor is it to say that the missile defense capabilities of the United States in the Asia-Pacific region are inadequate to maintain the integrity of the East Asian alliance system. Rather, the point is that what members of the East Asian alliance system have deployed can be upgraded to include the most up-to-date land- and sea-based missile delivery systems and that upgrades should be accompanied by certain deployment alterations. Specifically, upgrades should involve, at a minimum, a full deployment of THAAD missiles and the incremental expansion of more ship- and shore-based Aegis missile defense capabilities. At the same time, the United States must continue to commit itself to developing its missile defense capabilities, especially in such areas as the Ground-Based Midcourse Defense technology; lower-atmosphere missile defense capabilities, such as the Patriot Advanced Capability-3; and its detection technology, including its Space-Based Infrared System High Sensors.

The second area of security development is concerned with the cyber capabilities of the United States and its allies in Seoul and Tokyo, which have become an essential area of focus in building the defense capabilities of East Asian alliance system members. China has significant capabilities in this area and has employed them to engage in acts of industrial espionage (US Office of the Director of National Intelligence, 2021). Indeed, Chinese cyber experts have engaged in the hacking of all three members of the East Asian alliance system so they could acquire information on the technological capability of the United States and its allies and then develop and employ technology that it does not currently possess.[4] These kinds of hacking incidents will need to be defended against because they are very unlikely to stop any time soon since leaders in Beijing have made it clear that one goal of their national security strategy is to possess "information dominance."

It has been noted that information technology has been moved to the forefront of China's military strategy as it continues to develop its own technological capabilities in this strategic area (Koshino 2022). As stated above, this is part of Beijing's effort to achieve its goal of "information dominance," which is a serious threat to the activities of alliance system members, particularly their collective efforts to forge a coordinated response to China's growing power in the region. At this point in time, the United States, South Korea, and Japan, as well as all other potential targets of Chinese cyber intrusions, are at a disadvantage because there are no formally approved "international norms or rules that define how countries should or should not use the cyber and space realms for their security" (Koshino 2022, 52). This situation helps create vulnerabilities around the entire globe, but it is particularly troubling for members of the East Asian alliance system, who all operate in a context defined by imperfect coordination in their security efforts. Particularly troubling is the potential for this cyber vulnerability to become even more critical, especially in light of evidence that PLA-supported hackers will continue to target private companies and organizations involved in critical technological research and that Chinese-sponsored cyber criminals are likely to expand their hacking efforts to include civilian and government spaces more broadly.

Given that all alliance system members have experienced some form of cyberattack from China-sponsored hackers, they understand the seriousness of such incidents and agree that defending against them is a top security priority. However, beyond merely recognizing that this is a serious problem, the United States, South Korea, and Japan will need to work together to develop their respective capabilities to thwart Chinese-sponsored cyberattacks, which will require much higher levels of cooperation in the area of information sharing. Indeed, the first operating principle for alliance system members is to develop a system whereby appropriate officials in each country are apprised of all such incidents. Moreover, next steps should include leaders in South Korea, Japan, and the United States beginning cooperative efforts to develop their collective capability to thwart any negative implications stemming from such malicious cyber activity. At a minimum, such cooperation should include sharing technology to develop the individual and collective capabilities of alliance system members to defend against malicious cyber probes, but even more effective would be efforts to codevelop the technical capabilities that lead to collective deployment of counterespionage capabilities and also to guarantee the interoperability of anti-cyberattack technology.

The third area of focus rests on one of the hallmarks of the liberal international order that the East Asian alliance system helped to maintain throughout the postwar period: its facilitation of the dramatic expansion of world trade that occurred throughout the years after the Pacific and Korean Wars, which helped drive the rapid economic growth we witnessed in the Asia Pacific and the rise in prosperity that citizens in so many nations of this region experienced. Indeed, South Korea, Japan, and so many other nations throughout the Asia Pacific were manifest beneficiaries of the economic developments that were facilitated by the East Asian alliance system's maintenance of the region's peace and stability for so many decades. Unfortunately, the dramatic expansion of Chinese military power in the region, particularly in the South China Sea and other nearby bodies of water, have raised concerns about what the future holds for the enormous amounts of free trade that occur throughout the region and the unhindered free flow of goods that occurs there. The negative potential of China's rising influence behooves alliance system members to consider how to respond to such developments to ensure that the free flow of trade and commerce is maintained throughout the entirety of the Asia Pacific.

The Challenge of Maintaining the Liberal International Order   175

Naturally, enhancing the overall defense capabilities of East Asian alliance system members, both individually and collectively, is an important part of this effort, but focusing only on enhancing the general defense capabilities of alliance system members without paying specific attention to how the United States, South Korea, and Japan will help guarantee the openness of trade routes throughout the Asia Pacific will not be sufficient to maintain the region's liberal international order. Indeed, without it will be necessary to use member nations' combined defense capabilities to help guarantee an open trading system through the protection of sea lines of communication (SLOC), otherwise combined efforts will miss what is perhaps the most important aspect of building a stronger and more cooperative defense effort in the Asia Pacific. Specifically, to preserve the liberal international order in the Asia Pacific in the face of challenges from Beijing will require cooperation to guarantee the security of the maritime aspects of that order, which means that the United States and its allies in Seoul and Tokyo will need to take other specific actions to ensure that SLOCs throughout the Asia Pacific remain protected and open.

There are several actions that can be taken, and the first involves simply growing the maritime resources that South Korea, Japan, and the United States can deploy to begin catching up to the maritime resources China has put into the region's waters (Denmark 2020, 132). To accomplish this, the United States will need to assist its two allies in developing more robust and capable coast guard fleets, which means increasing the number of vessels that can be used by each country's coast guard and increasing the total tonnage dedicated to allied coast guards that will be responsible for engaging in enhanced maritime protection duties. While such coast guard enhancements are necessary, they are a minimum-level effort because the members of the East Asian alliance system will also have to complete other actions if they are to counter the maritime resources China has employed and guarantee the openness of SLOCs throughout the Asia-Pacific region.

One of these equally important actions concerns the scope of operations that alliance system members' updated and strengthened coast guards will need to engage in. Specifically, the South Korean and Japanese Coast Guards' activities will need to be expanded from traditional coastal patrol duties, such as performing rescues and protecting against drug and contraband traffic, to take much more active roles in protecting their respective countries' maritime claims throughout those bodies of water that surround their territories. This expanded range of duties will only be possible with the United States helping its two East Asian allies expand their maritime capabilities, but success at protecting the Asia Pacific's SLOCs will require one other task in this area of maritime security.

As we have discussed above, coast guard and other vessels from South Korea and Japan have had negative encounters with each other because of ongoing disputes over territory and a lingering propensity for mistrust. Consequently, increasing each's maritime resources without, at the same time, finding ways for South Korea and Japan to coordinate the employment of their strengthened coast guards and other maritime-based security assets in service of keeping SLOCs open has the possibility of feeding into these past unfortunate actions and raising tensions in South Korea–Japan relations. To prevent such avoidable and destructive events and better coordinate maritime activities, alliance system members will need to establish a Regional Maritime Domain Awareness Network whereby these three allies will cooperate to track maritime security events that affect all alliance system members throughout the entirety of this immense region (Denmark 2020). Without coordination and the sharing of such important maritime security information, members of the East Asian alliance system will not be able to respond in a coordinated and, thus, more effective fashion to developments that challenge the openness of the region's SLOCs while protecting their own territorial interests.

Another reason that a Regional Maritime Domain Awareness Network and other mechanisms of cooperation will be absolutely necessary for the United States and its allies to successfully enhance their defense capabilities, especially in the maritime area, is that they have historically played different roles within the East Asian alliance system and, as a result, have evolved different security concerns that have led them to respond to the security threats posed by an increasingly influential China in different ways. Despite common sources of threat, the distinct security concerns of South Korea and Japan have been reinforced by the fact that the rapid economic and domestic development each experienced in the last several decades has well-nigh equalized their overall relationship and capabilities. These changes make it even more important that efforts to increase the military capabilities of these two US allies be carried out in a way that is transparent and results in absolute clarity that the military enhancements are strictly to preserve the liberal international order that has governed interstate relations in this region for many decades.

Such cooperation and transparency measures are essential so that all members of the East Asian alliance system support every improvement that needs to be made to each member's respective military capabilities. While important for allaying the concerns of both of these US allies, they are also important to South Korea and Japan for different reasons. Specifically, Japan needs the support of its South Korean partner because, as Japan takes on more responsibility to preserve the liberal international order in the Asia Pacific, it must not accomplish such goals in a way that acts contrary to South Korea's essential security concerns. This refers mostly to Seoul's relationship with Pyongyang, which has been a strongly motivating force for Japanese prime ministers to beef up the capabilities of their country's Self-Defense Forces. Without allied consultation and approval, Japan must not take any independent action relative to North Korea that could increase the threats this rogue regime poses to South Korea.

On the other hand, such consultation imperatives are not exclusive to Japanese leaders but also concern presidential administrations in South Korea, especially with respect to countering the growing influence of China. Indeed, neither Seoul nor Tokyo should respond to Chinese provocations in a way that could result in a Chinese response that works disproportionately against the security or economic interests of any member of the East Asian alliance system.[5] In addition to this, leaders and citizens in both South Korea and Japan must begin to accept that they will need to take more active military postures in the region. This is important overall, but it is particularly important for South Koreans, who, even without Beijing provoking anti-Japanese reactions as it has in the past, have responded to Japan's attempts to increase its defense capabilities and security participation levels in a generally negative manner. Just as a more active military role for South Korea will be necessary for alliance system members to help to maintain the liberal international order in the Asia Pacific, it will be essential for the United States to assist both nations' leaders and publics to understand that more active military roles for both South Korea and Japan, in coordination with a more engaged United States, will only serve to bolster the ability of leaders in Seoul to promote their own security needs, particularly vis-à-vis Pyongyang and Beijing.

Such a high level of cooperation is necessary because US and allied efforts to strengthen the East Asian alliance system and preserve the Asia Pacific's liberal international order are much more likely to succeed if these alliance system members can avoid provocations and other actions that have raised the salience of unresolved historical issues and elevated tensions in South Korea–Japan relations. Again, there is no way to overstate the importance of the role that the United States will play in this process by working with its partners in Seoul and Tokyo to avoid actions that escalate tensions. Only by the United States investing its diplomatic and political capital to improve South Korea–Japan relations will alliance system members be able to remain focused on not giving China more ability to rewrite the rules of the Asia Pacific's international order. Moreover, as leaders in Seoul and Tokyo reduce tensions in their own partnership, they will be better able to coordinate their counteractions sufficiently to thwart Chinese efforts to rewrite the rules of the international order in the Asia Pacific.

To this end, the United States, South Korea, and Japan should set up a kind of adjudicative, or at a minimum investigative, body that can focus not specifically on how to solve this problem of disruptive unresolved historical issues in South Korea–Japan relations but rather on how to manage the fallout attendant to events or behavior that elevate the salience of these issues so that they become less disruptive to relations between these two essential US allies. The idea is for each country to appoint members to this body who have access to each country's political leadership, particularly the Ministry of Foreign Affairs and Trade in South Korea, the Ministry of Foreign Affairs in Japan, and the State Department in the United States, and then for members of this adjudicative/investigative body to convene when any event has occurred that has the potential to escalate tensions between South Korea and Japan.

For example, when the South Korean Supreme Court issued its ruling that stated that certain Japanese companies would have to offer compensation to workers who were forced into wartime labor, it led to a series of actions that succeeded in raising tensions between South Korea and Japan to such a level that each government curtailed its country's economic interactions with the other. If such an adjudicative/investigative body could have been convened immediately after this court ruling was issued, there is at least a chance that the negative fallout from the brinksmanship game that followed could have been halted, possibly avoiding the economic punishments that each side imposed on the other. What is most important is that investigating and adjudicating disputes over unresolved historical issues cannot occur without strong US leadership, which then places increased responsibility on the United States in its role as leader of the East Asian alliance system. Exactly what this responsibility means for a more actively engaged United States in the Asia Pacific is the topic of the final subsection of this chapter.

Economic Engagement and Messaging in US Regional Leadership

Preserving the liberal international order that has existed around the globe since the end of World War II will require that the United States recommit itself to its long-standing role as the apex power of the global system of alliances that established and maintained that international order. As stated above, in the Asia Pacific, this means reforming and strengthening the East Asian alliance system, which both leaders and citizens throughout the region vigorously support but perhaps nowhere more so than in South Korea and Japan. However, only with the United States helping alliance system members cooperate more effectively, particularly with respect to unresolved historical issues, can the system's foundation formed by South Korea–Japan relations be strengthened and function in the way that it must so as to guarantee the continuation of the region's liberal international order. Such US efforts are necessary, but unfortunately, they are not sufficient to guarantee that the United States has adequately reengaged in the affairs of the Asia Pacific to be the apex power that the region needs it to be. Accomplishing this will require two more sets of actions on the part of the United States, and the first of these involves US engagement in the economic activities of the Asia Pacific.

As part of its "pivot to Asia," the Obama administration championed the strengthening of US economic leadership in the region, and in pursuit of this goal, it designed and implemented the Trans-Pacific Partnership (Campbell 2016). The TPP was not simply ambitious; it was also path-breaking in its scope and provisions. This trade pact found its genesis in the impasses that were associated with the Doha round of multilateral trade negotiations, and, overall, it was a historic approach to trade agreements for many reasons. First, it came to include over a dozen countries with combined GDPs of nearly $30 trillion (Schott, Kotschwar, and Muir 2013), and, moreover, this trade pact would have been partner to higher levels of liberalization than at any other time, while at the same time offering better rules on how trade and investment could be made to serve the citizens of signatory nations than any other such trade agreement in history.

In addition to this, the trade pact was intended not simply to strengthen the economic connections the United States had with the nations of the Asia Pacific but also to "define economic relations along preferred American lines" (Denmark 2020, 67). Indeed, the TPP was intended to ensure

180 *Strengthening South Korea–Japan Relations*

that the rules and institutions governing trade in the region were led by the United States and its allies and could not be undermined by an increasingly powerful China. Despite the TPP's promise, both as a model trade agreement that did more to expand trade while elevating worker protections and environmental standards than any other trade agreement to date[6] and as a partnership that would help thwart China's efforts to undermine the economic interests of the United States and its allies in the Asia Pacific, one of the first executive actions taken by the Trump administration was to withdraw from the TPP, which carried many negative implications for the future of US leadership in the region.

Negotiating free trade agreements is no simple task, but given the incredible scope of the TPP and its extensive provisions for worker safeguards and environmental protections, getting nations to sign on was particularly cumbersome. Indeed, the TPP, like other trade agreements, did generate significant domestic political opposition, and leaders of signatory nations expended an immense amount of effort to earn their publics' support. This was no simple task: the TPP required that member states reform their domestic economies, which meant that all of this effort was lost when the Trump administration withdrew the United States from the agreement. This withdrawal wasted domestic political capital because it naturally caused concern among allies and partner nations throughout the region and also created a large credibility gap with respect to the trustworthiness of the United States as a committed regional leader.

We must also recall, as we stated briefly above, that the Obama administration's effort to get the TPP approved and implemented was not just targeted to economic outcomes but was also geopolitical in intent. Indeed, part of the motivation for Obama taking the lead in creating the TPP was to help counter China's growing economic influence in the Asia Pacific. Thus, when the Trump administration announced that it was pulling the United States out of the TPP, the negative implications were both economic and geopolitical. This Trump administration action led to an economic leadership vacuum in the Asia Pacific, one that the United States' number one competitor in the region was only too happy to step into. China is now the largest trading partner to US allies and partners throughout the Asia Pacific, but approving the TPP would at least have allowed the United States to set the rules for economic interactions for so many nations and, thus, enervate the negative implications to which China's rise has been partner. Unfortunately, instead of the United States enjoying large gains

The Challenge of Maintaining the Liberal International Order 181

from expanding trade and being at the apex of a set of trade rules designed to benefit the country and its allies and partners, Trump's action turned gains into losses and gave China more leverage to continue its reworking of the rules that govern the international order in the Asia Pacific.

Some of the original members of the TPP, Japan in particular, worked to keep that trade agreement alive after the Trump administration pulled out of the partnership, and these efforts resulted in the signing and implementation of the Comprehensive and Progressive Agreement for the Trans-Pacific Partnership (CPTPP), which was promulgated in November 2018. While more modest in scope than the original TPP, the CPTPP was successful in keeping many aspects of the original partnership alive. In fact, it was successful enough that China applied for membership, and while Beijing awaits a decision, it has not stood idly by but has instead joined a larger free trade organization, the Regional Comprehensive Economic Partnership (RCEP). This is the largest free trade agreement in the history of formal trade negotiations, and, while China is not the formal leader of this organization, its economic size and aggressive regional behavior make it a powerful force in how international trade administered by this formal agreement is likely to take shape. Moreover, it is important to add here that South Korea is a member of the RCEP but not of the CPTPP, although its previous president, Moon Jae-In, stated that it would be in South Korea's economic interests to join as soon as possible.

These developments tell us that, because the United States has not signed either agreement, it has reduced its ability to be an effective counterforce to China's increasing economic influence throughout the Asia Pacific. This is not an ideal position for the United States and its allies, but this state of affairs should not lead one to the conclusion that, at this point in time, there is little that the United States can do to address its loss of economic benefits from increased free trade with the nations of the Asia Pacific or to stem the decline in economic leverage that resulted from the Trump administration's decision to leave the TPP. Many trade and business organizations have recommended that the United States join the CPTPP immediately, but the Biden administration has not responded positively to this suggestion. Rather, it has proposed the formation of an alternative agreement that is much broader in scope, what the White House has called the Indo-Pacific Economic Framework for Prosperity (IPEFP).

This strategic plan encompasses much more than the CPTPP or the RCEP, including twelve original members and 40 percent of world GDP.[7]

182   *Strengthening South Korea–Japan Relations*

Also, while it contains a strong commitment to free and open trade throughout the Asia-Pacific region, it is also focused on achieving goals in such areas as addressing climate change and pandemics, deepening relationships with the region's nations, enhancing labor and environmental standards, increasing the region's security, and building a deterrence against China's ability to undermine the region's liberal international order. Taken together, these ideas represent a solid strategic framework for the United States to reestablish its leadership in the Asia-Pacific region, but the question remains whether it is sufficient to undo the damage that has been done through the Trump administration's withdrawal from the TPP and to counter the strengthening of the Chinese position in the region that has occurred with the setting up of new trade regimes; of these organizations, China is already an influential member of one and has submitted an application for membership to the other.

An economic reengagement strategy in the Asia Pacific will require, then, that the United States counter China's "offensive leverage," which in the economic realm is "an approach designed to decrease China's dependence on high-tech imports while making the world's technology supply chains increasingly dependent on China" (Pottinger 2021, 107). While China has a ways yet to travel to dominate the global supply chain in high-technology products, it has already positioned itself as a predominant actor in other areas of the global supply chain, and the United States and its allies around the world are already feeling the negative implications of dependence on China for supplies of so many essential economic inputs.[8] Clearly, the Biden administration has taken a significant step forward with the issuance of its February 24, 2021, Executive Order on America's Supply Chains, but the United States can take other actions to gradually achieve more secure supply chains for itself and its allies and rebuild its economic leadership in the region.

Clearly, China's zero-COVID policy dramatically reduced activity in its manufacturing sector, leading to severe shortages in the global supply chain, and while its recent loosening of this policy has led to some recovery in production, the downside of dependence on China was brought into relief during the COVID-19 pandemic. Recognizing this, however, does not address the problem of how the large number of nations that rely on Chinese companies for a wide array of products can begin to deal with their consequential levels of dependence. Clearly, there is no consensus on how nations can address this problem, even though many affected

The Challenge of Maintaining the Liberal International Order   183

nations will agree that reducing their economic dependence on China will be better for them in the long run. Any actions taken will be particularly tricky for South Korea—and also Japan—because any change to current economic relationships with China will require navigation between Scylla and Charybdis. Indeed, given that any attempt on the part of South Korea to establish alternative supply chain relationships can provoke retaliation from Beijing as it has in the past, any such action must be carried out in a subtle but real manner so as not to provoke Beijing into any retaliatory behavior.

While the United States has already begun addressing this problem of its dependence on Chinese supply chains, it should also consider how it can build new supply chain relationships elsewhere in the world. It is true that developing more capacity for US companies to become part of the US supply chain will help in this process, but this raises the question of whether or not the United States can satisfy its demand for economic inputs with strictly domestic sources. There may be some possibility for this in the long term but definitely not anytime soon. Thus, seeking other supply sources outside the United States is most likely necessary and, in addition, may go a long way to help solve another significant policy problem the United States has long been facing. The reference here is to addressing problems in the US immigration system, particularly with respect to the large numbers of migrants from Mexico and Central America who have been showing up on the southern border, either seeking entry to the United States through the asylum process or entering the country illegally.

The Biden administration's infrastructure plan contains a significant domestic jobs component, and its executive order on supply chains is a start at encouraging more domestic production. In addition to these efforts, the current administration can certainly do more to reduce US companies' dependence on Chinese supply chains. For instance, it could provide more incentives to US companies to divest from China and find alternative supply chains elsewhere. Specifically, the US Department of Commerce, the Office of the US Trade Representative, the Department of the Treasury, and other related federal agencies involved in domestic and international economic activities could offer tax breaks and subsidies for US companies to reestablish their supply chains, both in the United States and in such areas as North and Central America. If sufficient amounts of this incentivized reinvestment were to land in troubled countries of Central America, it is possible that, in addition to reducing US economic dependence on

184 *Strengthening South Korea–Japan Relations*

China, the United States could begin encouraging development south of its border, giving more economic opportunity to those nations from which it receives so many refugees seeking entry.

Incentivizing American companies to reduce their economic dependence on China while at the same time encouraging alternative investments to help develop reliable suppliers, both domestically and in parts of Central America, will help elected officials address a partisan-driven problem that currently divides the United States in a very significant way. Such action could begin to address the wretched socioeconomic conditions that exist in a number of Central American countries and possibly reduce the poverty and violence that affects so many citizens in this part of the hemisphere in a way that could even reduce their incentives to travel such a very long distance to seek entry into the United States. This will not be an easy policy to implement, and, even if done correctly, it will be no panacea for the supply chain problem or the immigration system problem the United States faces. Nonetheless, increasing US investment in Mexico and Central America could encourage more businesses to set up appropriate supply chain partners in these regions, which would help lead to more development in these nations, bringing more people into higher levels of well-being and building supply chains that would help the United States become less economically dependent on China.

Expecting South Korea and Japan to follow this specific strategy is most likely not realistic, especially given how much more economically connected they are to China and also how easily any dramatic change in Seoul's and Tokyo's economic relationships with China could spur a punitive reaction from Beijing.[9] Nonetheless, South Korea and Japan can begin with some very small divestment steps that would increase over time and lead to these two US allies ultimately reducing their economic dependence on China. While the United States should begin straightaway, South Korea and Japan can take very small baby steps toward this end, slowly reducing their economic dependence on China, which in the long run would make them less vulnerable to the kinds of punitive actions that China may heap upon them.

Finally, China's efforts to increase its power and influence involve an "information warfare" component that exploits the United States' social media services to generate and spread disinformation that aims to undermine not just the credibility of the United States as a global leader but also its commitment and ability to sustain itself in that role. Such Chinese

The Challenge of Maintaining the Liberal International Order   185

efforts render it clearly in the essential interests of the United States, both singularly and in cooperation with its allies in Seoul and Tokyo, to develop and spread an alternative message that counters the pronouncements and declamations that leaders in Beijing have been issuing for some time. This is essential not simply to act as a counterweight to the negative messages that Chinese leaders have been spreading at every turn but more importantly to expose China for what it is as a nation, an authoritarian country that shuns transparency while bullying other nations, companies, and organizations that do not follow CCP dictates or that dare to criticize it.

We pointed out above that numerous scholars and analysts have observed that many nations that have engaged closely with China have come away with heightened suspicions of Beijing's intentions and behavior. Such reactions are undoubtedly helpful to the United States, but merely hoping for more nations to register negative reactions to interacting with Beijing will not be sufficient to reveal why China is simply not trustworthy as an alternative global leader to the United States. In fact, the United States can point to many reasons that would undermine China's credibility in its efforts to supplant the United States as the Asia Pacific's apex power and rewrite the rules of the liberal international order that has helped govern interstate relations there and throughout the globe for so many decades. Naturally, a general version of such a message involves the CCP's aversion to democracy, liberty, openness, human dignity, or any other worthwhile human value if it interferes with China's state interests or in any way challenges the power of the CCP. It will be important for US leaders to promote this negative but nonetheless accurate image of China as it counters the negative messages leaders in Beijing frequently issue with respect to the United States. However, there are many other events and issues that the United States and its allies can use to undermine Beijing's efforts to promote its alternative vision to the current liberal international order.

For example, China's complete lack of transparency with respect to sharing information and refusal to offer anything close to a sincere level of cooperation with other nations to understand and fight the COVID-19 pandemic is a clear indication that Xi and the CCP are not to be trusted as world leaders. Chinese leaders behaved this way because transparency and cooperation may have forced Beijing's leaders to admit to some missteps, something they are never wont to do, but this lack of trustworthy behavior is even more troubling because Chinese leaders continually double down and defend such untrustworthy behaviors as inappropriate for other nations to criticize. Consider how Beijing retaliated economically against Australia by cutting off certain imported products because it suggested that there be an investigation into the Chinese government's handling of the COVID-19 virus, particularly in the early days.[10]

These kinds of Chinese actions do in fact undermine the attempts that leaders in Beijing have been making to promote their vision for a revamped world order that they insist is more inclusive and offers more hope for solving the world's problems and addressing the needs of the world's least developed nations. Indeed, there is a large gap between the evolving vision that China's leaders have been promoting, which they claim represents how their nation will improve the state of international affairs, and the exact actions that leaders in Beijing have carried out to implement Chinese foreign policy. The United States and its allies can send an alternative message by pointing out such inconsistencies and thereby raise concerns that any nation should have with respect to China heading an alternative world order. Emphasizing that such inconsistencies raise questions of China's trustworthiness as a rising power is important, but no issue reveals the problems of China's goal of becoming more influential in world affairs better than Chinese leaders' behavior toward certain groups within their own borders.

Many leaders around the globe have pointed to the inhumane mistreatment that the Uyghurs have received from Beijing, treatment that involves separating family members from one another and placing some in so-called reeducation camps. It also includes threatening family members with fines and imprisonment when Uyghurs living outside of China bring attention to the Chinese government's treatment of its Uyghur population. Clearly, this appalling and inhumane behavior attests to how far Chinese leaders will go to suppress any domestic challenge to the CCP, but Beijing's more recent actions in Hong Kong signal that China is not to be trusted as the leader of a new international order. It is not simply that China's leaders have systematically undermined the unique democratic and governmental norms that long existed in Hong Kong but more importantly that the Chinese government has flouted an international agreement that it signed and ratified by moving to abandon the One Nation, Two Systems formula for Hong Kong, a formula to which it agreed when the British returned Hong Kong to Chinese sovereignty.

Naturally, the United States would be greatly assisted in its efforts to promote a message of China's untrustworthiness if it could overcome its own partisan divisions and operate with more political unity. This is especially important for governmental decisions regarding foreign policy, particularly for actions the United States takes in response to other international threats, like the Russian military's horrific actions in Ukraine and the long-term impacts of China's rising power and influence. Perhaps a small step in addressing this problem would involve setting up a bipartisan working group that is focused on the US response to China and Beijing's efforts to undermine the current liberal international order, particularly in the Asia Pacific. This working group would naturally track Chinese behavior throughout the region and the globe, and it would also hear testimony from all manner of experts, but its most important task would be to ensure that, with respect to implementing a coherent foreign policy that would protect US and allied interests from the deleterious impacts of China's rise, the United States speaks with a strong and unified voice.

This will be a small but important step for the United States and its allies to take if they are to reduce the debilitating impacts that current political divisions have on US and allied efforts to reform and strengthen their alliances and do what is necessary to preserve the international order that has benefited the Asia Pacific and the globe for so many decades. As one analyst noted in the pages of *Foreign Affairs*, "the best way to respond to China is to make democracy work better" (Weiss 2019, 102).

Acknowledgments

It was the annual conferences held at the University of Wisconsin–Milwaukee, on the topic of South Korea in the New Millennium, supported by a generous grant from the Academy of Korean Studies, that allowed us to begin work on this book in earnest. These annual conferences allowed us to get insightful feedback from the participants at the many panel sessions, and we are especially grateful to Dr. Heo Uk and his leadership of this grant-funded project as well as his excellent staff at University of Wisconsin–Milwaukee. We are also grateful to these conferences' ongoing participants, especially Vanya Krieckhaus, Terry Roehrig, Min Ye, Wonjae Hwang, and Sunny Kim. Finally, we are thankful to the colleagues we have worked with in South Korea and Japan, especially Dr. Hyun In-Taek, former minister of unification; Dr. Kim Woosang, professor at Yonsei University; Dr. Nagahisa Toshio, chief research officer, PHP Research Institute; and Dr. Asano Masahiko, professor at Takushoku University in Tokyo.

This book would not have been possible without a generous grant from the Academy of Korean Studies, funded by the South Korean Government (MEST) (AKS-2012-AAZ2101).

Notes

1. Introduction

1. The reference here is specifically to the nations of East and Southeast Asia. Throughout this volume, we will refer to these two regions as the Asia Pacific or the Asia-Pacific region.

2. Some economists did not envision a bright economic future for the nations of this region because they believed excessive population growth would stunt economic growth (Myrdal 1968).

3. The clear exception is North Korea, but, for many, China remains a repressive regime even though the country itself is increasingly prosperous and its government is far more responsive to public needs than it was in the early years after its founding.

4. This is true for Japan (Patrick and Rosovsky 1976), South Korea (Amsden 1992), and the Asia Pacific overall (Bothwick 1992).

5. The theme of both the country-based and larger regionally focused studies has typically been the role played by the developmental state, which has been applied to Japan (Johnson 1982) and to other nations in Northeast and Southeast Asia (Hatch 2011).

6. In the interest of geographic clarity, the alliance system referenced above has been principally a Northeast Asian phenomenon, constituted by the United States' individual bilateral alliances with South Korea and Japan and by the relationship that has existed between Japan and South Korea. However, this alliance system and the extensive environment of peace and stability it helped establish and maintain have had a positive impact on the entire Asia-Pacific region.

7. This triangular system of alliances forms the underlying architecture of what scholars refer to as a hub-and-spoke system, where, over time, layers of additional institutions have been placed on the original East Asian alliance system (Yeo 2019).

8. Singaporean prime minister Lee Hsien-Loong (2020, 54) makes the point that the high levels of economic growth that occurred in China and facilitated its

rise in influence, both in Asia and around the globe, occurred under the environment of peace and stability provided by the system of treaties and security arrangements he refers specifically to as Pax Americana.

9. These Chinese goals (Ikenberry 2020) and the debates they have generated will be discussed in more detail in chapter 3.

10. One action taken by the Trump administration early on involved raising tariffs on steel and aluminum imports, which naturally targeted China, but also hurt the region's US allies, Japan and South Korea, and the United States' European and North American allies as well.

11. Moreover, the Trump administration's "America First" approach to foreign relations was also partner to the United States taking many more unilateral actions rather than seeking to form a consensus among allies.

12. The same can also be said of how the liberal international order in the Asia Pacific has also greatly benefited China, even though its current leaders endeavor to amend this order with new rules that better serve the interests of its current leader and the Chinese Communist Party.

13. Many scholars who have written about the strategic choices available to South Korea in particular but also to Japan have made such an assumption (Glosserman and Snyder 2015; Snyder 2018).

14. The most likely scenario where South Korea and Japan would be forced to consider an alternative to the East Asian alliance system consists of the United States abrogating its alliances with Seoul and Tokyo and completely withdrawing from the region. However, under the Trump administration's "America First" policy, although leaders in South Korea and Japan were worried about this administration's demands and its weak levels of commitment, they were not consumed with how to cope with a US withdrawal from the region. Moreover, the current Biden administration has clearly assuaged such concerns with its early efforts to rebuild its alliances around the globe.

2. The Origins of the East Asian Alliance System and Its Impact on South Korea and Japan

1. The word *arms* is used here deliberately because the East Asian alliance system is composed of a set of triangular relations, and the term arms refers to the two sides of the triangle that join at the apex and then connect to the base.

2. It was also greeted with suspicion by many Japanese leaders and citizens because it ostensibly contradicted the spirit of the postwar constitution, particularly Article 9, which prohibits Japan from using war as a foreign policy tool and from using its Self-Defense Forces to defend the United States off of its main islands. The specific language of Article 9(1) is as follows: "Aspiring sincerely to an international peace based on justice and order, the Japanese people forever renounce war as a sovereign right of the nation and the threat or use of force as means of settling international disputes."

3. US-Japanese security relations have evolved significantly since 1951 (Szechenyi 2014).

4. This is an unfortunate period of Korean history that became increasingly repressive and brutal to Koreans from the time it was established in 1910 until it ended in 1945. As a result, it continues to loom large in the historical memory of South Koreans and complicates the challenges leaders in Seoul and Tokyo face in their bilateral relations.

5. This amphibious landing essentially cut the invading North Korean army in half, leading to it ultimately being pushed back by UN forces to the Yalu River (Blair 1987).

6. MacArthur did suggest the use of nuclear weapons along the Yalu River on the Chinese–North Korean border, but this was rejected by Truman, who eventually replaced MacArthur with General Matthew Ridgway (Blair 1987).

7. We must keep in mind that the United States has also been expending enormous amounts of money to help rebuild its European allies.

8. A US Agency for International Development (USAID) study conducted between 1953 and 1961 noted that 90 percent of donor flows to South Korea came from the United States, making up as much as one-third of the country's national budget (Steinberg 1985).

9. General Park had served as an officer in the Japanese Occupation of Korea (Kim 2004).

10. While this hierarchy in South Korea–Japan relations did persist for several decades, it has changed, particularly in the last three decades (Kim 2017).

11. Two of these were most notable, the first occurring in the wake of the Tokyo Olympics, which was preceded by two years of strong economic performance only to be followed by over a year of economic downturn. The other downturn in Japan's business cycle is traced to the deleterious impacts of the rise in the price of crude oil that took place in the 1970s. While Japan weathered these "oil shocks" better than most industrial nations, it nonetheless experienced two economic downturns in this decade.

12. This is the principal tenet of the developmental state idea, which notes that elite bureaucrats developed and implemented industrial policies that promoted exports (Johnson 1982).

13. Our emphasis on the importance of international factors in Japan's rapid postwar growth is not meant to relegate the literature on Japan's domestic economic policies but only to note that there is evidence that indicates it was far less important than developmental state advocates assert (Beason and Patterson 2004).

14. Between 1997 and 1998, the Korean won lost nearly half its value vis-à-vis other currencies like the US dollar.

15. Specifically, between 1972 and 1995, this growth was over 250% from well under $7,500 to over $25,000. This increasing prosperity of South Korean workers led to more demands for the ability of labor to organize for their specific interests

and to take action to promote these interests. For a discussion of the obstacles that Korean workers faced in attempting to organize and form trade unions (Amsden 1992).

16. Democracy in this figure is measured using Polity data.

17. This is the commerce and coalitions framework, which reveals how expanding, or contracting, trade affects the economic prosperity and political wherewithal of groups in a country, leading to political change (Rogowski 1989).

18. One scholarly work showed that establishing an embassy led to a 5 percent increase in exports for Swedish firms (Ferguson and Forslid 2014), and another revealed similar export increases with the efforts of export promotion agencies (Lederman, Olarreaga, and Payton 2010). Finally, another investigation showed that exports increased when there were official state visits (Nitsch 2007).

19. An example here would be the French language and trade between France and its former African colonies.

20. There are many other currency unions, such as that defined by the East Caribbean dollar and two franc-based currency unions, one in West Africa and the other in the South Pacific.

21. Again, past research has shown this to be true for nations in general (Pollins 1989a, 1989b).

22. This analysis used data averaged over 2002 and 2003 for twenty-two exporting nations and two hundred importing nations (Rose 2007).

23. This is known as a nation's international status, and it is defined by the percentage of diplomatic missions in a nation's capital city compared to the nation whose capital has the largest number of diplomatic missions, and for this period that was the United States.

24. South Korea established formal relations with the United Kingdom in January 1949 and with France one month later. Two months later, in March, South Korea and the Philippines established embassies in each other's capitals.

25. In addition to embassies, the Correlates of War's "Diplomatic Exchange Data" also include the number of chargés d'affaires and ministers (legations) that South Korea sent abroad and the number of resident representatives it sent to such international organizations as the Association of Southeast Asian Nations (ASEAN) and the Organisation for Economic Co-operation and Development (OECD).

26. President Park also doubled the number of consuls his government sent abroad.

27. As can be seen from the table, the data do not contain the diplomatic efforts of South Korea's current and previous presidents, Moon Jae-In and Yoon Suk-Yeol.

28. South Korea's diplomatic efforts in Europe before the end of the Cold War did encounter some issues with respect to communist countries (Ahn 1980), but it did have more diplomatic success with these nations in the wake of the ending of the Cold War (Kihl 1991).

29. In fact, nearly three-quarters of South Korea's post-democratic-transition diplomatic relations occurred under these two presidents.

30. Among other things, this drop corresponds to the end of the Vietnam War and the loss of previously established diplomatic partners that the communist reunion of North and South Vietnam caused.

31. This security umbrella was sustained by the nuclear deterrent that the United States established and maintained, which also kept its allies from having to develop their own nuclear capabilities (Roehrig 2017).

3. China's Rise and the Asia Pacific's International Order

1. The weakening of the United States' position in the region is due not just to China's rising economic and political influence but also to the Trump administration's "America First" approach to US alliances. This has led to some disengagement with its allies in Seoul and Tokyo, weakening the influence the United States has traditionally had in the Asia Pacific.

2. In terms of sheer size, however, China's surpassed Japan in 2010.

3. China's per capita GDP is now four and a half times larger than that of India.

4. China's expanding commerce with South Korea and Japan—and with the United States, for that matter—also helped it more effectively attract foreign direct investment (Chantasasawat, Fung, and Iizaka 2004, table 6; Ohashi 2005).

5. The reason for this is that, since 2001, the United States has focused its attention on the successful execution of its global war on terror and, thus, has paid attention more to regions like the Middle East and Afghanistan than to East and Southeast Asia. This lack of attention to Asia was also partly due to the pressing problems caused by the 2008 financial crisis and the US and allied efforts to restore the jobs and losses of value that followed in its wake.

6. We should also note that China's naval ambitions extend beyond the Indian Ocean, with Beijing having begun negotiations with the government of El Salvador to establish a base at La Union Port as an illustration.

7. When Xi took power, he launched a third revolution in China in which he began reversing the openings initiated by Deng Xiaoping while setting out the principles for China's increasing influence in the current liberal world order (Economy 2018a, 2018b).

8. Some scholarly works admit that China's rise has led to a power shift while concluding that its intentions are status quo (Shambaugh 2005), while other scholars discuss the impacts of China's rise without addressing this question (Denmark 2020).

9. There are many contributions to the debate—indeed, too many to recount in detail here—but several are worthy of mention (see Art 2010; Denmark 2020; Johnston 2003; Kang 2010; Kasten and Saunders 2012; Lemke and Tammon 2003; Ross and Zhu 2008; Tellis 2020).

196   Notes to Pages 55–64

10. Some scholarly works divide China's strategic goals into three distinct time periods, with the current period being defined by an assertive promotion of its regional and global interests (Denmark 2020; Tellis 2020).

11. The Chair of the National People's Congress Foreign Affairs Committee, Fu Ying, added that the current system not only lacks the ability to solve these pressing world problems but also serves as a growing source of disruption and instability in the world (Zhao 2018).

12. There have been updates subsequent to the publication of this report, which we discuss.

13. For a list of the concepts that scholars and party officials have employed in their efforts to promote and clarify China's vision for its new world order, see Rolland 2020b.

14. Nations that participate in the Belt and Road Initiative can also benefit from China's Asian Infrastructure Investment Bank (Yeo 2019, Chapter 6). The Belt and Road Initiative is at the core of China's approach to international relations, which is development oriented, compared to the US approach, which is trade focused (Shiu 2020; Terada 2018).

15. Consultation, joint action, and mutual benefits are the three principles of China's Belt and Road Initiative (Shiu 2020). There are many illustrations of how China uses relations with BRI participant nations to expand not just its soft power but more importantly its military (hard) power around the globe (Rolland 2020a, 2020b).

16. This has generally been true for US relations with just about all of its allies (Beckley 2020).

17. The phrases *charm offensive* and *public diplomacy* have been used to describe these kinds of Chinese soft-power efforts to engage with South Korea and the other nations in the region (Shambaugh 2005; Kim 2019).

18. This included canceling certain K-pop concerts, which have become very popular in China, and restricting the activities of some of South Korea's largest companies (Kim 2019).

19. One view notes that Japan has moved away from its original policy of engagement with Beijing to a policy of hedging, of which its closer relations with the United States are part (Hornung 2014), but another view is that, despite Japan's efforts to tighten its relationship with the United States during the Trump administration, it is positioning itself to assume the role of a nation that can balance between the pressures they emanate from the United States and those of an increasingly important and powerful China (Katada 2020).

20. Policy actions include such things as the revision of history textbooks in a way that diminishes Japan's responsibility for the horrific conditions its military actions caused or politicians' official visits to Yasukuni Shrine, the shrine dedicated to Japan's war dead. Problematic statements include any high-ranking elected or bureaucratic official absolving Japan of any of its wartime responsibilities or reducing the role its military played in the destruction and loss of life that occurred throughout Asia before and during the Pacific War.

Notes to Pages 64–94   197

21. While it is more often than not the action of some part of Japanese officialdom that renders the problem of history salient, this is not the only manner in which unresolved historical issues become problematic in South Korea–Japan relations. To be fair, at times these troubles have been initiated by South Korean leaders for domestic political reasons. We discuss examples of such incidents in chapter 6.

22. The result was not only the end of Bush administration efforts on behalf of Japan and a softening of its initially harsh approach to China but also a rise in tension between South Korea and Japan (Blanchard 2013).

23. The Hwasong-12 missile had an original range of over 2,700 miles.

4. South Korean and Japanese Views of China and the United States

1. In the developmental state perspective, Japan had been labeled softly authoritarian, where "bureaucrats rule" and "politicians reign" (Johnson 1982), making advocates of this perspective conclude that bureaucratic influences will be much more important than electoral influences in the foreign policy decisions of South Korea and Japan.

2. This was true even during South Korea's authoritarian years under President Park Chung-Hee. Indeed, despite his extensive executive power, President Park thought it necessary to manipulate South Korea's electoral system so that he could guarantee himself sufficient support in the National Assembly.

3. Some important works show the impact of domestic factors on the foreign policy decisions of national leaders (Rosenau 1969; Wittkopf and McCormick 2008).

4. We will refer to some South Korean and Japanese data from the Pew Research Center from time to time in our analysis of public attitudes.

5. Originally, the nations about which Japanese were polled were Russia or the Soviet Union, China, and the United States before the end of the Cold War, and North Korea and South Korea shortly after this. Later, these Japanese public opinion surveys were expanded to include Southeast Asia, Europe, Australia, New Zealand, and the countries of the Middle East.

6. There is also the standard "don't know" category plus one where respondents note that they cannot say either way.

7. The data for the decade of the 1980s include the two surveys taken in 1978 and 1979.

8. These countries included the United States, North Korea, China, Japan, and Russia.

5. Public Attitudes and Relations between South Korea and Japan

1. We are grateful to former minister of unification Hyun In-Taek for his insights on this issue. The following discussion has benefited much from discussion with him about South Korea–Japan relations.

198   Notes to Pages 99–148

2. Interbrand is a global consultancy that produces the highly influential annual ranking of the Best Global Brands.

3. For years where multiple surveys were available, we took averages to calculate annual favorability rankings.

4. The main website for the Genron NPO surveys is https://www.genron-npo.net/en/.

5. The percentages do not add up to 100% because respondents selecting the Don't Know answer have not been included.

6. This recent row will be discussed in more detail in chapter 6.

7. The earlier data are an average of results reported for 2015 and 2016, and the later data are an average of results for 2018 and 2019.

6. Territorial Disputes, Human Rights, and Court Case Challenges in South Korea–Japan Relations

1. While the problem of forced labor goes back to the years before and during the Pacific War, it became very salient in South Korea–Japan relations in 2018 when the South Korean Supreme Court ruled that lawsuits against Japanese companies that engaged in forced labor could proceed. A subsequent court case overturned this decision. These cases are discussed in more detail in this chapter.

2. The 1965 agreement is known as the "Agreement on the Settlement of Problems concerning Property and Claims and on Economic Cooperation." It will be referred to herein as the Reconciliation Treaty.

3. South Korea's view of this territorial dispute remains very distinct (Lee 2021; Lee and Lee 2021; Yoo 2021), and it rests on assumptions that are very different from the assumptions that help form the Japanese view of this territorial dispute (Fukuhara and Sato 2021; Kaseda 2021; Usuki 2021).

4. In his first term as prime minister, he once denied the existence of sex slaves forced into service by the Imperial Japanese Army.

5. CUES refers to a 2014 naval agreement sanctioned by twenty-one nations to help ensure that potentially dangerous encounters at sea do not escalate into unwanted conflicts.

6. We should report that, while South Koreans are against Japan possessing nuclear weapons, the same polls indicated that a strong majority of South Koreans favor their own country possessing nuclear weapons (Genron NPO 2017).

7. These data are an average of the polls taken in 2018 and 2019.

7. US Leadership and the Evolution of Interstate Relations in the Asia Pacific

1. The Trump administration also removed the United States from the Paris Accords and the Comprehensive Plan of Action that was implemented with Iran and many other nations in July 2015.

2. In spite of the temporary reduction of tensions Trump's meetings brought to Seoul and Pyongyang, the South Korean public overall remained worried about North Korea's security threat and nuclear weapons.

3. Public opinion data that support this statement are presented later in this chapter.

4. Pursuing a collective self-defense policy will require at a minimum a different interpretation of the postwar constitution's Article 9 or perhaps an amendment to that article.

5. See table 6.5. Even in 2021, 44.1 percent of South Koreans saw Japan as a military threat.

6. This is not meant to understate the extent to which South Korean respondents saw the United States as more important for their country's future: those expressing this view were more than twenty percentage points higher.

8. The Challenge of Maintaining the Liberal International Order in the Asia Pacific

1. With its invasion of Ukraine, Russia has certainly challenged the US-led North Atlantic Treaty Organization (NATO) alliance. The ambitions of Russia under its current leader, Vladimir Putin, are, however, much more regional in scope than those of Xi's China, which are clearly global in reach.

2. Contrasting images are reinforced by the discovery of a surveillance balloon shot down off the coast of South Carolina.

3. This is a phrase used by former deputy secretary of state Robert Zoellick (Allison 2017).

4. For example, the Chinese hacker group that is supported by the PLA, Tick, has launched attacks against numerous Japanese companies and research institutions, including the Japan Aerospace Exploration Agency.

5. There are many examples of this kind of situation, such as where Japan reacts to a North Korean provocation in a way that increases the threats posed to South Korea or where either Seoul or Tokyo responds to China's growing threats against Taiwan without consulting each other and the United States.

6. The US position was to have the TPP implement and enforce the 1998 Declaration on Fundamental Principles and Rights at Work of the International Labour Organization (Schott, Kotschwar, and Muir 2013).

7. The original twelve members include Australia, Brunei, India, Indonesia, Japan, South Korea, Malaysia, New Zealand, the Philippines, Singapore, Thailand, and Vietnam.

8. This has been particularly true since the beginning of the COVID-19 pandemic, as China's strict anti-COVID policies have slowed and even stifled the recovery of its manufacturing processes.

9. We do not anticipate that either South Korea or Japan would focus on Central America for building new supply chain relationships; rather, they would look much closer to themselves, in Southeast and South Asia.

10. What is interesting about this Australian case is that Canberra's response to losing many of its Chinese export markets reveals clearly that refusing to acquiesce to Beijing's bullying has a strong potential to succeed, as affected Australian companies ended up finding other markets for the exports that their leaders cut off.

References

Ahn, Byung-Joon. 1980. "South Korea and the Communist Countries." *Asian Survey* 20 (11): 1098–107.

Alexandroff, Alan S., and Andrew F. Cooper. 2000. *Rising States, Rising Institutions: Challenges for Global Governance*. Washington, DC: Brookings Institution.

Allison, Graham. 2017. "China vs. America: Managing the Next Clash of Civilizations." *Foreign Affairs* 96 (5): 80–89.

Amsden, Alice H. 1992. *Asia's Next Giant: South Korea and Late Industrialization*. New York: Oxford University Press.

Art, Robert J. 2010. "The United States and the Rise of China: Implications for the Long Haul." *Political Science Quarterly* 125 (3): 359–91.

Bayer, Resat. 2006. "Diplomatic Exchange Data Set, v 2006.1." http://www.correlatesofwar.org/data-sets/diplomatic-exchange/.

Beason, Richard, and Dennis Patterson. *The Japan that Never Was: Explaining the Rise and Decline of a Misunderstood Country*. Albany: State University of New York Press.

Beckley, Michael. 2020. "Rogue Superpower: Why This Could Be an Illiberal American Country." *Foreign Affairs* 99 (6): 73–87.

Blair, Clay. 1987. *The Forgotten War: America in Korea, 1950–1953*. New York: Crown Books.

Blanchard, Jean-Marc F. 2013. "U.S.-China Relations under Bush and Obama." *Issues and Studies* 49 (3): 35–72.

Bothwick, Mark. 1992. *Pacific Century: The Emergence of Modern Pacific Asia*. New York: Routledge.

Brands, Hal, and John Lewis Gaddis. 2021. "The New Cold War: America, China, and the Echoes of History." *Foreign Affairs* 100 (6): 10–21.

Bukh, Alexander. 2020. *These Islands are Ours: The Social Construction of Territorial Disputes in Northeast Asia*. Stanford, CA: Stanford University Press.

Bush, Richard. 2010. *The Perils of Proximity: China-Japan Security Relations*. Washington, DC: Brookings Institution.

Callahan, William A. 2008. "Chinese Visions of World Order: Post-hegemonic or a New Hegemony." *International Studies Review* 10 (4): 749–61.

Campbell, Kurt M. 2016. *The Pivot: The Future of American Statecraft in Asia*. New York: Twelve Books.

Campbell, Kurt M., and Ely Ratner. 2018. "The China Reckoning." *Foreign Affairs* 97 (2): 70–81.

Canfield, Jonathan, and Mary Alice Haddad. 2021. "Japan's Alliance-Enhancing Security Developments." *Asia Policy* 16 (4): 167–93.

Cathcart, Adam. 2020. "China's Strategy and South Korea." In *An Emerging China-Centric Order: China's Vision for a New World Order in Practice*, edited by Nadège Rolland, 19–32. Special Report 87. Seattle: National Bureau of Asian Research.

Cha, Victor D. 1999. *Alignment Despite Antagonism: The US-Korea-Japan Security Triangle*. Stanford, CA: Stanford University Press.

Chantasasawat, Busakorn, K. C. Fung, and Hitomi Iizaka. 2004. "Foreign Direct Investment in China and East Asia." Working paper 233, Center for International Development, Stanford, CA.

Childs, N. K. 2018. "China's Carrier-Aviation Developments: Making a Difference." *Military Balance Blog*. International Institute for Strategic Studies, June 3, 2018. https://www.iiss.org/blogs/military-balance/2018/06/china-carrier-aviation-development.

Choi, Sung-Jae. 2005. "The Politics of the Dokdo Issue." *Journal of East Asian Studies* 5 (3): 465–94.

Chu, Yunhan. 2020. "It Is Time to See China for the Emerging Power It Is." *Global Asia* 19 (2): 25–31.

Chung, Jae-Ho. 2014. "China's Evolving Views of the Korean-American Alliance, 1953–2002." *Journal of Contemporary China* 23 (87): 39–59.

Chung, Jae-Ho, and Jiyoon Kim. 2016. "Is South Korea in China's Orbit?" *Asia Policy* 21:123–45.

Chung, Young-Iob. 2007. *South Korea in the Fast Lane: Economic Development and Capital Formation*. New York: Oxford University Press.

Clinton, Hillary Rodham. 2011. "America's Pacific Century." Speech delivered at the East-West Center, Honolulu, HI, November 10, 2011. US Department of State. https://2009-2017.state.gov/secretary/20092013clinton/rm/2011/11/176999.htm.

Cooper, Andrew F., and Daniel Flemes. 2013. "Foreign Policy Strategies of Emerging Powers in a Multipolar World: An Introductory Review." *Third World Quarterly* 34 (6): 943–62.

Cummings, Bruce. 1991. *The Origins of the Korean War*. Vol. 1, *Liberation and the Emergence of Separate Regimes, 1945–1947*. Princeton, NJ: Princeton University Press.

———. 1997. *Korea's Place in the Sun: A Modern History*. New York: Norton.

Daalder, Ivo H., and James M. Lindsey. 2018. "The Committee to Save the World Order: America's Allies Must Step Up as America Steps Down." *Foreign Affairs* 97 (6): 72–83.

Dallin, Alexander. 1985. *Black Box: KAL007 and the Superpowers*. Berkeley: University of California Press.

Deng, Jun, and Craig A. Smith. 2018. "The Rise of New Confucianism and the Return of Spirituality to Politics in Mainland China." *China Information* 32 (2): 294–314.

Denmark, Abraham. 2020. *U.S. Strategy in the Asian Century: Empowering Allies and Partners*. New York: Columbia University Press.

Dreyer, June Teufel. 2015. "The Tianxia Trope: Will China Change the International System?" *Journal of Contemporary China* 24 (96): 1015–31.

Economy, Elizabeth C. 2018a. "China's New Revolution: The Reign of Xi Jinping." *Foreign Affairs* 97 (3): 60–74.

———. 2018b. *The Third Revolution: Xi Jinping and the New Chinese State*. New York: Oxford University Press.

———. 2022. "Xi Jinping's New World Order: Can China Remake the New World Order?" *Foreign Affairs* 101 (1): 52–67.

Eichengreen, Barry, Dwight Perkins, and Kwanho Shin. 2012. *From Miracle to Modernity: The Growth of the Korean Economy*. Cambridge, MA: Harvard University Press Asia Center.

Erikson, Andrew S. 2019. "Power vs. Distance: China's Global Maritime Interests and Investments in the Far Seas." In *China's Expanding Strategic Ambitions*, edited by Ashley Tellis, Alison Szalwinski, and Michael Wills, 247–77. Seattle: National Bureau of Asian Research.

Fairbank, John King. 1992. *China: A New History*. Cambridge, MA: Belknap Press of Harvard University Press.

Ferguson, Shon, and Rikard Forslid. 2014. "Sizing Up the Impact of Embassies on Exports." IFN Working Paper 1012, Research Institute of Industrial Economics, Stockholm, Sweden.

Foot, Rosemary. 2020. "China's Challenge to the U.N. and the Global Order." *Global Asia* 15 (2): 19–23.

Fukuhara, Yuji, and Takeshi Sato. 2021. "Takeshima in Japanese Education, Media, and Culture." In *The Dokdo/Takeshima Dispute: South Korea, Japan and the Search for a Peaceful Solution*, edited by Paul Huth, Sunwoong Kim, and Terrence Roehrig, 222–43. Leiden: Brill-Nijhoff.

Funabashi, Yoichi, and Harry Dempsey. 2017. "Trump Threat Drives Japan and China Closer." East Asia Forum, 9 July 2017. https://www.eastasiaforum.org/2017/07/09/Trump-Threat-Drives-Japan-and-China-Closer.

Gates, Robert. 2020. "The Overmilitarization of American Foreign Policy." *Foreign Affairs* 99 (4): 121–32.

Genron NPO and East Asia Institute. 2016. *The 4th Japan–South Korea Joint Public Opinion Poll (2016): Analysis Report on Comparative Data*. Tokyo: Genron NPO and East Asia Institute.

———. 2017. *The 5th Japan–South Korea Joint Public Opinion Poll (2017): Analysis Report on Comparative Data*. Tokyo: Genron NPO and East Asia Institute.

204   References

———. 2018. *The 6th Japan–South Korea Joint Public Opinion Poll (2018): Analysis Report on Comparative Data.* Tokyo: Genron NPO and East Asia Institute.

———. 2019. *The 7th Japan–South Korea Joint Public Opinion Poll (2019): Analysis Report on Comparative Data.* Tokyo: Genron NPO and East Asia Institute.

———. 2022. *Will Improved Public Sentiment in Japan and South Korea Lead to Better Relations between the Two Countries?* Tokyo: Genron NPO and East Asia Institute.

Giles, Barry K. 1996. *Korea vs. Korea: A Case of Contested Legitimacy.* London: Routledge.

Gill, Bates. 2022. *Meeting China's Military Challenge: Collective Responses of U.S. Allies and Partners.* NBR Special Report 96. Seattle: National Bureau of Asian Research.

Glosserman, Brad, and Scott A. Snyder. 2015. *The Japan–South Korea Identity Clash: East Asian Security and the United States.* New York: Columbia University Press.

Goh, Evelyn. 2020. "China's East Asian Challenge: Managing a Complex Regional Order." *Global Asia* 15 (2): 52–56.

Gries, Peter. 2004. *China's New Nationalism: Pride, Politics, and Diplomacy.* Berkeley: University of California Press.

Gu, Weiqun. 1995. *Conflicts of Divided Nations: The Cases of China and Korea.* Westport, CT: Praeger.

Ha, Yong-Chul. 2003. *Bukbang Jeongchaek* [North policy]. Seoul: Seoul National University Press.

Hatch, Walter. 2011. *Asia's Flying Geese: How Regionalism Shapes Japan.* Ithaca, NY: Cornell University Press.

Hellman, Donald C. 1962. "Basic Problems of Japanese–South Korea Relations." *Asian Survey* 2 (3): 19–24.

Heo, Uk, and Terence Roehrig. 2014. *South Korea's Rise: Economic Development, Power, and Foreign Relations.* New York: Cambridge University Press.

———. 2018. *The Evolution of the South Korea–United States Alliance.* New York: Cambridge University Press.

Ho, "Tse-Ern" Benjamin. 2019. *PRC Turns 70: Five Elements of Its Grand Strategy.* RSIS Commentary 192. Singapore: Rajaratnam School of International Studies.

Hornung, Jeffrey W. 2014. "Japan's Growing Hard Hedge against China." *Asian Security* 10 (2): 97–122.

Huth, Paul, Sunwoong Kim, and Terence Roehrig. 2021. *The Dokdo/Takeshima Dispute: South Korea, Japan and the Search for a Peaceful Solution.* Leiden: Brill-Nijhoff.

Ikenberry, John G. 2020. "America's Asia Policy after Trump." *Global Asia* 15 (4): 1–5.

Johnson, Chalmers. 1982. *MITI and the Japanese Miracle.* Stanford, CA: Stanford University Press.

Johnston, Alistair. 2003. "Is China a Status Quo Power?" *International Security* 27 (4): 5–56.

Kang, David C. 2010. *East Asia before the West: Five Centuries of Trade and Tribute.* New York: Columbia University Press.

Kaseda, Yoshinori. 2021. "Takeshima in Japanese Politics and Foreign Policy." In *The Dokdo/Takeshima Dispute: South Korea, Japan and the Search for a Peaceful Solution,* edited by Paul Huth, Sunwoong Kim, and Terence Roehrig, 125–51. Leiden: Brill-Nijhoff.

Kastner, Scott L., and Phillip C. Saunders. 2012. "Is China a Status Quo or Revisionist State? Leadership Travel as an Empirical Indicator of Foreign Policy Priorities." *International Studies Quarterly* 56:163–77.

Katada, Saori. 2020. *Japan's New Regional Reality: Geoeconomic Strategy in the Asia Pacific.* New York: Columbia University Press.

Kawai, Kazuo. 1960. *Japan's American Interlude.* Chicago: University of Chicago Press.

Kihl, Young-Whan. 1991. "South Korea in 1990: Diplomatic Activism and a Partisan Quagmire." *Asian Survey* 31 (1): 64–70.

Kim, Hak-Joon. 1997. "The Process Leading to the Establishment of Diplomatic Relations between South Korea and the Soviet Union." *Asian Survey* 37 (7): 637–51.

Kim, Patricia M. 2019. "China's Quest for Influence in Northeast Asia: The Korean Peninsula, Japan, and the East China Sea." In *China's Expanding Strategic Ambitions,* edited by Ashley Tellis, Alison Szalwinski, and Michael Wills, 81–108. Seattle: National Bureau of Asian Research.

Kim, Samuel S. 2000. *Korea's Globalization.* New York: Cambridge University Press.

Kim, Sung-Chull. 2017. *Partnership within Hierarchy: The Evolving East Asian Security Triangle.* Albany: State University of New York Press.

Kim, Hyung-A. 2004. *Korea's Development under Park Chung-Hee: Rapid Industrialization, 1961–1979.* London: Routledge Curzon.

Koshino, Yuka. 2022. "China's Military Modernization in Space and Cyber and the Implications for the U.S.-Japan Alliance." In *Meeting China's Military Challenge: Collective Responses of U.S. Allies and Partners,* edited by Bates Gill, 49–64. NBR Special Report 96. Seattle: National Bureau of Asian Research.

Ku, Yangmo. 2018. "South Korean Diplomacy." In *Politics in North and South Korea: Political Development, Economy, and Foreign Relations,* edited by Yangmo Ku, Inyeop Lee, and Jongseok Woo, 91–110. New York: Routledge.

Kuo, Min Gyo. 2009. *Island Disputes and Maritime Regime Building in East Asia: Between a Rock and a Hard Place.* New York: Springer.

Kuznets, Paul W. 1977. *Economic Growth and Structure in the Republic of Korea.* New Haven, CT: Yale University Press.

Lederman, Daniel M., Marcello Olarreaga, and Lucy Payton. 2010. "Export Promotion Agencies: Do They Work?" *Journal of Development Economics* 9 (2): 257–65.

Lee, Chong-Sik. 1963. "Korea: In Search of Stability." *Asian Survey* 4 (1): 656–65.

Lee, Hee-Eun. 2021. "South Korea's Claim to Dokdo." In *The Dokdo/Takeshima Dispute: South Korea, Japan and the Search for a Peaceful Solution*, edited by Paul Huth, Sunwoong Kim, and Terence Roehrig, 103–24. Leiden: Brill-Nijhoff.

Lee, Hsien-Loong. 2020. "The Endangered American Century." *Foreign Affairs* 99 (4): 52–64.

Lee, Ji-Young, and Jaehyun Lee. 2021. "Dokdo in South Korean Education, Media, and Culture." In *The Dokdo/Takeshima Dispute: South Korea, Japan and the Search for a Peaceful Solution*, edited by Paul Huth, Sunwoong Kim, and Terence Roehrig, 201–21. Leiden: Brill-Nijhoff.

Lee, Kye-Woo. 2012. "Aid by Korea: Progress and Challenges." *Korea's Economy* 28:45–55.

Lee, Seung-Hyok. 2019. *Social Origins of the Current Diplomatic Tensions between Japan and South Korea*. EAF Policy Debate 114. Seoul: East Asia Foundation.

Lemke, Douglas, and Ronald Tammen. 2003. "Power Transition Theory and the Rise of China," *International Interactions* 29 (4): 269–71.

Lind, Jennifer. 2008. *Sorry States: Apologies in International Politics*. Ithaca, NY: Cornell University Press.

Ministry of Foreign Affairs and Trade. 2013. "Diplomatic Missions Established by Year" [in Korean]. http://www.index.go.kr/egams/stts/jsp/potal/stts/PO _STTS_IdxSearch.jsp?idx_cd=1676&stts_cd=167601&clas_div=&idx_sys _cd=&idx_clas_cd=1.

Mo, Jongryn, and Barry Weingast. 2013. *Korean Political and Economic Development*. Cambridge, MA: Harvard University Press.

Myrdal, Gunnar. 1968. *Asian Drama: An Inquiry into the Poverty of Nations*. London: Allen Lane, Penguin.

Nagahisa Toshio. 1995. *Gemu Riron noh Seiji Keisai Gaku: Senkyo Seido toh Boei Seisaku* [The political economy of game theory: Election systems and defense policy]. Tokyo: PHP Kenkyujo.

National Bureau of Asian Research. 2021. "The Rough State of Japan–South Korea Relations: Friction and Disputes in the Maritime Domain." Maritime Awareness Project, January 16, 2021. https://www.nbr.org/publication/the-rough -state-of-japan-south-korea-relations-friction-and-disputes-in-the-maritime -domain/.

Newnham, Randall E. 2002. "Embassies for Sale: The Purchase of Diplomatic Recognition by West Germany, Taiwan, and South Korea." *International Politics* 37:259–84.

NHK. 2018. "Kempo ni Kansuru Iken chosa 2018" [2018 opinion survey on the constitution]. Tokyo: NHK. https://www3.nhk.or.jp/news/special/kempon70 /yoron2018.html.

Nitsch, Volker. 2007. "State Visits and International Trade." *The World Economy* 30 (12): 1797–816.

North, Douglas C., John J. Wallis, and Barry R. Weingast. 2009. *Violence and Social Orders: A Conceptual Framework for Interpreting Recorded Human History.* Cambridge: Cambridge University Press.

Ohashi, Hideo. 2005. "China's Regional Trade and Investment Profile." In *Power Shift: China and East Asia's New Dynamics,* edited by David Shambaugh, 71–95. Berkeley: University of California Press.

Patrick, Hugh, and Henry Rosovsky, eds. 1976. *Asia's New Giant: How the Japanese Economy Works.* Washington, DC: Brookings Institution.

Patterson, Dennis, and Jangsup Choi. 2018. "Diplomacy, Trade, and South Korea's Rise to International Influence." *International Area Studies Review* 22 (1): 9–27.

———. 2019. *Diplomacy, Trade, and South Korea's Rise to International Influence.* Lanham, MD: Lexington Books.

Pempel, T. J. 1997. *Regime Shift: Comparative Dynamics of the Japanese Political Economy.* Ithaca, NY: Cornell University Press.

Pollins, Brain M. 1989a. "Conflict, Cooperation, and Commerce: The Effect of International Political Interactions on Bilateral Trade Flows." *American Journal of Political Science* 33 (3): 737–61.

———. 1989b. "Does Trade Still Follow the Flag?" *American Political Science Review* 83 (2): 465–80.

Pottinger, Matt. 2021. "Beijing's American Hustle." *Foreign Affairs* 100 (5): 102–14.

Power, Samantha. 2021. "The Can-Do Power: America's Advantage and Biden's Chance." *Foreign Affairs* 100 (1): 10–24.

Reeve, W. D. 1963. *The Republic of Korea: A Political and Economic Study.* London: Oxford University Press.

Reischauer, Edwin O. 1970. *Japan: The Story of a Nation.* New York: Arno.

Roehrig, Terence. 2017. *Japan, South Korea, and the United States Nuclear Umbrella: Deterrence after the Cold War.* New York: Columbia University Press.

Rogowski, Ronald. 1989. *Commerce and Coalitions: How Trade Affects Domestic Political Alignments.* Princeton, NJ: Princeton University Press.

Rolland, Nadège 2020a. *An Emerging China-centric Order: China's Vision for a New World Order in Practice.* NBR Special Report 87. Seattle: National Bureau of Asian Research.

———. 2020b. *Securing the Belt and Road Initiative: China's Evolving Military Engagement along the Silk Road.* NBR Special Report 80. Seattle: National Bureau of Asian Research.

Rose, Andrew K. 2007. "The Foreign Service and Foreign Trade: Embassies as Export Promotion." *The World Economy* 30 (1): 22–38.

Rosenau, James, ed. 1969. *Domestic Sources of Foreign Policy.* New York: The Free Press.

Ross, Robert, and Feng Zhu. 2008. *China's Ascent: Power, Security, and the Future of International Politics.* Ithaca, NY: Cornell University Press.

Schott, Jeffrey I., Barbara Kotschwar, and Julia Muir. 2013. *Understanding the Trans-Pacific Partnership*. Washington, DC: Peterson Institute for International Economics.

Schweller, Randall L., and Pu Xiaoyu. 2011. "After Unipolarity: China's Vision of International Order in an Era of U.S. Decline." *International Security* 36 (1): 41–43.

Shambaugh, David. 2005. "Return to the Middle Kingdom? China and Asia in the Early Twenty-First Century." In *Power Shift: China and Asia's New Dynamics*, edited by David Shambaugh, 23–47. Berkeley: University of California Press.

Shiu, Sin Por. 2020. "Tianxia: China's Concept of International Order." *Global Asia* 15 (2): 45–50.

Singer, J. David, and Melvin Small. 1966. "The Composition and Status Ordering of the International System, 1815–1940." *World Politics* 18 (2): 236–82.

Singh, Bhubhindar. 2018. "Introduction." *Asian Policy* 13 (2): 2–5.

Small, Melvin, and J. David Singer. 1973. "The Diplomatic Importance of States, 1816–1970." *World Politics* 25 (4): 577–99.

Smith, Sheila A. 2015. *Intimate Rivals: Japanese Domestic Politics and a Rising China*. New York: Columbia University Press.

Snyder, Scott A. 2009. *China's Rise and the Two Koreas: Policies, Economics, and Security*. Boulder, CO: Lynne Rienner Publishers.

———. 2018. *South Korea at the Crossroads: Autonomy and Alliance in an Era of Rival Powers*. New York: Columbia University Press.

Steinberg, David I. 1985. *Foreign Aid and the Development of the Republic of Korea: The Effectiveness of Concessional Assistance*. AID Special Study 42. Washington, DC: Agency for International Development.

Stolper, Wolfgang, and Paul Samuelson. 1941. "Protection and Real Wages." *Review of Economic Studies* 9:58–73.

Szechenyi, Nicholas. 2014. "The U.S.-Japan Alliance: Prospects to Strengthen the Asia-Pacific Order." In *U.S. Alliances and Partnerships at the Center of Global Power, Strategic Asia, 2014–15*, edited by Ashley Tellis, Abraham Denmark, and Greg Chaffin, 34–59. Seattle: National Bureau of Asian Research.

Tellis, Ashley. 2020 . "Pursuing Global Reach: China's Not So Long March toward Preeminence." In *China's Expanding Strategic Ambitions*, edited by Ashley Tellis, Alison Szalwinski, and Michael Wills, 3–46. Seattle: National Bureau of Asian Research.

Terada, Takashi. 2018. "The Competing U.S. and Chinese Models for an East Asian Economic Order." *Asia Policy* 13 (2): 19–25.

Tokuchi, Hideshi. 2021. "The Role of Japan in Sustaining Regional Order in East Asia." *Asia Policy* 13 (2): 32–38.

US Office of the Director of National Intelligence. 2021. *2021 Annual Threat Assessment*. April 9, 2021. https://www.dni.gov/files/ODNI/documents/assessments/ATA-2021-Unclassified-Report.pdf.

Usuki, Eiichi. 2021. "Japan's Claim to Takeshima." In *The Dokdo/Takeshima Dispute: South Korea, Japan and the Search for a Peaceful Solution*, edited by Paul Huth, Sunwoong Kim, and Terence Roehrig, 69–102. Leiden: Brill-Nijhoff.

Wang, Zheng. 2008. "National Humiliation, History Education, and the Politics of Historical Memory: Patriotic Education Campaign in China." *International Studies Quarterly* 52 (4): 783–806.

Weiss, Jessica Chen. 2019. "A World Safe for Autocracy? China's Rise and the Future of Global Politics." *Foreign Affairs* 98 (4): 92–102.

Wittkopf, Eugene, and James McCormick. 2008. *The Domestic Sources of American Foreign Policy*. Lanham, MD: Rowman and Littlefield.

Woo, Jongseok. 2018. "Legacies of Japanese Colonial Rule and the Korean War." In *Politics in North and South Korea*, edited by Yangmo Ku, Inyeop Lee, and Jongseok Woo, 111–29. New York: Routledge.

Wood, Christopher. 1992. *The Bubble Economy: Japan's Extraordinary Speculative Boom of the 1980s and the Dramatic Bust of the 1990s*. New York: Atlantic Monthly Press.

Wooldridge, Jeffrey M. 2013. *Introductory Econometrics: A Modern Approach*. 5th ed. Mason, OH: South-Western.

World Bank. 2013. "World Development Indicators." http://data.worldbank.org/products/data-portals.

Ye Min. 2017. *China–South Korea Relations in the New Era*. Lanham, MD: Lexington Books.

Yeo, Andrew. 2019. *Asia's Regional Architecture: Alliances and Institutions in the Pacific Century*. Stanford, CA: Stanford University Press.

Yoo, Hyon-Joo. 2021. "Dokdo in South Korean Politics." In *The Dokdo/Takeshima Dispute: South Korea, Japan and the Search for a Peaceful Solution*, edited by Paul Huth, Sunwoong Kim, and Terence Roehrig, 152–70. Leiden: Brill-Nijhoff.

Zhao, Suisheng. 2004. *A Nation-State by Construction: Dynamics of Modern Chinese Nationalism*. Stanford, CA: Stanford University Press.

Zhao, Xiaochun. 2018. "In Pursuit of a Community of Shared Future: China's Global Activism in Perspective." *China Quarterly of International Strategic Studies* 4 (1): 23–37.

Index

Page numbers in italics refer to figures and tables.

Abe Shinzo: with comfort women, 112, 125, 126, 149, 198n4; Dokdo/Takeshima and, 122–23; Moon Jae-In and, 108, 112; with reparations for forced wartime labor, 131–32; Senkaku Islands and, 68; South Koreans and views on, 105–6; with US, 82, 151

Aegis missile defense system, US with, 172–73

Afghanistan, 4, 97, 163, 195n5

"Agreement on the Settlement of Problems concerning Property and Claims and on Economic Cooperation." *See* Reconciliation Treaty

Air Self-Defense Forces, Japan, 62

all/everything under heaven (Tianxia), 57–58

"America First" policy, 5, 6, 149, 171, 192n11, 192n14, 195n1

America's Pacific Century, 145–47

anthrax, weaponized, 172

anti-cyberattack technology, 174

Armistice of 1953, 20, 22, 27, 30, 36, 67

Article 9, Security Treaty, 192n2, 199n4

Asan Institute for Policy Studies, 73, 102, 136, 156, 157

ASEAN (Association of Southeast Asian Nations), 194n24

"Asian Century," 7

Asian Infrastructure Investment Bank, China, 147, 196n14

Asian Women's Fund, 125

Asia-Pacific Economic Cooperation, 145

Asia-Pacific region, 191n1; China and challenge of US leadership in, 14, 154–61; economy, 191n2, 191n4; economy and messaging in US leadership, 179–87; US leadership in, 17–18, 147–54

Association of Southeast Asian Nations (ASEAN), 194n24

Australia, 186, 197n5, 199n7, 200n10

Belt and Road Initiative (BRI), China, 58–59, 147, 196nn14–15

Berlin Wall, fall of, 116

Best Global Brands, Interbrand, 99, 198n2

Biden, Joseph R., 14, 166; with Asia-Pacific region, 17; with East Asian alliance system, 154, 167, 192n14; GSOMIA and, 171; infrastructure plan and, 183; IPEFP and, 181; Moon Jae-In and, 153–54; with US allies, 153–54, 159

Board on Geographic Names, US, 119

BRI (Belt and Road Initiative), China, 58–59, 147, 196nn14–15

Brunei, 199n7

Busan Perimeter, 22

Bush, George H. W., 97

211

Index

Bush, George W., 4, 65, 148, 155–56, 197n22

Canada, 37
CCP (Chinese Communist Party), 54, 56–58, 146, 163–64, 185–86, 192n12
Central America, 183–84, 199n9
Cha, Victor, 2
charm offensive, 196n17
Chengdu J-20 aircraft, 51
Cheonan, sinking of, 66–67
China, 197n5, 197n8; anti-Japanese demonstrations in, 64–65, 79; Asian Infrastructure Investment Bank, 147, 196n14; Australia and, 200n10; BRI and, 58–59, 147, 196nn14–15; in country favorability studies, 101; COVID-19 and, 182, 185–86, 199n8; decadal analysis of Japanese feelings of closeness to US and, 76; decline of, 54; democracy and, 185, 187; diplomacy and, 57, 59, 60, 196n15, 196n17; Dokdo/Takeshima and, 68; East Asian alliance system and power of, 10–11, 47–52; economy, 3, 28, 47–50, 56–57, 88, 143, 146–50, 153, 170, 179–81, 191n8; with foreign direct investment, 195n4; GDP, 47, 195n3; with global ambitions, 199n1; hackers, 173–74, 199n4; with human rights, 55, 186; influence of, 15–16; "information dominance" and, 173; "information warfare" and, 184–85; Japan and, 61–62, 72, 74, 110, 170, 195n2; Japanese feelings toward, 75; Japanese views on US and, 74–82; with liberal international order, 55–56, 192n12; military, 6, 50, 50–52, 51, 56, 61, 78, 97, 137, 146–50, 153, 170, 172–74, 195n6, 196n15, 199n4; Nationalist Government, 19, 146; North Korea and, 22, 77, 84, 88, 98; public opinion data on US and, 13; as repressive regime, 191n3; rise of, xiv, 3–4, 6–7, 9–13, 16, 42, 91, 146–47, 187, 195n8; with sanctions-based tactics, 60; sex slaves, 124; with SOEs, 147; with soft power,

59, 60, 196n15, 196n17; South Korea and, 72, 99, 170, 199n5; South Korea and Japan impacted by, 12, 59–62; with South Korea–Japan partnership, 12–13, 46, 62–69; South Koreans favoring Japan vs., 101–2, 102; South Korean students in, 60; South Koreans with feelings of closeness to US or, 83; South Korean views on US and, 82–89; strategic goals, 196n10; supply chains and, 182–84; tariffs and, 84–85, 151–52; with technology, 151, 172, 173, 182; third revolution in, 146, 195n7; trade, 47–49, 60, 62; as trade partner for South Korea and Japan, 48–49, 49, 59; with tribute system, 53–54, 58; US and, 19, 151–52, 163–66, 168; with US leadership in Asia-Pacific region, 14, 154–61; Uyghur people and, 186; with vision of new international order, 11–12, 43–45, 52–59, 71
Chinese Communist Party (CCP), 54, 56–58, 146, 163–64, 185–86, 192n12
Chosun Ilbo (newspaper), 116
Chun Doo-Hwan, 39
Clinton, Bill, 78, 97
Clinton, Hillary, 145–46
coast guard: China, 61; Japan, 80, 119, 176; maritime resources, 175–76; South Korea, 119, 135, 176–77
Code for Unplanned Encounters at Sea (CUES), 135, 198n5
comfort women: Genron NPO poll on, 126, 127; lawsuits filed by, 125; reparations for, 124, 125, 130; as sex slaves, 14, 94, 108, 112–16, 120–22, 124–30, 149, 198n4; with South Korean–Japanese relations, 126–27, 127
Comprehensive and Progressive Agreement for the Trans-Pacific Partnership (CPTPP), 181
Comprehensive Plan of Action, 198n1
Confucianism: ideology, 57; tribute system and, 58
Confucius Institutes, 84
contamination, food, 79, 85
Cornell University, 77

Correlates of War, "Diplomatic Exchange Data," 36–37, 194n25

country favorability studies, 101–3

COVID-19 pandemic, 182, 185–86, 199n8

CPTPP (Comprehensive and Progressive Agreement for the Trans-Pacific Partnership), 181

CUES (Code for Unplanned Encounters at Sea), 135, 198n5

currencies: unions, 35, 194n20; value of South Korean, 193n14

cyberattacks, 174

cyber capabilities, 173

cyber counterspace weapons, 172

cyber security, 172–74

Declaration on Fundamental Principles and Rights at Work (1998), ILO, 199n6

democracy: China and, 185, 187; Genron NPO with, 103; human rights and, 145; Japan and, 103, 133; Polity data and, 194n16; South Korea and, 32–33, 39–40

Deng Xiaoping, 3, 47, 195n7

Department of Commerce, US, 183

Department of the Treasury, US, 183

Diaoyu (Senkaku) Islands, 61–62, 68, 79–80

diplomacy: China and, 57, 59, 60, 196n15, 196n17; forward-deployed, 145, 147; public, 196n17; trade and, 34–37, 41, 194n18

"Diplomatic Exchange Data," Correlates of War, 36–37, 194n25

diplomatic missions: international status and, 36, 194n23; Japan, 36–37, 37; South Korea, 38–40, 39, 40, 194n28, 194nn24–26, 195n29

disinformation, spread of, 184–85

Djibouti, 52

Doha round, trade and, 179

Dokdo/Takeshima (Liancourt Rock), 93, 115; China and, 68; leaders with politics and, 120–21; negative feelings about, 110–15; "peace line" and, 118; territorial dispute, 116, 117–23, 198n3

"don't know" category, of public opinion surveys, 138, 139, 197n6, 198n5

dumplings (*gyoza*), contamination of, 79

Dutch sex slaves, 124

East Asia Institute, 73–74, 103. *See also* Genron NPO surveys

East Asian alliance system: arms of, 20, 192n1; Chinese power and, 10–11, 47–52; cooperation and perceptions of threat and importance of, 160, *161*; cyber security and, 172–74; defined, 2, 191nn6–7; hacking of, 173–74; international order and, 2–4, 7; with maritime resources and security, 175–76; origins, 19–26; reform of, 17–18, 169–78; as security umbrella, 2–3, 26, 41–42, 195n31; with South Korean and Japanese rise to international influence, 26–33; strengthening of, 4–8, 15, 17–18, 98, 148, 154, 159, 165, 167–78, 192n14; structure of, 22–23, *23*, 192n1; supportive impact of, 33–42; with unresolved historical issues, 9–14, 16, 64, 66, 93–94, 110, 113–16, 178; weakening of, 5–8, 16, 63, 71, 133–34, 149, 150–52, 154–55; world trade and, 163, 174. *See also* Japan; South Korea; United States

East China Sea, 52, 79–80, 97, 147, 153

East China Sea Air Defense Identification Zone, 62, 68

economy: Asia-Pacific Economic Cooperation, 145; Asia-Pacific region, 191n2, 191n4; China, 3, 28, 47–50, 56–57, 88, 143, 146–50, 153, 170, 179–81, 191n8; with countries of importance, 141–43, *142*; financial crisis of 2008, 31, 195n5; IPEFP, 181; Japan, 20, 28–29, *29*, 36–37, 40–41, 92, 178, 184, 191n4, 193nn11–13; RCEP, 181; sanctions, 60–61; South Korea, *25*, 30–32, 40–41, 88, 92, 98–99, 178, 184, 191n4, 193n8, 193n14; "trade follows the flag" with, 34–35; US, 81, 143; with US leadership in Asia-Pacific region, 179–87. *See also* Gross Domestic Product; trade

214 Index

EEZs (exclusive economic zones), 79, 85
El Salvador, 195n6
Europe, 36, 53, 192n10, 193n7, 194n28, 197n5
European Union, 35
exclusive economic zones (EEZs), 79, 85
Executive Order on America's Supply Chains (2021), 182

financial crisis of 2008, 31, 195n5
fishing agreement (1965), 119–20, 122–23
food: contamination, 79, 85; garlic and kimchi wars, 84–85
Foreign Affairs (magazine), 187
foreign direct investment, 24, 78, 195n4
forward-deployed diplomacy, 145, 147
France, 194n19, 194n24
free trade, 35, 174–75, 180–81
Fu Ying, 196n11

garlic wars, 84–85
gas, natural, 61, 79
GDP. *See* Gross Domestic Product
General Security of Military Information Agreement (GSOMIA), 67–68, 134–35, 171
General Social Survey (GSS), South Korea, 74, 82–84, 86, 100–101
Genron NPO surveys: comfort women, 126, *127*; countries of economic importance, 141–43, *142*; democracy, 103; East Asia Institute and, 73–74, 103; forced wartime labor, *131*, 139, *139*, *141*; Japan with nuclear weapons, 136; radar lock-on incident, 136; South Korea and Japan as military threats, 137, *138*, 199n5; on South Korean and Japanese leaders, 105–7, *107*; South Korean and Japanese views of affinity and importance, 159, *160*, 199n6; South Korean–Japanese bilateral relations, 104–5, *106*, 107–8, *109*, 112–13, *113*, 127–28, *128*; South Koreans and Japanese on negative views of each other, 108–11, *111*, 121–22, *122*; South Koreans with favorable vs. unfavorable views, *87*; South Korean views of Japan, 103, *104*; trade relations, 132,

133; trilateral cooperation and perceptions of threat and alliance importance, 160, *161*; Trump administration, 155–56, *156*; website, 198n4
"gray zone" tactics, China with, 172
Gross Domestic Product (GDP): China, 47, 195n3; India, 47, 195n3; Japan, 28–29, *29*, 47; Russia, 47; South Korea, 30–32, *31*; TPP and, 179; trade and, 181; US, 47
Ground-Based Midcourse Defense technology, 173
GSOMIA (General Security of Military Information Agreement), 67–68, 134–35, 171
GSS (General Social Survey), South Korea, 74, 82–84, 86, 100–101
Gulf of Oman, 52
Gwadar, Pakistan, 52
gyoza (dumplings), contamination of, 79

hackers, China-sponsored, 173–74, 199n4
Hagiuda Koichi, 133
hedging policy, Japan, 196n19
Hellman, Donald, 116
Hong Kong, 55, 186
Horn of Africa, 52
hub-and-spoke system, 191n7
human rights: China with, 55, 186; claims, 118; democracy and, 145; Tokyo War Crimes Trials and, 116, 124; for Uyghur people, 186. *See also* comfort women
Hwasong-12, North Korea with, 66, 197n23

immigration, US and, 183, 184
Incheon, amphibious landing at, 22, 193n5
India, 47, 195n3, 199n7
Indian Ocean, 52, 195n6
Indonesia, 199n7
Indo-Pacific Economic Framework for Prosperity (IPEFP), 181
information: dominance, 173; GSOMIA, 67–68, 134–35, 171; with lack of transparency, 185–86; sharing, 174, 176, 185; warfare, 184–85
infrastructure plan, US, 183

Interbrand, Best Global Brands, 99, 198n2
International Atomic Energy Agency, 77
International Court of Justice, 123, 131, 138, 140
International Labour Organization, 199n6
international order: China with liberal, 55–56, 192n12; China with vision for new, 11–12, 43–45, 52–59, 71; East Asian alliance system and, 2–4, 7; with economic engagement and messaging in US leadership, 179–87; reforming and strengthening, 169–78
IPEFP (Indo-Pacific Economic Framework for Prosperity), 181
Iran, 198n1
Iraq, 4, 97

J-15 aircraft, 51
Japan, 197n8, 199n7; with bureaucratic influences, 197n1; China and, 61–62, 72, 74, 110, 170, 195n2; China as trade partner for South Korea and, 48–49, 49, 59; China impacting South Korea and, 12, 59–62; China with anti-Japanese demonstrations, 64–65, 79; China with South Korean partnership with, 12–13, 46, 62–69; defense cooperation by South Korea and, 135; democracy and, 103, 133; diplomatic missions, 36–37, 37; distrust and understanding with South Korea and, 104–14; with East Asian alliance system strengthened, 169–78; economy, 20, 28–29, 29, 36–37, 40–41, 92, 178, 184, 191n4, 193nn11–13; GDP, 28–29, 29, 47; hedging policy, 196n19; international status with changes, 38; LDP, 133; manufacturing and, 20, 28, 81, 133; military, 14, 50–51, 51, 61, 62, 67, 80, 93–94, 112–16, 119–22, 124–30, 135–37, 138, 151, 171–72, 176–77, 192n2, 198n4, 199n5; Ministry of Foreign Affairs, 178; North Korea and, 77, 151, 199n5; nuclear weapons and, 136, 198n6; in Pacific War, 8, 14, 64, 93, 94, 108, 110, 112–16, 118, 124–30, 149, 196n10, 198n4; Prime Minister's

Office surveys, 73–74, 85, 94, 123; with public opinion surveys, 197n5; rise of, 26–33, 54; with sex slaves, 14, 94, 108, 112–16, 120–22, 124–30, 149, 198n4; South Korea, comfort women and improved relations with, 126–27, 127, 149; South Korea and, xiv, 2, 4, 7–10, 14–17, 19–26, 43–44, 60, 91–94, 107–8, 109, 117–19, 122–25, 130, 139, 151, 166–67, 176–78, 193n4, 193n10, 197nn21–22, 198n2; South Koreans favoring China vs., 101–2, 102; South Korean views of, 100–104, 104; supply chains and, 199n9; supportive impact on, 33–42; surrender in 1945, 19, 21, 27, 54; with technology, 28, 33; with textbook revisions, 64–65, 79, 110, 120, 196n20; TPP and, 181; trade and, 36, 49, 131; US and, xiii, xiv, 2, 20–21, 59, 61, 62, 65, 82, 151, 153, 156, 192nn2–3, 193n3, 196n19, 199n4
Japan Aerospace Exploration Agency, 199n4
Japanese people: China and feelings of, 75; on China and US, 74–82; on countries of economic importance, 141–43, 142; decadal analysis of feelings of closeness to China and US, 76; decadal analysis of feelings of closeness to or distance from South Korea, 96, 96–97; on historical issues and bilateral relations, 127–28, 128; public opinion data of, 13, 71–74; South Korea as viewed by, 94–100, 95, 96, 100; South Korean leaders viewed by, 105–7, 107; with South Korean perceptions of affinity and importance, 159, 160, 199n6; South Koreans on improving relations with, 112–13, 113; with South Korean Supreme Court ruling on forced labor, 130, 131, 138–40, 139; with South Koreans viewing bilateral relations as bad, 104–5, 106; South Koreans with reasons for negative views of, 108–11, 111, 121–22, 122; South Korean views on trade with, 132, 133; US and feelings of, 81; on US presidents, 157–59, 158
Jin Yinan, 6

216   Index

Kaesong Industrial Complex, 67
Kennan, George, 168
kimchi wars, 84–85
Kim Dae-Jung, 40
Kim Jong Un, 66, 67, 151
Kim Young-Sam, 120
Kishida Fumio, 105, 106, 167
Koizumi Junichiro, 65
Korean Air Lines Flight 007, 101
Korean War, xiii–xiv, 2–3, 8–9, 11, 24, 27,
    143; diplomacy after, 39; economy and,
    31–32, 92; liberal international order
    after, 33, 159; manufacturing after, 28;
    trade after, 30
K-pop concerts, 196n18

labor, forced: court cases and wartime,
    129–43; Pacific War with, 14, 94, 116,
    129–32, *131*, 138–40, *139*, *141*, 178,
    198n1; reparations for, 129–32, *131*,
    138–40, *139*, *141*, 178, 198n1
language: of Article 9(1), 192n2; with
    China and new international order, 11,
    45, 53; trade and, 35, 194n19
lawsuits: comfort women with, 125; victims
    of forced wartime labor with, 140
LDP (Liberal Democratic Party),
    Japan, 133
leaders: Asia-Pacific region and US as, 14,
    17–18, 147–61, 179–87; opinions on
    US presidents, 156–59, *157–58*; with
    politics and Dokdo/Takeshima, 120–
    21; public opinion of South Korean
    and Japanese, 105–7, *107*; South
    Korean presidents and diplomacy, 39,
    40. *See also* presidents, US; *specific
    world leaders*
Lee Hsien-Loong, 7, 191n8
Lee Myung-Bak, 120, 134
Lee Teng-Hui, 77–78
Liancourt Rock. *See* Dokdo/Takeshima
Liberal Democratic Party (LDP),
    Japan, 133

Maas, Heiko, 170
MacArthur, Douglas, 20, 22, 36, 193n6
Malaysia, 199n7

Mansfield, Mike, xiii
manufacturing: China with COVID-19
    and, 182, 199n8; Japan and, 20, 28, 81,
    133; in North Korea, 27; South Korea
    and, 27, 84, 131–32, 133
Mao Zedong, 146
maritime resources, security, 175–76
Memorandum of Understanding (MOU),
    134
Mexico, 183, 184
military: China, 6, *50*, 50–52, *51*, 56, 61,
    78, 97, 137, 146–50, 153, 170, 172–74,
    195n6, 196n15, 199n4; coast guard,
    61, 80, 119, 135, 175–77; coup, 24;
    expenditures, *50*, 50–51, *51*, *52*; GSO-
    MIA, 67–68, 134–35, 171; installations,
    51–52, 195n6; Japan, 14, 50–51, *51*,
    61, 62, 67, 80, 93–94, 112–16, 119–22,
    124–30, 135–37, *138*, 151, 171–72,
    176–77, 192n2, 198n4, 199n5; mari-
    time resources, 175–76; navies, 52, 61,
    66–67, 78, 97, 135, 147, 195n6, 198n5;
    North Korea, 60, 66–67, 134, 137, 172;
    PLA, 6, 52, 172–73, 195n6, 199n4;
    radar lock-on incident, 135–36; Russia,
    101, 137; sex slaves and, 14, 94, 108,
    112–16, 120–22, 124–30, 149, 198n4;
    South Korea, 24, 50–51, *51*, 66–67, 119,
    135–37, *138*, 171–72, 176, 199n5; South
    Korea and Japan as threats to each
    other, 137, *138*, 199n5; THAAD missile
    defense system, 60–61, 172; US, 78, 172
Ming dynasty, 53
Ministry of Foreign Affairs, Japan, 178
Ministry of Foreign Affairs and Trade,
    South Korea, 178
missiles: Aegis defense system, 172–73;
    defense capabilities, 173; North
    Korea with, 60, 66, 134, 172, 197n23;
    THAAD, 60–61, 172
Mitsubishi Heavy Industries, 129–30
Mnuchin, Steven, 152
Moon Jae-In, 60–61, 100, 105, 194n27; Abe
    Shinzo and, 108, 112; Biden and, 153–
    54; on CPTPP, 181; GSOMIA and, 134,
    135; with reparations for forced war-
    time labor, 130–32; Trump and, 150

MOU (Memorandum of Understanding), 134

Murayama Tomiichi, 125

Nakasone Yasuhiro, 77

National Assembly, South Korea, 134, 197n2

National Bureau of Asian Research, 56

Nationalist Government, China, 19, 146

NATO (North Atlantic Treaty Organization), 171, 199n1

navies: China, 52, 61, 97, 147, 195n6; with CUES, 135, 198n5; Japan, 61, 67; South Korea, 66–67, 135; US, 78

New Zealand, 197n5, 199n7

Nimitz, USS, 78

9/11, 97

Nippon Steel, 129

Nixon, Richard, 74

Noda Yoshihiko, 80

Nonproliferation Treaty (NPT), 66, 77

North Atlantic Treaty Organization (NATO), 171, 199n1

Northern Limit Line, 67

North Korea, 100, 197n5, 197n8; China and, 22, 77, 84, 88, 98; in country favorability studies, 101; GSS data and, 101; invasion by, 22, 38, 193n5; Japan and, 77, 151, 199n5; manufacturing in, 27; military, 60, 66–67, 134, 137, 172; with missiles, 60, 66, 134, 172, 197n23; NPT and, 66; with nuclear testing, 61, 66, 76–77, 151, 155; as repressive regime, 191n3; as security threat, 155, 199n2; South Korea and, xiv, 20, 151, 177; Soviet Union and, 21, 22; US and, 151; Yongbyon testing facility, 76

NPT (Nonproliferation Treaty), 66, 77

nuclear weapons, 193n6, 195n31; development, 76; Japan and, 136, 198n6; NPT, 66, 77; South Korea and, 198n6; testing, 61, 66, 76–77, 151, 155

Obama, Barack, 14; Japan with confidence in, 156; with "pivot to Asia" policy, 4–5, 98, 134, 145–49, 179; South Korea with

favorability ratings for, 157; TPP and, 147–48, 179–82

OECD (Organisation for Economic Co-operation and Development), 194n25

Office of the US Trade Representative, 183

oil: prices, 193n11; resources, 61, 79

Okinawa, 21, 61, 79

One-China policy, US with, 65–66, 78

One Nation, Two Systems formula, with Hong Kong, 186

Organisation for Economic Co-operation and Development (OECD), 194n25

Pacific War, xiii, 2–3, 9, 11, 19, 24, 27, 143; Dokdo/Takeshima dispute and, 118; forced labor during, 14, 94, 116, 129–32, *131*, 138–40, *139*, *141*, 178, 198n1; Japanese military with sex slaves during, 14, 94, 108, 112–16, 124–30, 149, 198n4; Japanese repression in, 8, 64, 93, 110, 118, 196n10; liberal international order after, 33; Senkaku Islands and, 61

Pakistan, 52

Paris Accords, 198n1

Park Chung-Hee, 24, 38–39, 117, 193n9, 194n26, 197n2

Park Geun-Hye, 60, 87, 99, 100, 105, 112, 122–23; with comfort women, 125, 126, 149; MOU and, 134

Patriot Advanced Capability-3, 173

"peace line," 118

People's Liberation Army (PLA), 6, 52, 172–73, 195n6, 199n4

Pew Research Center, 74, 85–86, 197n4

Philippines, 30, 124, 194n24, 199n7

"pivot to Asia" policy, US, 4–5, 98, 134, 145–49, 179

PLA (People's Liberation Army), 6, 52, 172–73, 195n6, 199n4

politics: leaders with Dokdo/Takeshima and, 120–21; repressive regimes, 1; rights in South Korea, *32*

Polity data, democracy and, 194n16

Pollins, Brian M., 34

poverty, 1, 56, 184

218   Index

presidents, US: George H. W. Bush, 97; George W. Bush, 4, 65, 148, 155–56, 197n22; Clinton, 78, 97; favorability of and confidence in, 156, *157*; Reagan, 97; South Korean and Japanese views of, 157–59, *158*; Truman, 22, 193n6. *See also* Obama, Barack; Trump, Donald

Prime Minister's Office surveys, Japan, 73–74, 85, 94, 123

protests, anti-Japanese, 64–65, 79

public diplomacy, 196n17

public opinion: with common understanding, 15–16; on defense cooperation by Japan and South Korea, 135; "don't know" survey category, 138, 139, 197n6, 198n5; on Japanese military power, 136–37; Japan with, 197n5; on radar lock-on incident, 136; on South Korea–Japan relations, 14–16; of South Koreans and Japanese on US and China, 13, 71–74; on unresolved historical issues, 13–14, 113–14

Putin, Vladimir, 199n1

"quasi-alliance," 2, 4

radar lock-on incident, 135–36

RCEP (Regional Comprehensive Economic Partnership), 181

Reagan, Ronald, 97

Reconciliation Treaty (1965), 25, 117–19, 122–25, 130, 139, 198n2

refugees, 85, 88, 184

Regional Comprehensive Economic Partnership (RCEP), 181

Regional Maritime Domain Awareness Network, 176

reparations: for comfort women, 124, 125, 130; for forced wartime labor, 129–32, *131*, 138–40, *139, 141*, 178, 198n1; with Treaty on Basic Relations, 24–25; World War II, 20

reunification, of Korean Peninsula, 19–20, 21, 88

Rhee Syngman, 21, 22, 24, 38, 118

Ridgway, Matthew, 193n6

Roh Moo-Hyun, 40

Roh Tae-Woo, 39, 120

Rose, Andrew, 35

Russia, 197n5, 197n8; GDP, 47; GSS data and, 101; military, 101, 137; in Ukraine, 163, 187, 199n1

Ryukyu Island chain, 61

Samsung, 99

sanctions-based tactics, China with, 60–61

San Francisco Treaty (1951), 20, 116, 118

satellite technology, 134

Sato Eisaku, 117

sea lines of communication (SLOC), 2–3, 28, 175

security: cyber, 172–74; development and strengthening of, 172–74; GSO-MIA, 67–68, 134–35, 171; maritime resources, 175–76; NATO, 171, 199n1; North Korea as threat to, 155, 199n2; umbrella, 2–3, 26, 41–42, 195n31; US with, 149, *150*

Security Council, UN, 22, 47, 65

Security Treaty (Treaty of Mutual Cooperation and Security), 21, 192n2, 199n4

Self-Defense Forces, Japan, 62, 177, 192n2

Senkaku (Diaoyu) Islands, 61–62, 68, 79–80

"Senkaku nationalism," 80

Seoul Central District Court, 140

sex slaves, comfort women as, 14, 94, 108, 112–16, 120–22, 124–30, 149, 198n4

Shimane Prefecture, 123

Singapore, 7, 191n8, 199n7

Sino-Japanese War (1894–95), 61, 79

SLOC (sea lines of communication), 2–3, 28, 175

Socotra Rock, 85

SOEs (state-owned enterprises), 147

soft clashes, 84, 85

soft power, China with, 59, 60, 196n15, 196n17

South China Sea, 51–52, 80, 97, 147, 153, 174

Southeast Asia, 2, 145, 191n1, 191n5, 195n5, 197n5, 199n9

South Korea, 197n5, 199n7; with bureaucratic influences, 197n1; China and, 72, 99, 170, 199n5; China as trade partner for Japan and, 48–49, *49*, 59; China impacting Japan and, 12, 59–62; China with Japanese partnership with, 12–13, 46, 62–69; decadal analysis of Japanese feelings of closeness to or distance from, *96*, 96–97; defense cooperation by Japan and, 135; democracy and, 32–33, 39–40; diplomatic missions, 38–40, *39*, 194n28, 194nn24–26, 195n29; diplomatic successes of presidents in pre- and post-transition periods, 39, *40*; distrust and understanding with Japan and, 104–14; with East Asian alliance system strengthened, 169–78; economic aid received by, *25*, 193n8; economy, *25*, 30–32, 40–41, 88, 92, 98–99, 178, 184, 191n4, 193n8, 193n14; GDP, 30–32, *31*; GSS, 74, 82–84, 86, 100–101; Japan, comfort women and improved relations with, 126–27, *127*, 149; Japan and, xiv, 2, 4, 7–10, 14–17, 19–26, 43–44, 60, 91–94, 107–8, *109*, 117–19, 122–25, 130, 139, 151, 166–67, 176–78, 193n4, 193n10, 197nn21–22, 198n2; Japanese views of, 94–100, *95*, 96, 100; manufacturing and, 27, 84, 131–32, 133; military, 24, 50–51, *51*, 66–67, 119, 135–37, *138*, 171–72, 176–77, 199n5; Ministry of Foreign Affairs and Trade, 178; National Assembly, 134, 197n2; North Korea and, xiv, 20, 151, 177; nuclear weapons and, 198n6; political rights, *32*; RCEP and, 181; with reunification, 88; rise of, 26–33; sanctions-based tactics against, 60–61; students in China, 60; supply chains and, 199n9; supportive impact on, 33–42; Supreme Court, 129–32, *131*, 138–40, *139*, 178, 198n1; with technology, 33, 98, 131–34; with THAAD missile system, 60–61, 172; trade and, 30, *31*, 36, *49*, 60, 62, 84, 88, 131–32; US and, xiii–xiv, 2, 21–22, 40, 60, 89, 150, 153–54, 157, 193n8; wealth, *32*, 33; working class, *32*, 32–33, 193n15

South Koreans: on China and US, 82–89; comfort women, 14, 94, 108, 112–13, 115–16, 120–22, 124–30, 149, 198n4; countries most favored by, *99*; on countries of economic importance, 141–43, *142*; with favorable vs. unfavorable views, *87*; with feelings of closeness to US or China, *83*; on historical issues and bilateral relations, 127–28, *128*; Japan as viewed by, 100–104, *104*; Japanese leaders viewed by, 105–7, *107*; Japanese opinions on improving relations with, 112–13, *113*; with Japanese people viewing bilateral relations as bad, 104–5, *106*; Japanese people with reasons for negative views of, 108–11, *111*, 121–22, *122*; with Japanese perceptions of affinity and importance, 159, *160*, 199n6; Japanese views on trade with, 132, *133*; Japan vs. China favored by, 101–2, *102*; Pacific War and forced labor of, 14, 94; public opinion data of, 13, 71–74; with Supreme Court ruling on forced labor, 130, *131*, 138–40, *139*; on US presidents, 157–59, *158*

Soviet Union, 19, 21, 22, 197n5
Space-Based Infrared System High Sensors, 173
Special Measures Agreement, 150
State Department, US, 178
state-owned enterprises (SOEs), 147
Status of Forces Agreement, 21
steel and aluminum tariffs, 152, 192n10
students, China with South Korean, 60
Suga Yoshihide, 153
Sukhoi 33 aircraft, 51
Sumitomo Metals, 129
supply chains: China and, 182–84; South Korea and Japan with, 199n9; tariffs and global, 152; technology, 182; US, 182–84
Supreme Court, South Korea: contrasting views on decision by, 130, *131*; how South Korea and Japan should respond to ruling, 138–39, *139*; ruling on reparations for forced wartime labor, 129–32, *131*, 138–40, *139*, 178, 198n1
surveillance balloon, 199n2

Taiwan, 2, 55, 61, 64, 78, 97, 153, 199n5
Taiwan Straits Crisis, 77–80

220   Index

Takeshima/Dokdo. *See* Dokdo/Takeshima
tariffs: on garlic, 84–85; increased, 5, 84, 149, 151–52; on steel and aluminum imports, 152, 192n10
technology: anti-cyberattack, 174; China with, 151, 172, 173, 182; hackers, 173–74, 199n4; Japan with, 28, 33; missiles, 66, 173; satellite, 134; sharing, 174; South Korea with, 33, 98, 131–34; supply chains, 182; US, 151, 173
terrorism: 9/11, 97; war on, 4, 5, 97, 195n5
textbook revisions, Japan with, 64–65, 79, 110, 120, 196n20
THAAD (Terminal High Altitude Area Defense) missile system, US with, 60–61, 172
Thailand, 199n7
Terminal High Altitude Area Defense (THAAD) missile system, US with, 60–61, 172
third revolution, in China, 146, 195n7
Tianxia (all/everything under heaven), 57–58
Tick, hacker group, 199n4
Tokyo Olympics, 193n11
Tokyo War Crimes Trials, 116, 124
Toyota, 99
TPP (Trans-Pacific Partnership), 147–48, 179–82, 199n6
trade: China, 47–49, 60, 62; China with Japan, South Korea and, 48–49, *49*, 59; commerce and coalitions framework with, 194n17; CPTPP, 181; deficits, 5, 149, 151; diplomacy and, 34–37, 41, 194n18; Doha round, 179; expansion, 19, 28; free, 35, 174–75, 180–81; GDP and, 181; how South Koreans and Japanese view, 132, *133*; IPEFP, 181; Japan and, 36, *49*, 131; language and, 35, 194n19; Office of the US Trade Representative, 183; RCEP, 181; restrictions, 108, 132, 140; SLOC and, 2–3, 28, 175; South Korea and, 30, *31*, 36, *49*, 60, 62, 84, 88, 131–32; South Korean Ministry of Foreign Affairs and Trade, 178; TPP, 147–48, 179–82,

199n6; "white list" for, 108, 131, 132; world, 163, 174
"trade follows the flag," 34–35
Trans-Pacific Partnership (TPP), 147–48, 179–82, 199n6
Treaty of Mutual Cooperation and Security (Security Treaty), 21, 192n2, 199n4
Treaty on Basic Relations (1965), 24, 25
tribute system, China with, 53–54, 58
Truman, Harry, 22, 193n6
Trump, Donald, 14, 100, 153, 196n19; "America First" policy and, 5, 6, 149, 171, 192n11, 192n14, 195n1; with bullying tactics, 150; Comprehensive Plan of Action and, 198n1; East Asian alliance system and, 154–55; Kim Jong Un and, 151; NATO and, 171; negative views of, 157; Paris Accords and, 198n1; support for and concerns about, 155–56, *156*; tariffs and, 151–52, 192n10; TPP and, 147, 148, 180–81, 182; with US allies, 149–50

Ukraine, Russia in, 163, 187, 199n1
UN. *See* United Nations
Unha-3 rocket, North Korea with, 66
La Union Port, 195n6
United Kingdom, 194n24
United Nations (UN), 19; North Korea and, 193n5; Security Council, 22, 47, 65
United States (US), 197n5, 197n8; Aegis missile defense system, 172–73; with allies, 149–50, 153–54, 159, 164; "America First" policy, 5, 6, 149, 171, 192n11, 192n14, 195n1; America's Pacific Century, 145–47; Asia-Pacific region and leadership of, 14, 17–18, 147–61, 179–87; Board on Geographic Names, 119; China and, 19, 151–52, 163–66, 168; China with Asia-Pacific region and leadership of, 14, 154–61; in country favorability studies, 101; decadal analysis of Japanese feelings of closeness to China and, *76*; Department of Commerce, 183; Department of the Treasury, 183; with East Asian alliance system strengthened, 169–78;

economy, 81, 143; Executive Order on America's Supply Chains, 182; with financial crisis of 2008, 195n5; GDP, 47; immigration and, 183, 184; influence of, 15–16, 163–64; infrastructure plan, 183; Japan and, xiii, xiv, 2, 20–21, 59, 61, 62, 65, 82, 151, 153, 156, 192nn2–3, 193n3, 196n19, 199n4; Japanese feelings toward, *81*; Japanese views on China and, 74–82; military, 78, 172; with missile defense capabilities, 173; North Korea and, 151; Office of the US Trade Representative, 183; with One-China policy, 65–66, 78; with "pivot to Asia" policy, 4–5, 98, 134, 145–49, 179; public opinion data on China and, 13; with security, 149, 150; South Korea and, xiii–xiv, 2, 21–22, 40, 60, 89, 150, 153–54, 157, 193n8; South Koreans with feelings of closeness to China or, *83*; South Korean views on China and, 82–89; State Department, 178; supply chains, 183–84; with tariffs, 149, 151–52; technology and, 151, 173; THAAD missile system and, 60–61, 172; TPP and, 147, 199n5; Trump administration, 155–56, *156. See also* presidents, US

US Agency for International Development (USAID), 193n8
Uyghur people, 186

Vietnam, 195n30, 199n7
Vietnam War, 195n30

"white list," for trade, 108, 131, 132
working-class wealth, South Korea, *32*, 32–33, 193n15
world trade, growth of, 163, 174
World War II, 20, 36, 43, 47, 55, 179
World Wide Web, 146

Xi Jinping, 45, 54, 87, 99; COVID-19 and, 185; with global ambition for China, 199n1; on rise of China, 146; with third revolution in China, 146, 195n7

Yasukuni Shrine, 77, 93, 110, 196n20
Yellow Sea, 52, 80, 85
Yeonpyeong Island, shelling of, 67
Yongbyon testing facility, North Korea, 76
Yoon Suk-Yeol, 105, 167, 194n27

Zoellick, Robert, 199n3

ASIA IN THE NEW MILLENNIUM

SERIES EDITOR: Shiping Hua, University of Louisville

Asia in the New Millennium is a series of books offering new interpretations of an important geopolitical region. The series examines the challenges and opportunities of Asia from the perspectives of politics, economics, and cultural-historical traditions, highlighting the impact of Asian developments on the world. Of particular interest are books on the history and prospect of the democratization process in Asia. The series also includes policy-oriented works that can be used as teaching materials at the undergraduate and graduate levels. Innovative manuscript proposals at any stage are welcome.

ADVISORY BOARD
William Callahan, University of Manchester, Southeast Asia and Thailand
Lowell Dittmer, University of California at Berkeley, East Asia and South Asia
Robert Hathaway, Woodrow Wilson International Center for Scholars, South Asia, India, and Pakistan
Mike Mochizuki, George Washington University, East Asia, Japan, and Korea
Peter Moody, University of Notre Dame, China and Japan
Brantly Womack, University of Virginia, China and Vietnam
Charles Ziegler, University of Louisville, Central Asia and Russia Far East

BOOKS IN THE SERIES

The Future of China-Russia Relations
Edited by James Bellacqua

North Korea and the World: Human Rights, Arms Control, and Strategies for Negotiation
Walter C. Clemens Jr.

Contemporary Chinese Political Thought: Debates and Perspectives
Edited by Fred Dallmayr and Zhao Tingyang

Power versus Law in Modern China: Cities, Courts, and the Communist Party
Qiang Fang and Xiaobing Li

China Looks at the West: Identity, Global Ambitions, and the Future of Sino-American Relations
Christopher A. Ford

The Mind of Empire: China's History and Modern Foreign Relations
Christopher A. Ford

State Violence in East Asia
Edited by N. Ganesan and Sung Chull Kim

Challenges to Chinese Foreign Policy: Diplomacy, Globalization, and the Next World Power
Edited by Yufan Hao, C. X. George Wei, and Lowell Dittmer

The Price of China's Economic Development: Power, Capital, and the Poverty of Rights
Zhaohui Hong

Japan after 3/11: Global Perspectives on the Earthquake, Tsunami, and Fukushima Meltdown
Edited by Pradyumna P. Karan and Unryu Suganuma

Korean Democracy in Transition: A Rational Blueprint for Developing Societies
HeeMin Kim

Modern Chinese Legal Reform: New Perspectives
Edited by Xiaobing Li and Qiang Fang

Democracy in Central Asia: Competing Perspectives and Alternative Strategies
Mariya Y. Omelicheva

Strengthening South Korea–Japan Relations: East Asia's International Order and a Rising China
Dennis Patterson and Jangsup Choi

China's Encounter with Global Hollywood: Cultural Policy and the Film Industry, 1994–2013
Wendy Su

Growing Democracy in Japan: The Parliamentary Cabinet System since 1868
Brian Woodall

The Soldier Image and State-Building in Modern China, 1924–1945
Yan Xu

Inside China's Grand Strategy: The Perspective from the People's Republic
Ye Zicheng, Edited and Translated by Steven I. Levine and Guoli Liu

Civil Society and Politics in Central Asia
Edited by Charles E. Ziegler

About the Authors

Dennis Patterson is professor of political science and Executive Director of Academic Programs for Regional Sites, Office of the Provost, at Texas Tech University. He has lived in Japan and is the coauthor of *The Japan That Never Was: Explaining the Rise and Decline of a Misunderstood Country* (SUNY Press) and *Diplomacy, Trade, and South Korea's Rise to International Influence* (Lexington Books) as well as over sixty peer-reviewed articles in such journals as *International Studies Quarterly, Legislative Studies Quarterly, the British Journal of Political Science, Asian Survey*, and other peer-reviewed journals of disciplinary significance.

Jangsup Choi is associate professor of political science at Texas A&M University–Commerce. His research interests include political behavior, campaigns and elections, and Asian politics, with a special interest in political outcomes as explained by institutional arrangements. His recent publications have appeared in such journals as *International Area Studies Review, Politics and Religion, Studies in Ethnicity and Nationalism, Islam and Christian-Muslim Relations, Korea Observer*, and the *Korean Journal of Area Studies*.